WILD WOMEN

By Moira Hodgkinson

CoA Publishing

London, UK

First Paperback Edition
Printed and bound by The Children of Artemis, London, 2017

Cover design and photograph by The Children of Artemis
Author photograph courtesy of Elric Sullivan

Children of Artemis
BM Artemis, London, WC1N 3XX

ISBN 978-1-9998551-0-9

Wild Women is dedicated to Tim Hewitt.

I would like to thank a few people for helping to make this book possible: my husband Chris for his enduring patience and allowing me to stay focused on my writing, my daughter Phoebe, likewise, and my mum for bestowing in me a love of stories and the desire to share them. I am indebted and very grateful to Dave and Cath who took my mad idea and brought it to life with passion, dedication and hard work. Thanks ever so much to Elle who graciously modelled for the cover and to Elric Sullivan for my author photograph. Finally, thank you so much to all of you, my readers, I look forward to hearing from you.

WILD WOMEN

PROLOGUE

'Just get your hands in there, Sal, a little bit of dirt won't hurt, no matter what your mum says.' Gran's opinion of my mother hadn't changed much over the long years. 'These things are best done with the hands.'

She hollowed the earth deeper with her bare hands, rich soil merging with roughened skin. I find her earth-stained hands comforting but my mother holds them in disdain.

The two of them couldn't be more different if they tried. Gran wears long, flowing earthy coloured clothes from second-hand shops while Mum is a complete fashion victim. Gran works hard as a tarot reader and healer and Mum rebelled to find work as an assistant bank manager. Gran is honest and kind with a good sense of humour and she brought me up with laughter and love. Mum is a drama-queen; she never swears, rarely laughs and hates the outdoors. Gran has a way with people, plants and animals and she's full of good advice. Mum continually makes poor decisions and ends up in trouble, which is why we came to live with Gran when my father died. Then Mum moved in with one terrible boyfriend after another, the most recent of whom was also the worst.

'That's deep enough, love.' Gran's voice brought me back to the present and I turned to the hole in the ground and the wooden box next to it.

'No tears, Sally.' Gran chided. 'Time enough for that at the dark moon, tonight she's full, so let's remember the good things, eh?'

'You're right, Gran.' I took a deep breath and picked up the box, running my hands over the polished surface. I'd thought about this moment all day but suddenly I was speechless. Gran's hand settled on my shoulder and a subtle surge of energy ran through me. I breathed rhythmically, silently asking the Goddess to help me too.

Lady Bast, help me find the words for this little soul, help me get through.

'Lady Bast, watch over my dear Judy. Cherish her as I have and – and – take her – take her into your heart.'

Gran took up the thread, her words coming naturally where my own had floundered. 'We thank you, Judy, for your loyalty, love and companionship. We honour your spirit and give you rest with the Old Ones.'

I nestled the box carefully in the ground, packing the space around it with flowers and herbs and I placed a photograph of Judy on top. Gran laid the turf back down, patting it into place. She stood up, taking my smooth hand in her wrinkled one, and moved to the altar. A small table was set with all my ritual tools and the sad addition of a silver cord.

'Sally, it's time.' Gran said quietly.

Heavy hearted, I picked up the cord and scissors and shut my eyes briefly, determined not to cry. 'Lord of the forest, Lady of the moon, may ever the cord be loosed and the spirit be free. May we meet, remember and love one another again, in this world or beyond.' I snipped through the cord, laying one piece over the grave in a spiral, the other on the altar. I'd sleep with it under my pillow tonight, along with Judy's little red collar.

'So mote it be.' An unexpected voice came from the shadows and we both spun round in surprise to see our visitor.

'Is that Judy?' My mother asked.

'Mum? How could you know that?' I sniffed. Not knowing if I should move towards Gran or Mum, I took the safer option and stayed rooted to the spot. I wished my gorgeous feline familiar hadn't died, that she was waiting to comfort me so this awkward meeting of stubborn women wouldn't feel so heavy in the still of the night.

Mum shuffled and looked down at her feet. 'I can't explain it; I just felt something telling me to come here.'

'Out with it.' Gran said stonily. 'What are you really doing turning up at the poor lass's requiem for Judy like this?'

'Gran, please, stop it!' I shouted. I hate to see them bicker even though I was used to it.

'I'm going in.' Gran's voice was cold and distant. 'I'll see you inside, Sal.' She grabbed her athame off the altar and marched across the garden to the back door, slamming it shut.

'What are you doing here, Mum?' I hadn't seen her in six months. 'I've just buried the cat I've loved for twelve years, I'm not in the right frame of mind for your drama.'

'Can we sit down, love,' she asked? I followed her to the living willow seat nestled amongst fragrant honeysuckle. The full moon's light made the bright red patent of my mother's shoes glimmer and shine. My worn and mucky Dr Martens were shabby and tired in comparison.

Mum turned to me, brushing her hand briefly over my cheek. A tiny stubborn part of me wanted to draw back but a bigger part of me felt comforted. She steadied herself and took a deep breath. 'I filed for a divorce yesterday.'

Well, that was a bolt from the blue!

'I know, it's been a long time coming.' She smiled weakly and looked away.

'How did you get away from the slug?' The slug, my so-called step-father, was a prime example of the cowardly wife-beaters I'd come across whilst doing admin for a women's shelter last month.

'I haven't told him, I just put a bag in the car and went to work as usual this morning. I thought about it all day and then I drove straight here.' She shook her head, laughing suddenly. 'All this time and she was right, I just didn't want to admit it.'

'We've both been telling you for years, Mum. You shouldn't have moved in with him in the first place.'

'I know, and it was stupid of me. That man is the biggest mistake I've ever made.'

My eyes were leaking so now it was my turn to look away. Through the kitchen window I could see Gran at the table, glass of red wine in hand, surrounded by pots and pans and clouds of e-cig

3

vapour. She smoked, she swore and she drank, but this loving woman had always been there for me while my mother's contact had been sporadic and selfish.

'I'm so sorry, Sally.' Mum brushed away her tears. 'I knew I'd never be happy with him, but by then it was too late.' She shook her head. 'I was stuck with it Sally, I was so scared.'

I'd heard it all before but working at the women's refuge had taught me compassion and understanding. Gran's kindness played a large part in that too, but nothing made up for Mum's intermittent contact once she moved out of the house. The slug was just the latest and nastiest of her bad life choices.

'You've taken the first steps.' I tried to sound reassuring. 'Things will get better from here.'

'I don't expect it to be easy,' she went on, 'but I hope I can start building bridges between us now I'm free.'

'You want to stay here?' I felt a tingle of warmth at the thought of it. 'I think I'd like that, Mum, but I don't know if Gran will warm to the idea.'

'Yes, I've got my work cut for me there.' Mum straightened up and pulled a small package out of her handbag. 'Here, I got you something.'

My Gran had given Judy to me as a companion when Mum and I first came to live in the village. I was barely a teen and Judy, still a kitten back then, helped me adjust to life in Gran's house and I would miss her dreadfully. And now Mum was offering this small box at the end of Judy's life, some pathetic trinket to buy my affection?

'I've always denied my witchiness.' She said, shaking her head and looking up at the moon to avoid my eyes. 'I guess it scared me a little and I got teased at school: the way Mum dresses, the tarot readings… you know what kids can be like.'

I let out a huffing sigh. I knew exactly what she meant; I'd gone through the same hellish torment at school myself. I fumbled with the wrapping paper while Mum tried to explain.

'But I still have flashes of intuition, times when I need to knock on wood or say hello to magpies. I have felt so unsettled for the last few days. And it was definitely not connected to Paul, for once. I wanted to come and see you, Sally.'

'Oh Mum!' I sobbed loudly and she held me close, kissing my forehead before heading inside to break her news to Gran.

It was a struggle to remain composed, looking down at Judy's collar, especially with Mum's revelation about the divorce. Her relationship with the slug had been doomed when the first bruises landed. It had been four nasty, hard years and her reluctance to admit what was going on played a large part in the arguments between her and Gran but I think really they were just too different to get along. Maybe now the walls between them would start to come down.

The altar was lit only by the stars and moon and I took out the box to look at the contents again. Judy had been my companion and my comfort for so long, I couldn't bear the thought of not having her in my life. I opened the box again and smiled at the gift. A new cat collar, its tag engraved with my name and phone number. Tucked in with it were the details of a local animal shelter.

I looked up at the moon, feeling the soothing energy of the Goddess offering strength and courage. The loss of my cat had brought new situations to light and I looked forward to seeing how things would turn out from here. I packed up the altar tools and made my way back indoors while Mum walked inside.

I have no idea for how long I lingered outside, once I got in the aroma of vanilla candles and sandalwood greeted me in the dining room. Gran poured me a glass of wine and I plonked myself between her and Mum. We sipped our wine in silence until Mum's mobile lit up. She read the text with a worried expression.

'It's Paul. Where am I and when am I coming back?' She sounded terrified and her hands were shaking as her fingers hovered over the phone.

'Don't you dare!' Gran swiftly laid a hand over Mum's to stop her replying. 'He won't come here for you, not for love nor money. You can stay here for as long as you need to.'

I don't know what the two of them had been talking about when I'd left them alone but it must have been a deep and hard conversation to have led to this turn-around. 'What have I missed?' I asked. 'Have you two patched things up?'

'Not by a long shot, Sally.' Mum scoffed.

'But we're working on it,' Gran said, the glint of a smile on her wrinkled face. 'Aren't we?'

'You two are like sugar and spice.' I mused aloud. 'So different to each other but you go together well when the recipe is right.'

'Oh, stop being daft and drink your wine, Sal.' Gran hid a sly grin and I caught a glint of moonlight shining through the window. In two weeks the orb would be new, the perfect time to start looking for a new familiar. I held the little box in my hands and went up to bed, tucking it under my pillow with the silver cord and Judy's red collar and that night, I dreamed the dream of a thousand cats.

CHAPTER ONE

'I don't know why you read this rubbish, Jasmine.' Magda cast her beady eyes over the horoscope column of the local paper Jasmine had spread out on the table. Magda picked up a glass and filled it with grapefruit juice. She took a sip and then grimaced at the sour taste. 'Pour me a mug of tea, love.'

'Yes, Mother.' Jasmine replied, surprising herself with how easily she slipped back into the role of dutiful daughter, even though she'd only returned to the family home as a temporary stop-gap until she found her feet again. 'The only reason you never read horoscopes,' Jasmine continued, 'is because you don't like what it says for your star sign.'

Magda sniffed haughtily. 'You know I've always preferred the tarot. Horoscope columns are for muppets who can't read the signs for themselves,' she said, turning back to the ancient stove where a large pot of liquid bubbled away, clouds of steam rising from it to fill the kitchen with a thick haze of minty fog. She plunged a large wooden spoon into the concoction, stirring it deosil, ever deosil, the witches' word for clockwise, the direction of good luck. 'I'm supposed to believe that out of billions of people on the planet, there are only twelve types? Such a load of old rubbish.'

'Here's yours, Mum. Virgo: an unexpected invitation leads to a hot date with an unusual character and a surprise business proposal may be on the cards. On the cards, ha.'

'See?' Magda said, not taking her eyes from the pot even when a sharp rapping knock on the back door rang out loudly. 'I'm going to write and complain to the paper about this stupid horoscope. I could do better myself. It's utter drivel. I work for myself so the career thing's wrong to begin with, Village life never throws up any surprises and nobody from around here is likely to ask me out on a hot date, and even if they did, I'd refuse: I'm too old for that kind of thing. Mark my words, lass, it's a load of old boll –,' the knock came again, insistent.

'Gran!' Magda's grand-daughter, twenty-three year old Sal, yelled from the top of the stairs, 'you'll have to answer the door yourself for a change, I'm still in my pyjamas!'

'Jasmine, will you get it, love? I can't leave this now or it'll boil over. Got to stir it to infuse it.'

Jasmine huffed under her breath at her mother and reluctantly stood up. 'It's either one of your weird customers after a potion or it's – oh no. Mum, what if it's him?'

For split second Magda felt her blood run cold and a horrible flash of anger coursed through her veins. She could feel her skin tensing up with goose bumps as she filled with venom for the man her daughter had run away from, coming home just yesterday with nothing but a few carry-all bags to her name. Jasmine had arrived unannounced late at night, right in the middle of the burial ceremony for Sal's poor old familiar cat. It had been four years since Jasmine had cleared off to Manchester with Paul. Magda had pleaded with her to leave him when the first bruises started to show, but by the end of the second year she had given up trying and a frosty silence had laid between them ever since. That nasty piece of work had spoiled everything and if he thought for one minute he could come here and … No. This wouldn't do at all. Magda realised her thoughts had gone in the wrong direction entirely and she brought herself sharply back around. One should never treat aggression with anger. She took a deep breath, feeling a fresh air of calmness enter her lungs, and another one. Calm, yes, but definitely resolved. She rolled up her cardigan sleeves, ready for business.

'I'll get the door, you stir this; deosil, mind.' Magda wiped her hands on the raggedy apron tied round her waist and drew herself up to her full height. Admittedly, five-foot-five is not exactly tall but when Magda was in full swing, five-foot-five could appear scarily intimidating. 'I don't think he's likely to have driven a hundred-and-forty miles to follow you here, if he even knows where to find you at all, but if it is him, I'll see him off. Don't worry love, I promise I won't hit him unless he throws the first punch.'

8

'It's not the slug,' Sal called again from upstairs, using her pet nickname for her so-called step-father, 'it's Granger, I can see the top of his baldy little head from up here.'

'Granger? Well, that's a relief.' Magda visibly relaxed, now refusing to give over the stirring spoon. With her free hand she shoved a somewhat nervous Jasmine towards the door. 'You can let him in Jasmine, though I wonder what on earth he's doing here at this time on a Sunday morning. He should be getting ready for work.'

'Who in God's name works on a Sunday?' Jasmine asked.

'Exactly.' Her mother snorted.

At Magda's house, an unexpected visitor could mean a pensioner wanting ointments for leg ulcers or a frumpy house wife coming for a tarot reading. Growing up in this house as a young girl, Jasmine had sometimes been amused by the people who visited her eccentric mother: other times, maybe even most of the time, she had been terrified of the freaks who came calling. Herbal lotions, tarot readings, poppets to stop a wayward lover from straying; Magda did it all. Jasmine shuddered at the unwanted memory of one particular chap, a short, dumpy man tainted with grease and oozing nastiness, appearing on the door-step clutching a small glass vial full of rusty nails and vinegar. At least, thought Jasmine on reflection, it had looked like vinegar at the time but now she was older and understood a little more, she realised that it was probably something far less sanitary and palatable than vinegar. She had scampered upstairs to hide in her room and when the man left some time later, the house stank of sage and Jasmine, even as a child, was familiar enough with her mother's habits to know she hadn't like the man either, not one little bit. The sage was to cleanse his essence and repugnance from the house. The expression on his ugly, craggy face and the narrow meanness of his piggy little eyes as he'd pushed past her into the house sent a chill down her spine. Jasmine shut the image from her mind with deliberate finality as she put her hand on the large, cold door knob.

'Hello, how can I – oh!' Jasmine opened the door and stood

back agape as a friendly looking man bustled in, smiling at her. Now she recognised the name: he was not just any-old caller but her mother's friend, perhaps her closest one, the Reverend Granger.

'Jasmine!' The man with the baldy little head said, clasping her happily on the shoulders and nodding his head enthusiastically. 'How lovely to see you, must be what? Four or five years at least, eh?'

She shut the door behind him and poured a cup of tea from the still-warm pot, handing it to him as he babbled gently before striking out at her with the questions she should have been expecting.

'Your mother didn't tell me you would be coming up.' Granger shot a beady-eyed stare at Magda who pointedly failed to turn away from her stove top. 'Will you be staying long? How's life in the big city?'

'Complicated. I'm – taking a break – shall we say?' Jasmine shuffled the newspaper awkwardly in front of her, pretending to read. Anything to deflect his well-meant but awkward quizzing.

'Never mind that, Granger, what brings you here this early on your working day?' Magda came to the rescue and scooped up some of the goo from her pan, shoving the spoon beneath his nose. 'I want an honest opinion, my friend: what do you think of this?'

'I do work the rest of the week, too, as you know very well.' Granger sipped the brown gloop cautiously then wrinkled his nose in a grimace. 'Oh good Lord, Magda, that is quite possibly the most revolting thing I've ever had in my mouth. What's it for? Coughs and colds?'

'Dinner. Thought I'd get on it with now so it has time to infuse but I may have over-done the mint.'

'Yes, you have indeed. Now, I am a bit busy this morning what with it being a Sunday and-all, so I'll come straight out with it. I need you to do me a bit of a favour. Please?' Granger put on his most winning smile and leaned his head over to one side foppishly.

Magda shrugged, non-committal, slurping luke-warm tea loudly while Jasmine sat quietly pouring over the television guide in the paper. 'A favour? Might do, Vicar, might do.' Magda hunkered

down at the table and glared at her old friend, Revered Granger.
She saw a glint of humour in his eyes. This could prove to be an
interesting interlude and after a restless night worrying over her
daughter's unexpected return to the proverbial nest, Magda was not
about to turn down the chance of an interesting interlude. 'What's in
it for me?' She said finally.

'I want you to be my token person representing a minority
faith.' Granger leaned forward and whispered. 'I've got to host
a meeting with that idiot vicar of St Mary's after the service this
afternoon. Interfaith cropped up in one of our discussions a few
months ago and he's found some minority faith followers in his
Parish. I only went and forgot all about it and there's nobody else I
can ask, so no pressure, you see?' A hint of desperation in his voice,
Magda noted, quickly stopping her coy smile from reaching her lips. It
was part of the game they played, this vicar and witch, each of them
never quite letting the other know exactly how deep their friendship
ran. She was his devil's advocate and he enjoyed the banter and he
– well, he was all right, she supposed. For a vicar.

'So this other vicar is giving you a run for your money and
now you want a weirdo of your own to show-off?'

The vicar fiddled with his white collar, his cheeks an
unflattering beetroot colour. 'Well, I wouldn't put it quite like that
myself, but, yes. Would you mind awfully? He suggested a semi-
official interfaith meeting and the, what do you call them? The
greylings? The women's group I mean: they're doing another one of
their horrible little buffets with dry sandwiches and yesterday's stale
sausage rolls left over from Mrs Beers' abominable bakery. Please say
you'll come. I've already asked the Singh's but they've got Sukhjinder's
Auntie staying for the weekend.'

'Oh, I see. I'm your second choice then am I?' Magda put
a hand dramatically over her heart, pretending to look offended.
Granger put his hands together in a pleading gesture once more,
matching her drama and fluttering his eyelids rapidly. 'Well, as luck
would have it, I've made a right pig's ear of this casserole and I could

do with palming it off on some un-suspecting hungry souls. The ladies of the Wilveringham Women's Group will do nicely.'

'Jolly good, that's settled then.' Granger pushed himself away from the table and cleared his throat. 'There's nothing, you know, odd in there, I take it? No aphrodisiacs or anything?'

Magda shook her head and saw the vicar to the door with a two-finger salute. 'Not a drop of it, Witch's Honour. What time's your shin-dig kicking off then?'

'One-thirty. You'd be very welcome too, Jasmine, be lovely to see you and have a proper catch up. And Sally, of course, wherever she is. Always seems to be busy when I call round, but never mind.' He stepped out of the kitchen into the slightly frosty morning and then turned back briefly as he remembered something. 'Oh, and would you be a dear and wear something nice, Magda? And I don't mean that dodgy old Stephen King t-shirt of yours.'

'That's my favourite t-shirt, why I've never…' She could feel her eyes drawing together crossly and she made a point of relaxing her face. 'What are you getting at?'

Granger rolled his eyes and shook his head in despair. 'Just dress nicely and be on time, all right?'

'Keep your opinions on my wardrobe to yourself, will you? I've got things to do, I haven't laid my cards out yet and I know you've got better things to do at this time of a Sunday morning too, other than darkening my doorstep. Go on, scram or you'll be late for your own service.' So saying, she pushed Reverend Granger through the door with a cheeky smile and closed it behind him.

Sal poked her head around the door to the inner hallway. 'Has he gone? Good.' She looked from her mother to her grandmother, not sure which of them she ought to sit next to. She settled for leaning against the trusty old Aga stove, warming her behind. 'I can't bear the way he's always trying to get me into the church.'

'Ha! You don't mean that and you know it. Besides, he's got to have someone to convert,' Magda laughed, 'after all, he gave up on me years ago. He's a decent sort, really.'

'Eww, what's that stink, Gran?' Sal wrinkled her nose and poked a spoon into the gigantic pan which was still steaming away as its contents cooled. 'It smells like something died in there.'

'Your gran is making minted lamb casserole for the village women's group at the church this afternoon.' Jasmine announced, pulling the television guide out of the paper. 'I'm going to have a long soak in the tub and then I intend to spend the day consoling myself with weepy movies and a box of chocolates.'

'Here, hang this over the tap to help soothe those bruises of yours.' Magda pulled a white-linen sachet of herbs from a drawer. Jasmine took the sachet and sniffed it suspiciously. 'Don't pull that face, it's only rosemary. You may be in your forties but I'm still your mother and sometimes I still know best.'

Sal watched her mother from the kitchen, tramping off into the hallway and up to the bathroom. She picked up a wooden spoon and gave the suspicious looking pot another stir, coughing as the action released yet more puffs of minty vapour into the room.

'Gran, do you think Mum will stay?' She said quietly, deliberately not looking up to meet Magda's eyes. 'I know she's only going to be here a few days or so, but after that, she'll find somewhere nearby, won't she? I mean, she won't go back to Manchester?'

'Well, she's circled a couple of adverts in the property section by the looks of it, but with your mother, I'm afraid it's hard for anyone to say what's really going through her mind.' Magda shook her head slowly. 'She was never really happy here, even growing up. Couldn't wait to get away to the bright lights of a busy city. I think she used that first real crush of hers, whatever his name was, Pete Something, as an excuse to leave Wilveringham. Then it was one bad boyfriend after another and one new city after another: Birmingham, Nottingham, Leicester, Manchester. Pete, John. It didn't seem to matter who or where as long as she had some reason to stay away from home. Your father was the only good one she ever had.'

Sal nodded sadly, remembering what little she could of her father with fondness and love. His dark, curly hair, the roguish twinkle of his brown eyes, an infectious laugh that had made her giggle with glee. She wiped her face with the back of a hand, brushing away the first pricks of tears that threatened to sting her eyes. 'Yeah, he was a good one all right.' Her emotions got the better of her as always then and Sal wiped her face again. 'Oh, Gran, why did Judy have to go now, just when Mum's come back?'

'Judy was twelve, Sally, that's a good enough age for a cat.' Magda drew Sal close, planting a kiss on her forehead and wrapping her up in a hug. 'And things do seem to happen all at once, that's just the way of things, I'm afraid.'

'I had the weirdest dream last night.' Sal stopped sniffing and pulled away. 'There were hundreds of tiny red men, all dressed in bright red mankinis, dancing backwards and forwards in straight lines. They had no faces, no eyes, just red potato-heads. There was no music, only some monotonous clapping and the red men all bowed at the end of the dance and a massive queen bee flew down and ate them all up. Judy was there and she pounced on the bee and ate it and when she burped, all of the little red men came flying out of her mouth and sat on her back while she scampered around. Then someone banged a gong and I woke up.'

'Hardly weird compared to some of my dreams, but I'm not going to analyse it for you, Sally.' Magda laughed. 'Sometimes a dream is just a dream.'

Sal let out a heavy sigh. 'Anyway, what's this about a church do and the Women of Wilveringham? Did I hear Granger say something about a t-shirt? I do hope you're not starting to get conventional on me, Gran.'

'If I ever do, you have my permission to kick my backside firmly and swiftly back to the wrong side of normality. He wants to show me off as the only pagan in the village. I'm his token fringe religious person for some interfaith thing. It'll be the most boring thing I've done all year and Granger says I'm to dress nicely but at least I can palm that horrible casserole off on the ladies-wot-lunch and the straggly little vicar from St Mary's.' Magda brushed a gnarly hand through her long and frizzy, salt-and-pepper hair. 'Right, pass the cards love, time to see what they have lined up for me.'

Sal spied her gran's tired and worn looking deck of tarot cards sitting on the top shelf of the kitchen dresser, tucked in-between the paprika and a fragrant bunch of drying lavender. She took the cards down, passing them to Magda, and then she cleared pots and pans and breakfast dishes to make space on the table. She watched as Magda breathed slowly and deliberately, shuffling the cards and then laying out the top three. Magda peered at them for several long and silent minutes before huffing loudly and muttering something indecipherable but which sounded to Sal a lot like horoscope, nonsense and quite possibly, traitorous cards!

Sal gave in to temptation and looked over her gran's shoulder. Though her knowledge of the tarot was not as good as Magda's, she recognised the Wheel of Fortune, the Lovers and the Ten of Pentacles and could hazard a rough guess that the line-up indicated chance encounters, a potential romance and a future full of business opportunities. It was unusual for the tabloid horoscope column and Magda's tarot cards to be in agreement but it was certainly looking like Magda was in for some unexpected fun at the church event. As she washed up the breakfast dishes, Sal toyed briefly with the idea of tagging along herself, just in order to keep Gran company, of course. Finally she dismissed the notion in favour of a long walk by the canal; she wanted to see what plants she could still forage before the weather turned too cold and everything died down as the coming wintry weather hit the ground in a barrage of rain and wind.

Sal finished the last of the dishes and sat down with the paper, turning to the jobs pages and dismissing one vacancy after another. There were a couple of admin posts that she would apply for but nothing else called to her, nothing that would be as rewarding as the work she'd done for the women's refuge before it closed last month. She folded the newspaper and smiled to herself at the sound of Magda tromping through the house with deliberate noisiness whilst going through piles of laundry.

'Looking for something nice to wear, Gran?' Sal called up from the stairwell. She dodged and laughed as one of Magda's numerous green silk scarves drifted down the stairs to land on her head. Sal tied it around the lion's head on the banister post, a tinge of sadness in her heart as she remembered there was no cat left in the house to batt and play with the dangling ends.

'Something nice, indeed! I'll give him something nice.' Magda shouted down, distracting Sal from her musings. 'Have you seen my Stephen King t-shirt lately, Sal?'

CHAPTER TWO

It took Magda only ten minutes to walk from her home on the edge of the village to the church hall in the centre of it. Five of those minutes had included a catch-up chat with Stacy, the young woman who worked at and owned the high street grocery. She called in to collect two large bottles of mead she had ordered the week before. Mead was her drink of choice for rituals and with Samhain and a full moon looming in front of her, Magda needed to replenish her supplies. Walking from Stacy's little shop to the church took virtually no time at all and as she approached the old building she noticed a thing of beauty. A gleaming, well-kept motorbike was parked in one of the on-street parking bays immediately outside the church. She stopped beside it for a moment and sighed, reminiscing about her one-time dalliance with motorbikes, back when she'd still been on the young side of twenty. An idea popped into her head and Magda looked around, vaguely wondering if the bike's owner was nearby and if he or she might be persuaded to take her out on it for a wild ride around the village. There was no sign of any bikers in the vicinity unfortunately and besides, this witch was due at church; it wouldn't do at all to be late.

Magda pulled the ends of a floaty crimson scarf to fall evenly around her neck, made sure the mead was safely out of sight in her roomy hand-bag and entered the church. She had always rather liked St Anne's with its ornate carvings in wood and stone, the arches in the ceiling and the serenity of its stained glass windows. The first time she'd stepped through its doors as a young woman with a baby and a reputation for being a witch after only a week in the village, she'd been hounded straight back out again. She'd been trying to return the purse of a woman who had dropped it on her way in. The Reverend Granger had immediately followed her out, declaring that if his parishioners thought for one minute his church was the sort that would not welcome everybody with open arms, no matter what their beliefs, then he was not going to be their vicar for very much longer.

That had been the start of her long friendship with the man and they had done each other all kinds of favours since then, so she was happy to put on a smile for him today – happier still to be getting rid of her horrible casserole.

Toward the back of the church were a collection of function rooms and Magda headed for the one with voices coming from it. The room held twenty or so guests, seated or standing in small groups holding cups of tea or coffee and making polite conversation. She didn't recognise anyone and was relieved to have brought the lamb casserole, it gave her a good excuse to stand about at the table laden with refreshments. Granger wasn't kidding about the bakery's left-over pastries. She took a bite of a dry, over-cooked sausage roll, found a tissue hiding in her bag under the mead and discreetly spat the pastry back out again. She shook her head, placing down her dish of soggy casserole, hiding the tissue back in her purse for later disposal and wondering if it was too early in the day for a crafty sip of mead.

A hand on her shoulder startled her, warm and firm. Granger. The vicar beamed happily at her and gestured to the people gathered in the room. 'Magda, thank you for coming. You will make yourself known, won't you?' He asked hopefully. 'Especially to the visitors from the St Mary's area, one of whom in particular expressed quite an interest in your, err, well. You know. What you do. He's over there. The one with the hair.' Granger pointed vaguely towards the back of the room where all she could see was the back of people's heads. 'Right, must dash.' Granger left her to her own devices. He ought not to keep doing that, Magda thought, she could get into a lot of mischief in a room full of conventional people.

Almost all of the men in the group were bald or nearly so, but there was one who stood out a mile with a full head of long and wavy white hair. She gasped with a mixture of surprise and delight as Mr White Hair turned his face around and nodded a silent greeting to her before going back to his conversation. It was a pleasant looking face. Was that his deep, gruff voice she could make out among the background hub-bub of noise in the airy meeting room? He was tall, he was broad, his face adorned with a beard of – dare she say it? – biblical proportions, dressed in jeans and a white pirate-style shirt with a leather waistcoat over it and Magda assumed, correctly as it would turn out, that he was the owner of the bike she'd stopped to admire outside. A flush of excitement, a tingle, a giggle, rose up inside her, the first time in years she had felt anything like this. Her head reeled dizzily as she realised this man was Pan made flesh. She felt a young girl's twitter of lust, nothing more, and it was not a twitter that was becoming in a woman of her sixty-eight years.

Hang on, her eyes widened wildly. What was that in her stomach? That queer feeling of churning? It took her a moment to identify it and when she did, Magda clutched her bag tightly under one arm and brought her thoughts under control: she was in a church, after all. Butterflies. No! She wasn't having any of it. She was well and truly over all that at her age and she urged the fluttering to keep quiet. Despite what the cards had said about a potential romance, she'd realised some years ago that those heady days of lust and passion were over for her. A new friend, however, a new friend she would like. Especially a friend with a bike. She'd have to butter him up with a compliment or two and talk him into it. How likely was it that he'd brought a spare helmet?

'Mrs Howard,' a woman in her late middle-ages, indistinguishable from hundreds of others, addressed her and Magda grimaced inwardly. 'I didn't expect to see you here, my dear.'

'Mrs Beers,' the 'old witch' replied, knowing that was exactly what the baker thought of her. Old Witch indeed. 'How very good of you to put on such a fine spread for the vicar's guests, and freshly baked this morning, I'm told. You know I'm here as a special guest, of course? I'm his person of a minority faith.'

'Faith? Is that what they're calling it these days?' Mrs Beers mumbled through gritted teeth, making sure she wouldn't be overhead and at the same time keeping her plastic smile firmly in place in case anyone was watching. 'I thought running around in the buff was called a public disturbance.'

'And I thought your left-over sausage rolls were the most vile and tasteless thing I have ever put in my mouth. Freshly baked, my backside.' There, Magda smugly replied, take that for a witty retort. Mrs Beers held out her hand and the two women gave one another a smiling hand-shake and Magda reflected that she'd really had enough of playing nicely with the old bag. But being the only 'old witch' in the village meant that while Mrs Beers, who was chairperson of the Wilveringham Women's Group, could get away with outright hostility from time to time, Magda was nearly always under scrutiny and had to be seen to be doing the right thing. She was grateful that her regular clients brought new customers to her through word of mouth and though she would never be rich, she managed to get by after a fashion through selling her potions and lotions and reading the cards.

With Mrs Beers wandering off to fawn over a visiting lady vicar, Magda introduced herself to a couple of the other guests, shaking hands, introducing herself and gradually working her way closer to Pan.

'Hello, good to see so many people here.' She said, at last close enough to draw his attention away from the cluster of other guests. 'I wonder if you could tell me if there's an agenda this afternoon or is it a meet and greet kind of thing? I'm afraid I was called in at the last minute this morning and didn't get all of the details.' She couldn't help noticing, as she spoke, that he smelled very slightly of engine oil and patchouli.

'Not sure, I'm afraid I'm in the same boat as you.' He put down his cup of tea and held his hand out to her. 'Pleased to meet you, by the way. I'm Stuart Redman.' Her Pan, Mr Tall and Beardy smiled, looking at her t-shirt.

'Oh that's brilliant!' She nearly squealed out loud in delight but stopped herself in time.

His eyes lit up and crinkled in the corners but it was a little difficult to tell for certain what expression he was really making underneath the great white bush that covered almost his entire face. What would it be like to run her fingers through that significant

20

amount of chin hair? The very thought of it made her eyes boggle so Magda blinked rapidly to clear it from her mind.

They shook hands, his large strong one completely dwarfing her dainty, earth-stained one. 'Pleased to meet you Stuart Redman, I'm Frannie Goldsmith.' She chuckled loudly. 'You must be a fan, too?' She pointed at her Stephen King t-shirt, holding a drape of crimson scarf out of the way, waiting for Pan to start laughing along with her little joke. For an unexpected encounter she hadn't even really wanted until she felt those butterflies in her stomach, this was going quite well.

Until suddenly it wasn't. Pan dropped her hand and shook his head, taking his big blue eyes away from the Stephen King motif across her ample chest. 'Like I haven't heard that one before. My name is actually Stuart Redman.' Mr Tall and Beardy Pan was not laughing, so Magda shut her mouth quickly before another guffaw could escape and embarrass her even more. She tilted her head, eyes wide, asking the question with a raised brow. He nodded, lips tight. 'Stuart Redman, really.'

Well done, Magda, messed that one up didn't you? You and your supposed wit! She opened her mouth to try and fumble her way through an apology but, Stuart Redman or not, her handsome Pan was already walking away. Curse her wretched t-shirt! She ought to take it off right now and chuck it in the bin, her bruised pride along with it. She resisted the temptation. As much as she would enjoy putting on a minor scandal, Magda didn't want to give Mrs Beers the satisfaction – ammunition like that would be enough to last her a good six months or more. Magda pushed her way through the people who suddenly seemed to be crowding around her and headed out of the hall with her weighty hand-bag, wondering how rude it would seem if she took a break outside for fresh air this soon.

'Ah, there you are, hurry up; this way!' Granger stepped into her path and took hold of her arm, leading her back into the hall. 'Did you meet the druid then? Very lovely man, Mr Redman, despite the beard, isn't he?'

21

So not only was he a biker, he was also a fellow pagan, a druid no less, and she'd managed to offend the poor man the moment she opened her mouth. Just her luck. She would have to console herself with a wee dram of mead but even that would have to wait because Granger was dragging her to stand beside him and he coughed loudly to get the attention of the gathering.

'Thank you all for coming this afternoon,' the vicar began, 'as this is only the first part of our inter-parish inter-faith event, today is purely a social occasion. I'd like to invite you all to our orchard next Friday for a barbecue and bonfire party. Donations of prizes for a raffle will be welcome, the proceeds of which will go toward the air ambulance fund. My old friend Magda Howard, our resident Pagan, will lead us in a short blessing to the apple trees which have provided us with such an abundant harvest this year. Mrs Howard?'

'Oh, well, as I'm sure you all know, apples are seen as a treasured and sacred fruit in many religions so I'll be delighted to lead you in an apple tree blessing of course, a good old-fashioned wassail.' Magda smiled and looked around at the surprised faces of the crowd who obviously hadn't heard about the planned barbecue and blessing. Magda hadn't heard about it either but she was used to being put on the spot by Granger and besides, the barbecue might be just the opportunity she needed to make an apology to Pan, Stuart Redman, always assuming he would be there.

'I'll get you back for this, you know.' She leaned over and whispered under her breath to the vicar, who had a cheeky glint in his eyes. As he walked away and left Magda to her own devices, a gentle looking young man wearing a yarmulke approached her.

'I'm Bram,' he said shyly. 'I'm doing a piece on interfaith connections for my theology degree, I wonder if you'd mind me asking a few questions about your religion, Mrs Howard?'

'Not at all, Bram.' Magda allowed him to lead her to the refreshments and pour her some coffee. She enjoyed talking about her beliefs and learning about those of others so she was happy to oblige but it didn't escape her notice that Pan was nowhere in sight. She turned back to Bram and nodded happily, it would be nice to have the company of an intelligent new acquaintance for a little while. Some things were meant to be and some things, she resigned herself to it, some things were not and that was all there was to it.

*

Sal poked about with her walking stick in the thick undergrowth and bushy mess of scrubby plants that sprang up alongside the canal towpath and wondered if all the mugwort was over with for the season. She smoothed a hand over her lower abdomen as a hard cramp of period pain crept through her. The pain passed quickly and Sal focused on her foraging again, disappointed with herself for leaving it so late. Mugwort was a well-known tonic for menstrual disorders and she had been having a hard time with her cycle for several months now. She really ought to have been foraging for quite a few things over the last few months but never seemed to find the time. An erratic career, if she could even call it that, doing administration work through a temping agency, hadn't left her with much spare time. Moving from one work place to the next every month or two wasn't easy and Sal found it draining, especially her most recent assignment. Her free time out of work was normally spent helping Gran stirring her brews, blending creams, crushing herbs or sterilising glass bottles and there was always a string of visitors coming to the house for tarot readings.

She pulled her stick out of the bushes and gave up her hunt for the elusive plant, rambling slowly along with only her thoughts for company. Not even a bumble-bee or a butterfly stirred in the air at this time of year and there were no water birds on the canal today. She supposed she ought to be content with her own company and usually she was, but today she could have done with a bit of friendship to take her mind off things. Maybe she ought to have gone with Gran to the church event but although she could cope with Reverend Granger in small doses and knew his faux conversion attempts were exactly that, she had never felt comfortable with him in the same way that her gran did. There was nothing wrong with him, she mused, and he had been a good friend to her gran for a long time, but he was constantly badgering her about getting a steady job and settling down. Sal was not sure if either of those things were what she wanted. She didn't object to the idea of working for a living and working hard for it, if the right job came along, but it never seemed to. One meaningless, unproductive temping post after another for two years now. She was fed up with the mountains of paperwork, filing documents and doing accounts for a living and wanted to do something worthwhile, something that mattered. The job with the women's shelter had still been office based, but at least she'd been working for a place which helped people who really needed it. It was the first assignment in a long while that had left Sal feeling anything like job satisfaction and she was upset that a lack of funding to support the shelter had brought about its closure.

This train of thought was not getting her anywhere and she returned to her search for mugwort. Teasels, blackberry branches, grasses and reeds grew up at the side of the path creating a diaspora of wild and luscious foliage. Most of it was over now, turning brown. Like my life; Sal shook her head. What would Gran be saying to her right now? The plants are not dead, just conserving their energy, waiting and plotting and putting down roots. Should she be planning ahead herself, then? Planning what? There was no plan, no clear idea of what she wanted to do for a living. Now twenty-three and with no qualifications to speak of, Sal had fallen into an office job years ago and had drifted from one dull position to the next with nothing to distinguish between them and nothing to show for it. She hadn't even managed to make any real friends in all that time, except for Sophie. Sophie and Sal and that one long, hot summer's night last year when the sweet night scent of honeysuckle filled their lungs and they had sat giggling and tipsy in the willow garden seat, getting to know each other, getting themselves giddy and getting excited and Sal's fingers entwined with delight in soft silken strands as she plaited Sophie's blonde hair, the two of them smiling and laughing until Sal had made a mistake and then… Then Sophie had vanished from her life as quickly as she had come into it and it was as though they had never met.

Sal picked up a little speed on her walk. Dandelion. Perhaps if there was no mugwort to be had, she could at least dig about for some dandelion root to take home for Gran. The dotty woman loved it as a coffee substitute. Sal grimaced every time Gran drank the vile stuff, she preferred a decent Costa Rican latte any day of the week. She'd been introduced to high standards of coffee by Soph – by a friend. Nothing more than a friend.

The autumn was drawing on towards winter and Samhain was only a few weeks away now, though there were still some bright red rowan berries clinging tightly to a few branches. Sal heard Gran's voice in the back of her mind, telling her to plant her own roots and seek out the nourishment in the earth. Start growing yourself, my love! Focusing on herself would have to wait; for now all she wanted to focus on growing was a decent job doing that elusive good work she craved. If she had half of Gran's talent with herbs, she would do something similar but alas, she didn't have a flair for it and besides, she wanted a more secure source of income after years of living without one. Sal paced along the towpath, heading back to the grim reality of mundane life with every step and each time she looked at the rough grasses and wild flowers in the hedges, a pale golden leaf would catch the light of the late afternoon sun and it would gleam like gold. Like the honey coloured hair of a woman she had once wanted to kiss.

*

Jasmine lay back in a bath full of bubbles, her face resting in a haze of steam and a mashed avocado face mask. Her tears made tracks in the green coating and slid down her cheeks, splashing with quiet pops into the bath where it mingled with the rosemary scented water which was now turning cold. She hadn't intended to come back home, not really. She had nowhere else to turn to and the old saying is true: home is the place where they have to take you in when you turn up on the doorstep with nothing but an overnight case and another disastrous relationship to escape from. At least it was true for her; her mother Magda, village witch, busy-body and all-round do-gooder, wouldn't turn away anyone in need, least of all her own daughter.

Jasmine felt guilty at taking advantage of Magda yet again and the soft pop of tears falling from her face increased. She was no good at being an adult; even Sally seemed to be doing better at it than she was. Sally was one of the reasons she kept on coming home when she found herself in trouble. Keeping in touch regularly had never come naturally to her and it was only when things fell apart that Jasmine was filled with a sudden need to know that her daughter was all right, even if nothing else was. The last week with her abusive excuse of a man had been overwhelming and when she was swamped a few days ago with a nagging feeling in the pit of her stomach that Sally was grieving, she knew she had to come back. Leaving Paul had been one of the hardest things she'd ever done and she told herself she was only going to be away overnight because of that psychic twinge about Sally. If that was really the case though, she knew deep down inside that she would have packed a smaller bag.

She would phone her branch manager on Monday and see if she could get compassionate leave. She didn't look forward to explaining her situation but Mr James was one of those employers who was determined to be a supportive manager. She could also ask about the possibility of a transfer somewhere nearby. Living in the village for any significant length of time didn't hold the slightest appeal for her but it was a good move for now. Of course, the fact that Magda still lived in the old house didn't hurt. Jasmine found the village stifling and dull, she needed the brightness and bustle of a large city and thrived on it, but there was nevertheless something comforting about coming home. The old house was the only real home she had ever known and when Sally's father had died, Magda took them both in happily and they had spent a couple of good years there together, grieving, recovering and starting to live again.

Then Jasmine's soul began to stir and wander so she went back to work at the bank in Stoke for a year and lived in the city itself for six months with the very lovely Philip who she had met at the branch. After that, Jasmine started transferring to branches throughout the country as her life and her loves dictated. A free spirit, she'd thought, not tied down to anyone or anything, not even when she was with Philip, brief though that had been in the end. She developed a horrible knack of choosing poor boyfriends after that. But it was Paul who really changed me, she thought now, sinking deeper into the tub and letting the hot water and the bubbles slip over her face until she was submerged completely and the avocado floated off her face.

She was broken, utterly. She didn't know if she could be repaired but she had to try because he had dragged her so far down that the only way now was up. The strains of an old pop song drifted into her head and Jasmine quickly started singing it out loud to make sure this tiny, short moment of hope didn't run away before she could revel in it. 'For me and me now, the only way is up, baby!'

She lifted herself out of the bath and wrapped up in a worn lilac towel.

'Honestly, mother,' she said out loud, 'are you still so poor selling herbs that you can't afford a decent towel?' Jasmine was not ashamed of talking to herself. It was answering back that she was embarrassed about so she kept that down to a minimum. A hot soak and a long think seemed to have done her good, the rosemary had eased her aching back and the bruises would soon fade. No looking back, she had promised herself yesterday as she'd crammed as many knickers, dresses and shoes into the bag as she could fit, this was a fresh start. Again. This time she would make it work. After this many years of heart-break, she was determined that she would make it work.

Feeling more uplifted and happier than she had in years, Jasmine shrugged into her dressing gown and put a hand on the bathroom door to open it. A noise. What was that? A thud. A single noise that sounded like something being knocked over downstairs. All her fear and goose bumps came rushing back and Jasmine called out loudly. 'Who's there? Is someone here?'

There was no answer. Perhaps Sally had returned from her walk or was it her mother coming back from church? The ridiculous notion of her mother going to church amused her but not enough to belay her nerves as the prospect of somebody unknown inside the house loomed in front of her.

She plucked up her courage and cautiously turned the doorknob and went through the door. She started downstairs, calling out another loud hello. Shouldn't have done that, she supposed, in case it was Paul coming to fetch her back but the chances were slim. He wouldn't know where to come, surely? He had never been here with her, not once in the four years they had been together. Standing at the threshold of the kitchen, Jasmine heard the faintest tinkle of a bell. At least she thought she heard it. When she went into the kitchen there was an overturned jar of herbs on the dining table, gently rocking back and forth as if it had only just been spilled. A slight chip had come off one edge and Jasmine picked it up, puzzled.

'Judy!' But it couldn't be Judy; Sally's cat with its tinkling collar, because Judy was six feet under and had been since the previous night.

Jasmine checked through the whole house systematically. All the doors and windows were tightly closed and there was no sign of a stray cat or a trapped bird flapping about that could have tipped over the jar. The house was old, it made its own unique noises as old houses are bound to do and Jasmine told herself, out loud, to stop being so paranoid. The noise was nothing more than the ancient wooden floorboards creaking and the jar had been blown over by a gust of wind.

'But that bell,' she looked at the jar as if it was going to answer her back, 'now that is curious.'

CHAPTER THREE

'Pass the sauce Mum.' Sal reached over the table, holding out her hand. She was finding this all a little bit strange. Like old times, but strange nevertheless to have all three of them together, sitting down to dinner at Gran's large table as if it was something they did every day. The conversation seemed to flow well enough, though that may have had more to do with Magda's home-made blackcurrant wine than it had to do with them all being at ease with each other. Having her mum living with her at Gran's again made for a slightly strained household but there was a large part of her that was enjoying it, even if Mum did have a lot of lost time to make up for.

'So it didn't go well then?' Jasmine asked, picking up a jar of mint sauce.

'No, not mint.' Sal shook her head and a new jar was thrust at her. Cranberry? It would have to do, though it was a month or two early in the year for cranberry. 'Is this left over from last Yule?'

'I was mortified,' Magda continued her story. 'And after that, the vicar only went and got me up front of everyone and announced some wassailing barbecue next weekend which he wants me to lead!' Gran was in her element, Sal noted, holding court while she recounted the day's events and passed a massive variety of dishes full of steaming hot food around the table, making sure everyone had a little bit of everything. 'Not that he called it a wassail but still, fancy that!'

'You mean he didn't ask you first?' Jasmine wanted to know, taking a dish of potatoes and piling the vegetables onto her plate. 'What will you do?'

'I'll have to do it, I suppose. I couldn't really say no, could I? Not in front of all those people.' Magda held her head a little bit higher, as if some huge honour had been bestowed upon her. 'Besides, it'll be fun.'

'Besides,' Sal teased, 'your handsome biker might be there, eh, Gran?' She earned a stern look for that little comment. 'You do know you've gone red?'

'How do you know he was handsome? I never said.'

'You didn't need to, Mum.' Jasmine raised her eyebrows. 'It's written all over your face.'

'Oh stop it, you two wind-up merchants.' Magda scolded lightly. 'Honestly, you're acting like a couple of teenage girls. Here, one of you finish off the last bit of broccoli.' She held out a serving dish and Sal reached for it but her mother was quicker. Perhaps too quick. She'd noticed that her mum looked as if she'd lost weight but could she really be that hungry?

'Sure you've got enough there, Mum?' Sal raised her eyebrows and Jasmine looked at her plate in mild embarrassment to see it piled high with enough food for two, possibly even three. Suddenly Jasmine dropped her cutlery and started to cry in loud, choking sobs, her hands flying up to cover her face.

'It's all right, I didn't mean it. I'm sorry.' Sal was bewildered; she had been expecting tears, plenty of them, from her mother at some point but not over broccoli. She pushed her own plate aside and hutched over to put an arm around her mother. It felt awkward and uncomfortable to be consoling her mother, shouldn't it be the other way around? She looked at Magda for guidance.

'What's this really about, love?' Magda stood up and came around the table to sit next to her daughter and take over, rubbing Jasmine's shoulders and patting Sal's hand in reassurance. Sal breathed a silent whisper of relief. 'Come on, let it all out.'

'He never let me fill my plate.' Jasmine cried out the words, barely audible among the noise of tears. 'I know it sounds stupid, but I swear, if I put on a pound of weight he – he, oh! I just couldn't do anything I wanted to. I wasn't allowed to see my friends, staying late at work was a definite no-no, he made me stop wearing make-up unless I was out with him. He controlled everything I did. And one time we,' she broke down again and the sobs wracked through her body. Sal, still wrapping her mother up in her arms, felt every vibration and realised with a shock just how very thin she was. She shot a worried look at Magda who shushed her concerns with a finger-tip over her lips, out of sight above Jasmine's head.

'You don't have to tell us, my love.' Magda made soothing hushing sounds and held Jasmine close, wrapping Sal into the embrace as well and they quietly, gently rocked Jasmine, soothing her back and forth, back and forth. Grandmother, daughter, granddaughter, all three of them feeling the pain and the shame and willing it to get better. And it would get better, Sal was sure of it. As soon as her mother shook off the last vestigial hurts and humiliations that man had inflicted on her, things would turn around and she'd see her mother become a strong woman, perhaps more so than ever. Sal and Magda had seen it happen before, time and again, after Jasmine returned home from one broken relationship or the next and she would take a few weeks to pull herself together again. This time she seemed worse and it would take her longer but she would get there, wouldn't she? My mum is broken, Sal thought sadly and hugged her tighter. Broken into a hundred fragmented pieces that needed to be found and glued back together. Then coated with varnish and kept safe. Sal wanted desperately to help, to be the glue that fixed her mother back together again.

It was Jasmine who broke it off, struggling free of the enveloping arms of her family. She breathed deeply and picked up a napkin to wipe her face dry. 'Oh dear, I'm sorry.'

Sal shook her head. 'You don't need to apologise, not to us.'

'It was our second anniversary and I hadn't got on his nerves as much that week, I suppose.' Jasmine was interrupted by a tutting noise from both her mother and her daughter. 'So he drove us to Chicco's, this gorgeous Italian place, and I dressed up nicely, make-up, good shoes. Paul said I looked lovely and we sat down with the menu but when the waitress came to take our order he asked for a plain salad for me when I'd already said I wanted something else. I feel so stupid for letting him get away with it.'

'Control freak.' Magda huffed. She tucked her long grey hair out of the way behind her ears, revealing the plastic pixie ear tips she liked to wear to annoy and bewilder Mrs Beers. 'If I ever get my hands on him…' Magda left that thought hanging in the air and though it was out of character for her gran to ever wish harm on anyone, Sal knew exactly what the dotty old witch would like to do to him and she would be the one holding him down if she was given half the chance.

'I tried to change my order but he found my foot under the table and ground at me with his heel till the skin broke and my foot bled. I couldn't say anything; we were in public for crying out loud. He always ordered my food for me after that. He reckoned I was putting on weight – I wasn't – but it was easier to go along with it, like everything else.'

'Oh Mum,' Sal wished she'd kept her mouth shut about the plate. 'I had no idea, I'm so sorry.'

'It's all right, Sally.' Jasmine gave her a thin smile. 'You didn't know. I'm the muppet who put up with it, aren't I?'

'Well, you're shot of him now love and you're nothing but skin and bones.' Magda patted her hand and passed her a jug of gravy. 'So eat your heart out.'

Sal had one last squeeze of her mother's hand and then listened to Gran talking in that calm, soothing manner of hers which left anyone listening to it feeling as if they were in the company of their best friend and confidante. She let the conversation drift over her while she ate and smiled, adding in the odd word here and there as the tears dried up and the food was gradually demolished.

'When was the last time you rode one?' Jasmine asked, moving onto cheesecake for dessert and pouring herself another glass of blackcurrant wine.

'Not since my twenties, I think.' Magda replied. 'I must say I rather fancied it when I saw that beast of a bike outside the church but it's not to be. Even if Stuart Redman is at the apple orchard wassail, I don't think he'll be offering me a ride any time soon after my stupid joke.'

'You've got all week to come up with a good apology, Gran.'

Sal said, catching up with the conversation.

Magda shook her head. 'No, I shall be trying to come up with some tasty concoctions for the wassail bowls. Besides, he scarpered as soon as the vicar nominated me for his shenanigans. If that's not a clear signal, I don't know what is.'

'Well, I think that's a shame.' Jasmine said. 'One of us needs to have a bit of fun in her life and it's not going to be Sally, is it? Sorry to be so blunt, Sally, but you are the only twenty-three year old recluse I know.'

'Mum!'

'No, I'm getting tipsy now, so there's no stopping me.' Jasmine held up a half-empty wine bottle and topped up her glass. 'All I mean Sal, is that you haven't exactly got a very busy social life, have you? No fun on my agenda at the moment either: I felt really positive and determined this afternoon but I still need gluing back together, just like you said Sally, so it has to be your Gran.'

'I never said anything about glue.' Sal began, but her mother was on a roll.

'I hope your handsome Pan is there, on his Harley, and I hope he whisks you off into the distance and sweeps you off your feet. We will both be happy to see at least one of the Howard women enjoying herself.'

'And I didn't say I thought of him as Pan.' Magda and Sal exchanged a look between them but neither of them knew quite what to make of Jasmine's psychic twinges. They were always very careful never to bring the subject up with Jasmine as it seemed to scare her a little. Gran had once told Sal that having a mother as a witch was what drove Jasmine away from the village; she hated the bullying and name-calling at school and the furtive glances from people across the street as well as the whispers and the rumours. Sal could understand that and had suffered much the same herself but it had the opposite effect on her, it drove a wedge between her and her peers that left her feeling closer to Gran, the only person she could talk to about it. Without any sports to occupy her, no school friends or hobbies

33

and living in a small village, Sal had grown up with time on her hands and she filled it with learning about her gran's herbs and potions, finding all of it fascinating. She was impressed with the way people would nod respectfully at Gran a week or so after a visit. A faintly heard word of thanks or a bunch of flowers left on the doorstep spoke to Sal of valuable work, something done with pure and honest intentions to help people and make them feel better, either physically with the creams, teas and salves, or emotionally with a tarot-come-counselling session. Gran made people better; Mum didn't understand that and rebelled against the gentle witchery of the family to build herself a good career in the mundane and acceptable world. Such a shame that she always went and spoiled other aspects of her life with her bad taste in men.

'I said I'd like you to help me clear things away Sally.' Jasmine, still a little red eyed and now somewhat unsteady on her feet, held out an empty glass serving dish and Sal blinked rapidly.

'Of course, sorry.' She took the dish and the three of them went to work, swiftly cleaning and clearing away pots and plates.

'Oh no, look at this!' Magda's voice held a note of dismay and Sal turned to see her holding an enamel jar with a slight chip on one edge. 'How did that happen?'

'Oh yes,' Jasmine cried out, 'I forgot to tell you about that.' She relayed the incident and Sal listened intently.

'Judy.' Tears pricked at her eyes when her mum told them about hearing a cat's bell. 'Do you think it's her, Gran?'

'Who knows, Sal, my girl?' Magda gently placed the jar back where it belonged on the shelf beside the dried rosemary and a tin of bay leaves. 'Weird damn creatures, cats. It wouldn't surprise me in the least.'

'Do you think you will get another one, Sally?' Her mother asked. 'I didn't mean to pressure you into it, with the gift I mean.'

'Mum, Judy has barely gone cold.' She suddenly felt angry and frustrated. Her mother was like an alien creature who didn't know how to behave among humans. It wasn't her fault, though, Sal told herself. No, the poor woman's been manipulated and controlled for so long she can't think clearly for herself anymore. Sal calmed herself down and thought of something supportive to say instead of dredging up an argument.

'I appreciate you thinking of me and getting me a collar for a new cat.' She said. 'I do miss having a cat around the place.'

'Gosh, is that the time?' Magda said loudly. 'Nice night for a little moon gazing before bed, eh, my loves?'

'Not for me,' Jasmine indicated her empty glass. 'I may have had a splodge too much of the old vino, so I'll say goodnight.'

Magda and Sal linked arms and went into the garden, leaving Jasmine to make her way upstairs. The night was chilly with the promise of rain and wind and Sal let go of Magda's arm to sit by herself at the sad mound of earth she had covered in sea shells and pretty pebbles and a polythene wrapped photograph of her with Judy, her feline familiar. Oh Judy, my beautiful cat, I do miss you. I still haven't found a new job and the temping agency are a joke; Mum's come back home with her head hanging in shame once again and I think Gran's going to get a motorbike, at her age, I tell you! What should I do, Judy?

'Penny for them?' Magda called to her softly and Sal joined her on the garden seat, the willow arbour adorned with sweet smelling honeysuckle.

'Just thinking about Judy.' She said, shuffling her scruffy boots on the ground. 'And jobs and Mum and all that kind of stuff.'

'Ah, yes.' Magda sighed. 'All that kind of stuff. Well, the moon is waning, Sal, so it's a good time to get rid of it all. A worried soul doesn't do anybody any good.' And with that the old woman went over to the stone bird bath in the centre of the garden that she and Sal used as an outdoor altar and took a small plastic tub out of her cardigan pocket. She tilted her head to Sal, gesturing for her to come over.

The container held a mixture of herbs and dried flowers. Not quite sure what she was supposed to be doing with it, Sal delved her fingers into the mix, picking out a small handful. She sniffed it, cautiously because she never knew what her gran could have put in there, but all she got was a hint of rose and the general odour of dried greenery. She sprinkled it on the grass around the altar, walking widdershins, the direction of banishing, and looked up at the moon, still almost round but now fading on one side. She let the mood take over and shut her eyes, standing tall and breathing deeply, raising her arms to the glowing orb and calling out in a loud, clear voice.

'Oh shining lady of the moon and tides, I call to you now. Let me be rid of all those things in my life I do not need, make way for new inspirations, new dreams and goals. Lady bring me dreams of my destiny, my purpose.' She lost track of it now, not sure what she was supposed to be asking for, just knowing that she needed guidance, especially for a new job. She stood silently for a few minutes thinking about that and asking for peace of mind for her mother too. A gust of cold wind blew rose petals and dried herbs in a miniature tornado a few inches above the grass and Sal watched it dance and flutter and settle again as the breeze died down. Her eyes widened and she dared a quick look over at Gran, meeting her eyes.

'Nothing magical about that, lass.' Magda said simply. 'Just as a dream is sometimes only a dream, sometimes a breeze is only a breeze.'

*

'So you haven't got anything for me this week? Nothing at all?' Sal's pen hovered over her notebook expectantly but all it had made were doodles in each corner. 'Right. Yes, Mrs Brookes, no, no, that's all right. Thanks anyway.'

She put down the pen and closed her notebook. She would have slammed it shut in annoyance but it was only a small paper-back book so it wouldn't have added any drama to the moment. If Mrs Brookes couldn't find her another position with the temping agency soon she'd be out of options and out of cash.

'I applied for twelve jobs in the last fortnight, Gran. Twelve.' She sidled over to the large white marble table top in the kitchen where her gran was preparing batches of chamomile moisturisers and comfrey ointments. 'Not one interview from any of them and the agency is next to useless lately. What am I going to do?'

Magda kept quiet, stirring her pot of greasy green liquid, sending a puff of steam into the air. 'Gran?' Sal said, waving her hand in front of her gran's face. 'I mean it, I haven't been paid since last month and I know you say we'll manage but how? I can't keep sponging money from you all, let's face it, you barely break even most of the time.' Sal pulled a tray of glass jars and bottles in assorted sizes out of the oven, using thick gloves to tip the water inside them down the sink and then setting them aside to cool.

'Sally Howard,' Magda turned off the heat under the pan she was stirring and let the wooden spoon splosh back into the massive jam pan full of green oil, 'can you please put some trust in the Old Ones and be positive for once?'

Sal always knew she was in for a lecture when her gran called her Sally. Her mum was normally the only one who did that. 'Don't start.' She tried desperately to stave off the impending hour of dullness she was about to endure. 'I'm seriously worried and we need to talk about it. We can't pay the bills with fresh air and free potions, you've got to start charging people properly, Gran, and I have to spend every spare minute filling out application forms because the Old Ones won't give me a job if I sit back on my laurels and do nothing. I haven't got time to sit here sterilising bottles all day without getting paid.'

'As you say, dear.' Magda said, turning off the stove top and lining up rows of gleaming glass jars and bottles. 'Here, hold this funnel for me. Put that muslin over it, that's right, here we go.'

Together they managed to get the green oily liquid strained into the spotless bottles and scooped soft creamy lotions into jars. The next hour was spent screwing on lids, mopping up spillages and putting things away. As they worked hard together to tidy up and clean, Sal found a small supply of lady's mantle and wondered aloud if that might help her cramping pains. Magda immediately went into a flurry of action, picking out other herbs to go with it.

'I spent ages trying to find some mugwort on the canal bank yesterday.'

'Yes, you could use mugwort or you could have white dead nettle, yarrow, evening primrose and a host of other plants too. Why didn't you just ask me?'

'I don't like to create yet more work for you to do.' Sal said. 'Besides, the walk did me good and it got me out of going to church yesterday.'

A few minutes later, Magda handed Sal a full jar of the mixture she'd concocted.

'Make this into a tea and have it two or three times a day when you need it.'

'What's it going to be called?' Sal always liked the names Gran came up with for her remedies. 'Perioditea?'

'Ooh yes!' Magda was delighted and clapped her hands with a giggle. 'That's perfect. Perioditea.' She scribbled the name and the list of herbs she'd used onto a label and stuck it proudly across the front of the jar.

'If this works you could make a fortune, Gran.' In the back of her mind where she couldn't see it, something started to happen. She didn't know it yet, but it was the start of something big.

'A fortune, Sal?' Gran snorted. 'Ha! Chance would be a fine thing, I'd be very grateful of a fortune right about now.'

'Honestly, there are hundreds of women who would kill for this. You'd be onto a winner.' Sal mused, wondering how she might make her own fortune if she didn't find a job quickly. She mulled it over while she worked hard with Magda to clean and pack away the vast array of spoons, trays, unused bottles, the seven pestles and mortars, the blender and the grinder. The kitchen was spick and span when they finished and all that remained was laboriously hand writing the labels for everything. As she wrote slowly in her best hand-writing, she heard a small scuffling sound coming from the desk in the corner where she kept her laptop. She looked up, half expecting to see her cat turning around three times before curling up on top of the printer where she sometimes liked to sleep. Sal shut out the memory but now that her attention was drawn to it, she wondered why Gran didn't just print off labels for her jars.

'It would look more, well, you know. More professional.' She told Magda. 'And think of the time it would save. You could put sigils or runes in the corner of each label, Gran, or little pictures of specific herbs for each remedy with the text over the top, it'd look awesome. You could even use – shock horror – different colours.'

'Could I? Hmm.' Magda pulled a face. 'I suppose I shall have to give it a try then, but you know me and technology. Hint, hint.'

'Really?' Sal was thrilled. 'I'll finish these for now and next time I'll come up with something on the computer and if you like it, we'll see how it looks in print.' Something shifted again then, deep inside the core of her being. She didn't know what it was, she couldn't see the shape of it yet but she felt it now. A stirring, a pop, a chain reaction of – of what, she couldn't say yet. It left her with a serious look on her face and a slow pause of movement, a still and quiet time between times.

'Mum.' Jasmine's voice interrupted the moment before Sal could understand or really even grab hold of that shift inside of her. 'Can I come in?'

'What ever do you mean? Of course you can.'

'You used to tell me off if I stayed in the kitchen while you worked.'

'Yes, when you were a pesky little brat who wanted to taste everything and didn't know the difference between poisonous plants and healing ones.' Magda huffed at her. 'Do something useful and put the kettle on, we're just about done for today but I'll have to chase you both out later. I've got Mrs Brown-Smythe coming over soon for a bit of something to help her husband's chesty cough.'

'You should just open a shop and keep proper hours, Mum.' Jasmine said without thinking. Sal frowned: there it was again. A twinge of something, a thought, an idea; a concept she couldn't quite hold on to. Something was brewing in there but now was not the time to go delving into it. 'I used to hate it when strangers kept knocking on the door at the weekend, or when I was trying to do homework after school.'

'Did you speak to your boss, Mum?' Sal could taste the hint of an argument on the air and decided to change the subject. They might be getting on well with each other on the surface, but she dreaded the day when the big row that was looming finally bobbed up to be aired.

'Unfortunately, work are not as understanding as I would like. I've got two week's compassionate leave and if I want to go back after that they've got a position in Hastings. If I don't take that, it means going back to my branch in Manchester which is obviously not an option. I don't want to move anywhere until I'm, well, I won't say better, but a bit more normal at any rate, so it looks like I'm going to be out of work.'

'Welcome to the club.' Sal sighed and shook her head. 'Sorry to hear it. What will you do now?'

'I don't know.' Jasmine looked lost and haunted, a worried expression on her face. 'I only planned far enough ahead to drive here and get away from that piece of dirty scum. I'll have to see if I can get something else, maybe one of the other banks in Stoke will have an assistant manager's position I can apply for. It'll probably mean a pay cut but I've got some savings set by to tide me over, so at least I can support myself for a while and pay a few bills while I'm here.'

'Good girl!' Magda beamed and patted her on the shoulder. Sal was pleased to hear it too, it was one of her grandmother's best pieces of worldly advice: always have a running-away fund that your partner doesn't know about.

'There is something else though, Mum,' Jasmine continued. Sal sighed, with a mother like hers, this came as no surprise. She waited anxiously, picking at her fingernails where dirt from the plants and herbs had seeped into the skin.

'Paul texted me again this morning, telling me to come home, I expected that. But I got another message from one of the counter staff at work, Erica. She said he's been into the branch asking after me. She didn't tell him anything but still…'

'Jasmine,' Magda rolled up her sleeves all the way up to her elbows and her eyes became narrow slits. She took a long drag on her e-cig and exhaled slowly. 'If that man thinks for a second he's coming here to drag you away, he's got another thing coming. We shall see to it that he never even steps foot over the threshold.'

Sal's gaze flitted nervously from one woman to the next, her skin prickling slightly and she sipped the last, cold dregs of her perioditea. Her mother was not going to like this one little bit. She knew what rolled up sleeves meant and she knew of old that particular look of determination on her gran's face. The last time the sleeves and the look had combined, it had been because somebody had had the dim-wittedness to smash Gran's car window and steal her bag from the passenger seat. The robber had been caught, tried and convicted, of that and several other local crimes, inside of a week. The old witch was about to get her mojo on.

She was about to get up to Magic.

CHAPTER FOUR

'Salt, spring water, rose thorns, yes, Gran, for the last time, I've got everything.'

'Well, just check again, would you?' Magda bossed. 'I can't be going backwards and forwards at my age if you've forgotten anything.'

'Your age?' Sal moaned. 'You were perky enough a few days ago when you wanted to get on the back of that bike.'

'Oh just bring the box, Sally.' Jasmine put a stop to the bickering. 'I can't believe I let you rope me into this, you know it's not my sort of thing. Mind you, if it were up to me, I'd be burning an effigy of the …'

'Bit drastic, burning poppets needs the right frame of mind, positive intentions. We'll stick with this for now.' Magda called from the doorway. 'Sal, there should be some mead in my hand-bag, can you fetch a bottle out for us, please?'

'Why have you got mead in your hand-bag?' Sal fetched her gran's bag and found two full, unopened bottles in there. 'Got it.' Fortunately Sal knew that although the old crone liked a drink, she was not at risk of becoming an alcoholic so she wasn't concerned at finding a secret stash. Unsure if her gran had plans for the second bottle, she decided to leave it in the bag for now.

Cold, thick rain fell in a heavy barrage and Sal pulled the hood of her cloak over her head and braved the weather, armed with a small array of ritual tools. 'I still don't know why this can't wait until the rain's passed over.' She had argued in favour of waiting till morning but her mum, if she was going to be doing this at all, wanted it done as quickly as possible. Sal had to admit that the thought of the slug turning up unannounced at the house gave her the creeps, so she braced herself for a good soaking and the three of them paraded around the perimeter of the house and garden in the middle of the night in the pouring rain. It could have been worse, she supposed, Gran could have insisted on them all being completely skyclad and that wouldn't have been pleasant in this weather. The old house was full of cloaks hanging from the back of nearly every door, stowed in cupboards or sometimes draping from the top of the banister rail amid the collection of flowing scarves and Sal had chosen one at random, slinging it on over the top of her jeans and a long-sleeved top. Sal had seen her mum glancing out of the window earlier and then grabbing a thick coat and putting her own cloak over the top of the coat, designer jeans and silk blouse. Sal wished she'd also had the foresight to put a coat on but settled for drawing the cloak around herself a little more tightly.

The house and garden were not overlooked at all, being right on the edge of the village, though the main row of houses on this road, which turned into the village high street a little farther along, was just visible. They were lucky to have such an ideal place for a traditional witch's cottage, close to local amenities while maintaining privacy for the most part. With fields at the back of their gardens and the canal running close by, the cottage was perfectly placed for all their needs. Her mother wouldn't see it that way, of course, she of the cities and bright lights and bustling social life and reliable broadband connections. Sal wondered how things might change in the house now that Mum had come back to recover. She seemed to be coping surprisingly well so far, though as far as Sal knew, she hadn't left the house on her own yet. Hopefully this protection spell would help her to feel less threatened.

Sal put the box down by the side of the stone altar and laid out her gran's ritual things. There was salt, local spring water, a dish of rose thorns and hawthorns, a small mirror and a pot of loose incense blended with dragon's blood and frankincense. Jasmine held an umbrella over the altar, Sal lit a charcoal disk and Magda mumbled something indecipherable while they waited for the charcoal to heat up.

'Can't you hurry it up a bit? I'm freezing.' Jasmine complained. She was treated to a glare from Magda. Sal took a pinch of incense and let it fall onto the glowing charcoal, instantly releasing clouds of fragrant smoke which caught and swirled under the umbrella. Magda tipped the salt into the water, stirred it with the tip of her athame and handed the censor of incense to Jasmine, holding it by the chains. Sal took the thorns and emptied them into a leather pouch, knotting it to a cord around her waist. Each of them had their part to play and with Magda leading the way, sweeping her besom as she went, they walked the perimeter of the grounds, encompassing house and garden, sweeping away anything unwanted, smudging the entry points, gates, doors and windows with the incense, and sprinkling the water. Magda intoned a protective chant while she walked slowly and the others took it up.

'Circle of protection, circle of reflection, a charm of protection against you, Paul Fox, a sacred boundary you may not cross.'

As they walked past each of the doors to the house, Sal knelt down to take a few thorns from the leather pouch and pushed them into the ground. She did it with determination and a clear image in her mind that a physical boundary was being forged, a barrier he wouldn't be able to pass through. Not wishing him ill, not causing him harm, just keeping him off their premises to keep her mother safe. The mirror was set just inside the covered porch outside the front door to reflect away negativity.

'We place this mirror as a charm against harm.' Magda said out loud. 'May the Goddess who watches over all women keep this place safe from all who would wish us ill.'

Pushing past trees and hedges, getting scratched by brambles and tripping over the hems of long cloaks, they navigated the grounds in the dark, getting wetter and wetter with each step. Despite Jasmine's best efforts, she had to ditch the umbrella in order to squeeze behind the tool shed and the incense went out, but still she followed Sally and Magda until they'd completed a full circuit of the entire property.

Sal's pouch was empty of thorns and her water bottle held only a few drops. She sprinkled the remains of it on the ground to soak into the grass along with the rain. Silently she held her hand out to her mum who passed her the censor of soggy incense to put back on the altar. She looked to her gran for a sign that they were finished; she hoped so, the hem of her cloak had soaked up muddy rain water and become heavy and cumbersome and she was cold and tired but it looked as if Magda wasn't done quite yet. The bottle of mead was still on the altar and Magda opened it, passing it to each of them in turn with a kiss and then she poured a little of it out on the earth.

'To the Old Ones, so mote it be!' Sal echoed the familiar phrase but her mother only muttered it under her breath.

'Join hands.' The old witch commanded and they did as she asked, raising arms high to the sky, faces revealed by fallen hoods to catch the last rays of dark moonlight and the last drops of rain. 'By all the power of earth and sea, by all the might of moon and sun, the spell is cast, our will is done, to this house he will not come.'

Sal repeated the phrase with her three times, felt herself being led slowly in a circle round the stone altar. She swayed with Magda as they circled, going with the flow of energy that was buzzing all around them and though her mother walked around with them, hands held still high in the air, Sal noticed her voice was quiet, her movements stifled, uncertain. At a cry from Magda, they dropped their hands and silently returned to the house and the lounge, where Sal shook off her drenched flip-flops and the damp cloak and sat down to warm up.

'This was a stupid idea,' Jasmine hissed at her, glancing to check if Magda was within earshot. 'I can't believe she dragged us out in this weather. Look at the state of my new jeans.'

Sal was surprised her mother had brought it up. 'Think yourself lucky it was raining or she might have insisted we do it skyclad.'

'She's half-mad, Sally,' Jasmine said seriously. 'Why on earth do you stay here?'

'I stay here for the same reason that you came back.' Every muscle in her face clenched up as she spoke in defence of her gran.

'She may not be conventional but that's a hell of a lot more fun than being normal, believe me. I'm happy here, Mum, and so would you be if you gave her half a chance. And the village too, it's got a charm of its own if you can see past the gossipy women's group.' Sal wasn't in love with village life but she still preferred living here to being cooped up in a city. Here she could be herself, be by herself, she could breathe and think and listen and just – just be.

Jasmine pulled off her cloak, an old one her mum had optimistically made for her years ago. She had very rarely worn it but nevertheless a comforting tang of incense clung to it, along with a few of Magda's long grey hairs. She threw it over the back of the sofa and sank down, willing the soft cushions to open up and swallow her, taking her away, far away.

'She's right, you know, Jasmine.' Magda startled them both and Sal made a little squeaking sound in fright. 'There's more to Wilveringham that you'd think. Sal, put the kettle on, would you please? I've got something herbal to soothe your nerves if you want it, Jasmine.'

'Thank you, Mum, but if I wanted herbal medicines I would have asked.'

'Hmm, suit yourself then.' Magda felt slighted but didn't rise to it. 'What was I saying? Oh yes, we've even got a yoga class now at the village hall on Fridays.'

Sal left them to it and headed to the kitchen where she busied herself with mugs, cocoa and marshmallows. She picked up a fresh tea-towel and dabbed with it at her soggy hair while the kettle boiled and in the quietness, her mind wandered back to her fruitless, endless job search. She just needed something worthwhile that paid a fair wage. Was that too much to ask for? The morning's newspaper was still on the kitchen table and she leafed through the pages absently, not really reading it but a few words caught her eyes. Premises to let, outskirts of Stoke, suitable for small retail, catering or similar business. She was no cook by any stretch of the imagination but the idea of running her own business sounded appealing. She couldn't see what that business might be but nevertheless, working for oneself had a certain allure – keeping your own hours, setting your own goals, being your own boss. Sal threw the paper onto the counter as the kettle started to whistle. You'd need a decent business head on your shoulders though, and that was something she definitely didn't have, even if the idea of running a shop was inspiring.

She put instant cocoa and hot water into mugs, stirred in cream and emptied a bag of marshmallows and some cookies onto the tray. No, she couldn't be cooped up behind a shop counter all day, she'd go insane. But, she thought, taking the tray into the lounge, there was an idea brewing. Something was definitely going on in the back of her brain if only she could just grasp it.

'Ooh, thanks love, here let me.' Magda took the tea tray off her hands, setting it down on the low coffee table. 'I could do with a bit of something else in mine, Sal.'

'Of course, how silly of me to forget.' Sal darted back to the kitchen and returned with a fresh bottle of Irish cream, pouring a generous measure into two of the mugs.

'Not for me.' Jasmine put a hand over her own mug. 'You know I don't really drink and that blackcurrant wine of your gran's the other night reminded me why.'

The cocoa went down well with a hint of alcohol but Sal could understand why her mother didn't drink much. She'd had more than her fair share of hangovers herself and despite the herbal pharmacy at her disposal, courtesy of Magda, she had never yet found a remedy that worked.

Sal sank back into the comfortable arm chair and felt her eyelids becoming heavy as the warm drink worked its way through her body. Voices drifted hazily around her and though she caught the odd word or two, she paid them no attention, content to let the sound wash over her in a nonsensical jumble of phrases. She closed her eyes and drifted into a dream, an incoherent, disjointed dream as they so often are.

A brush of fur against her fingers, a touch of ginger, the

sound of a tiny bell, the small frightened squeak of a young animal.

The touch of skin against her hands, the fragrant scent of lemon balm, warm skin, a satisfied sigh of relaxation, her hands kneading muscle.

A vibration of metal beneath her hands, the smell of worn leather, a sensation of motion seeming to glide through the air, jolting over a cobbled street, the thrumming noise of a motor in her ears.

A brush of fur against her fingers, wide green eyes, lavender oil, roaring engines, and a card turned over on a velvet covered table… the empress of the tarot.

And then a noise, a crying, mewling noise of loss and despair, the acrid aroma of something burning, a thunderous, metallic crashing noise. Sal couldn't see what caused the sound but she could see a woman sitting in a willow arbour, her hair like straw, like gold, like honey; bees buzzing around the honey but bees were bees and bees could make honey but they couldn't make money. In her dream she knew this, for the woman told her so. The woman stood up and walked away, lifted a finger and beckoned her. The woman wore a torn grey dress, she looked flimsy and sad. The woman's hair was black and short now, as black midnight and as short as a warm and sultry midsummer's night. She pointed to the horizon where pots and jars and bottles sat gleaming in the sunlight but Sal couldn't follow the woman, no matter how much she tried to, for she was chained to the seat and there was a lock in the chains that she couldn't pick. Sal was chained and she had no key. No key, no key… 'You have to find the key. Is it me or is it thee, or is it together that shall we be?'

Sal woke up alone and cold in the still of the night, slightly disturbed by something she had dreamed. She reached out instinctively to feel the warm fur of the cat who should be lying next to her, curling up in the crook of her bent knees. She found only a cold, damp patch of fabric beneath her fingers and realised she'd fallen asleep in her armchair, draped in a cloak that was heavy with the evening's rain. She yawned, stretched, fetched a glass of water and went upstairs, feeling out of sorts. Dreams of cats burping out little red men were nothing compared to the weirdness the Sandman had left her with tonight. Did it mean anything? Did it? She wrote down what fragments she could remember in her notebook and would press her gran for answers in the morning.

A dark weight seemed to press upon her as she climbed into bed, trying to recapture the threads of the dream she'd been having but it wasn't coming back to her. Something to do with different things she could hear, see, smell and touch and that had been all right but then there had been something else, something sinister and malevolent, lots of bees and a woman without a key, and Sal lay awake, fretting about money and jobs, until the first light of dawn cast its promise of a new day through the sliver of the window where the curtain edges didn't quite meet. She slept again then, a dreamless, restful sleep and when she woke in the full morning light, she had no recollection of her dreams at all and still no clear thoughts about her future. There would definitely be a cat in it though, as much as she missed Judy, she couldn't bear to think of herself living in a world in which there was no cat.

CHAPTER FIVE

The day of the vicar's bonfire crept up on Sal too quickly. She had spent all morning scurrying around in the kitchen with her little tribe, getting ready for the event with four different types of spiced cider and non-alcoholic apple based drinks. The mulled cider made to her gran's old recipe was her favourite so far.

'You say your dad gave you this recipe?'

'Handed to him by his mother, who got it from her grandmother.' Magda confirmed.

'So this must be at least, what, six generations old by now?' Sal took another sip of the brew and nodded in appreciation. 'It's very good,' she said, 'I could drink a fair bit of that, Gran.'

'Yes, here's to the ancestors.' Magda didn't bother dipping a spoon into the giant pot full of the spiced cider to taste it. She knew it would be good and besides, she couldn't be doing with half measures. She used a mug instead and leaned back against the old Aga with it, taking a long puff of her e-cig to release a fresh and modern apple vapour into the air. When Sal had convinced her to try the electronic variety last year, Magda had missed real cigarettes but now she revelled in the wide variety of different flavours that were available. She liked to pick ones that were in tune with the current season.

'It smells like a brewery in here.' Jasmine came in from the cold, laden with carrier bags. 'Where do you want these?'

'Anywhere for now, I'll go through it all in a sec and get things onto serving plates.' Magda said. 'Just let me finish this.' She indicated her e-cig and saw Jasmine pull a disapproving face. 'Oh lighten up, my girl, it's not real baccy.'

'Did you ask Stacy if she's coming along tonight?' Sal wanted to know. Although there was a good ten years between them, she and Stacy, the village's grocer, got on well and spent a bit of time together once in a while. Stacy was the closest thing Sal had to a good friend in Wilveringham and as making friends didn't come easily to her, she valued the older woman's company. It was a shame the grocery wasn't a bigger store, she might have finagled a job out of it, still, the high street shop did well enough to help support Stacy and her partner, Mark.

'Yes, as soon as Mark gets back from Stoke.' Jasmine said. Sal wasn't sure exactly what Mark did for a living but knew he worked for an engineering firm and did something mechanical and oily. He was a gruff but friendly person and he made Stacy happy and Sal was glad for that. With her own life so devoid of close company, it was always good to know those around her were happy and cared for.

'Right,' Magda announced, 'I think everything's just about ready. Let's see about those printed labels now, Sal.'

This was something Sal had been working on a little at a time over the last few days and she proudly displayed sheets of colourful scroll-work labels and both her relatives looked on with admiration.

'This is superb work, my love.' Magda approved and Jasmine nodded in agreement. 'Looks really professional, especially with those brown bottles we picked up from Wares.'

With such short notice to produce gallons of cider and apple juice, the women had not been able to brew it themselves and resorted to stocking up with ready-made cider, some artisan speciality brands from Stacy's shop and the rest was a more bog-standard variety from the supermarket in Stoke. Now the liquids had been imbibing with herbs and spices and fruits, strained and bottled up with labels. It all looked very impressive and Sal was pleased to see Gran brimming with pride. Sal had done four styles of label, one for each of the drinks they'd made, with fancy lettering and watermark branches, blossom and apples beneath the text in a range of colours, each label distinct but within an overall theme.

'And you're sure that apart from the initial batch to pass around, it is all right if we try and sell the rest?' Sal had been working hard with her gran all week to source and sterilise bottles, shop for cider, apple juice, herbs and spices and it hadn't been cheap. The church was putting some funds towards to it but only enough to cover costs. Anything left over after the first round of drinks was up for sale and they could keep the cash as payment for the time they'd put in. Thinking ahead to another week without any work lined up for her, Sal had done some calculations to make sure there would be a decent amount left over to sell. A donation back to the church out of any sales would be in order but hopefully the rest of it might make up enough to cover the rent and board she owed her gran.

Brewing and stewing and producing a good quality batch of mulled and spiced cider at the end of it, which she thought was presentable enough to sell to the public, had also put a little bit of flesh on the bare bones of the idea that been slowing materialising but Sal didn't have time to dwell on that now. She helped her mum unpack the shopping and pack up some freshly made pastries and tarts onto plates. They quickly threw cling-film over the lot and started loading up the car with bags, boxes and bottles. Jasmine was the designated driver at Magda's insistence, as she was the only one not drinking.

The village orchard belonged to the church and Revered Granger was quite proud of it. Providing jobs for several of the locals, the orchard had a good crop of apples every year which were sold not only to the local shops but to large scale cider breweries, including the famous Harrison brand once upon a time.

'So why have you never done a wassail before, Vicar?' Jasmine asked, genuinely curious and surprised her mother hadn't cajoled him into it already.

'It's Reverend, actually.' Granger corrected. 'But you can call me Peter if you like. I had to fill out risk assessment forms for this, I'll have you know, and raise the funds for it. Thank you, by the way, for doing most of the hard work.'

'Oh it's been good fun, most it anyway.' Jasmine sipped her warm cinnamon apple juice and looked around her awkwardly. She recognised one or two faces but most of the people crowded around the gnarled old trees were strangers. Villages were odd places, she mused, with the only constant faces being the ones of her mother's generation. None of her school friends, not that she had many, had stayed and she knew Sal's friends from the village had moved away too. Apart from the reverend and Stacy, who had inherited the village shop when her dad died a few years ago, there wasn't anyone she remembered. Perhaps that was why she found herself clinging to Granger for company now instead of trying to mingle and meet people. He was a very likeable person but whatever he saw in her mother's friendship was beyond her. Jasmine had always been slightly embarrassed by her mother but things seemed different now, maybe attitudes were changing as the villagers gradually died out or moved on and the place was filled with newcomers from cities with broader outlooks, coming to places like this as a way of escaping the rat-race.

'I'm so glad Magda agreed to this, I did rather put her on the spot, I'm afraid.'

'Oh no worries, there,' Jasmine smiled. 'She likes to be the centre of attention, in case you hadn't noticed.'

The old gentleman nodded sagely. 'Yes, she does like that. She always seems to think outside the box, as it were.'

'Only because she was never inside the box to begin with.' Jasmine frowned and looked down at her feet. Her shoes were getting ruined by the grass, she noticed, and then she wondered if that mattered anymore. It wasn't as though she had to dress nicely for work next week, let's face it.

'I gather you've been having quite a hard time lately, Jasmine.'

Not liking the way this conversation was heading, she squirmed under his scrutiny but could see no way out of it without being rude. She sipped her warm non-alcoholic cider and kept her mouth shut. What had her freak of a mother been telling everyone this time?

'I don't want to pry,' he said, 'but my door is always open, should you need it. The old adage is often true about sharing problems and apparently I'm a good listener.'

She still didn't say anything but Granger moved round so that he faced her directly, his kind eyes wrinkling at the edges. 'Don't forget that, will you? Any time.' He put his hands on her shoulders and she met his eyes now, suddenly finding that her own were starting to spring forth with tears. She hated that she cried so easily these days. Granger wiped her cheeks with his thumb and patted her shoulders once more.

'Now, why don't we see if that old witch of ours is around here somewhere?' He said with a more jolly tone of voice. 'I'm sure I asked to her to lead this blessing thing and it's high time we got started, Jared has already lit the fire and Mrs Beers has got her ladies' group to foil wrap a sack of potatoes so we're all set.'

Magda was busy pouring cider and alcohol free apple drinks into six rather large goblets, four of which were on loan from St Mary's. One of them was enamel and with a bit of luck, it would survive the night without being smashed or chipped. She deliberated over alcohol or not for that one – it could be in the hands of tipsy adults or clumsy children either way, so equally likely to get dropped and broken in both cases.

Sal had added their haul of goods from Stacy's shop to the range of food laid out on tables from the church hall and saw Granger heading their way.

'Gran, let me finish that,' she said, taking one of the goblets, 'you've got company. Can you remember the words?'

'Of course I can, I may be old but I'm not senile.' Magda huffed at her. 'Ah, my friend, are we ready?'

Magda and the reverend were almost identically dressed: he in a long, flowing black cassock and she in a long, flowing dark blue robe. They both looked very much the part of the ministerial professional and Sal felt proud of her gran for being held in such esteem, at least by one member of the local community, that she was invited to do something significant like this for the whole village.

The crowd gathered round in the dusky light and as Granger and Magda took turns to speak about the importance of harvest, community and friendship, the last of the daylight gave way to the darkness of night. The bonfire was starting to blaze finely and torches and lanterns lit up among the crowd. It seemed to Sal that the entire village had turned out for this, judging by the amount of people gathered. Some of them were only here for the free baked potatoes and hot-dogs of course, but Sal liked to think a larger percentage were here to enjoy the community spirit of it all. She stood by the goblets with her mum and Mrs Beers, whose bakery had provided the majority of food for this evening, passing around the beverages as Gran wound up her blessing to the ancient and venerable trees of the orchard.

'And so, my friends, fellow residents and visitors to Wilveringham, we behold the apple tree! Oh hail to thee, old apple tree, that blooms well, bears well. Hats full, caps full, three bushel bags full, an' all under one tree. Hurrah! Hurrah!'

The crowd roared right along with her – hurrah, hurrah – in a mighty cheer with claps and shouts and whoops and one of the orchard workers, Sal recognised him as one of Stacy's regular customers, had brought a shot-gun. He fired it now with a cracking boom up into the air above the trees. Children screamed with surprise and more cheers rose up into the night air. Sal knew this wasn't quite the right time of year for a wassail, but she didn't care, she was enjoying herself and when the empty goblets returned to her, she refilled them and was met with smiles and thanks, even from one of Mrs Beers' sycophantic hangers-on. The blazing warmth of the bonfire cooked dozens of potatoes, sausages and burgers that were devoured in minutes by the gathering multitudes and Sal chatted with a few people she vaguely knew while trying to find her family. Jasmine was talking to the reverend and Mrs Beers, so that ruled her out for company and Magda, she noticed, well, Magda looked as if she was about to be enjoying the company of a certain bearded biker who was heading her way. Could that be her mysterious Stuart Redman? No wonder the crone wanted a ride on his bike. Sal smiled inwardly and left them both to it, wandering back to the table and before long she was swamped with people wanting to buy a bottle or two of cider and apple juice to take home. By the end of the night, only a few lonely bottles of cider were left and Sal was grateful that so much cash had been handed over that she'd have to leave counting it all until daylight.

Magda stood by the bonfire, warming her hands and sipping her luke-warm spiced cider. She had spotted a certain someone in the crowd and mused on the folly of her Stephen King joke. Surely she wasn't the only person who had read that book? Never mind, it was over and done with now and Magda knew from experience there was no point in dwelling on the past, she wasn't going in that direction. Her family's future concerned her far more right now, with Sal and Jasmine both looking for work. There was no way she could support them both with the scattered and unreliable income she made reading cards and touting a few potions here and there. She did all right for herself and thankfully she owned the old house outright but unless something came up soon for her troubled brood they would struggle to pay bills and put food on the table. Still, she supposed it wouldn't be more than a week or so until Sal's agency secured her another assignment and Jasmine would not doubt be off before long on another one of her reckless relationships and moving out again. Always a worry, that was. Magda hoped that perhaps this time she'd stick around a bit longer, get herself back to normal. Would she benefit from a bit of counselling, Magda thought? Thirty quid a time, twice a week? No, there was no way they could afford that right now. She decided she would have to come up with some alternative way of helping her daughter and then she was roused sharply from her reverie as her elbow was grabbed from behind.

'Bwah ha!' Magda uttered in surprise and her whole body shook with the sudden touch, arms flinging up, spraying cider all over herself and she pivoted round wildly. 'Who the bloody hell… oh.' It was Stuart Redman. Of course it was, complete with a face full of Magda's still-warm cider that was now dripping in great golden streams through his thick beard.

'Oh damn it, I'm so sorry, you took me by surprise.' She garbled her words, struggled to find a clean tissue in her hand-bag and generally felt that this would be a good time for the ground to swallow her up. She found a ratty handkerchief and thrust it in his face to mop up the cider before she realised what she was doing. She froze mid-fumble, her fingers caught in his beard, eyes wide with horror at her impulsiveness. Think, woman, think! How are you going to explain this?

She didn't have to, as it turned out. Stuart Redman, the lusty-looking Pan with a motorbike, took a gentle hold of her hand and pulled it away from his beard, soggy tissue and all.

'It's fine, I'll save it for later.' He smiled at her. 'Vicar was right about you.' He said, smiling more broadly now.

'Why, what did he say?' Magda was confused for a second. 'Wait, I don't get it. Are you actually...?'

'Yes,' he said, 'my name is Stuart Redman but I was winding you up too. Reverend Granger said you had a bit of a thing for Stephen King. I've never read The Stand and I've never heard the Frannie Goldsmith thing before, if I'm honest. Thought it was bloody genius, though.'

'You did? Then why?' Still confused, Magda retrieved her hand, somewhat reluctantly, from his warm one and threw the offending tissue into the fire beside them along with her now empty paper cider cup.

'It was the vicar's idea, he coached me a bit before I met you. That fella's got a weird sense of humour. I didn't mean to embarrass you.' The biker shrugged apologetically and at last the penny dropped.

'Granger! I should have known.' It had been a while since the last time Magda had been so relieved to have not offended somebody. She scanned the crowd around the bonfire and spotted the vicar tucking into an enormous hot-dog, surrounded by a group of the greylings, the women's group spearheaded by none other than Mrs Beers. Magda nodded her head at the vicar, catching his eye. 'Yes, you little bugger.' She wagged a finger at him and he returned her nod, raising his glass to her. 'You got me. Ha ha.'

'That woman's been driving him up the wall all evening.' Said Pan. No, not Pan, Magda reminded herself. He was Stuart Redman in the flesh and even if she were not Frannie Goldsmith, there was still a spark of chemistry bubbling between them if she was any judge. She hoped that spark would include the spark of a motorbike roaring into life with her riding pillion and feeling that glorious white hair of his flying back towards her as they shot off along the open road.

'Yes, she's our very own socialite. So you haven't read the book?' Magda asked. 'I can lend it to you if you like.' She had four copies.

'Sounds good to me, Frannie Goldsmith.' He replied amiably, his eyes creasing up at the corners as he smiled.

'It's Magda,' she held out a hand still sticky with dried cider. 'Magda Howard.'

'Magda.' He grinned, revealing perfectly neat white teeth. 'Shall we sit for a while?' He ambled over to the low stone wall of the orchard, a little away from the motley collection of visitors, and shimmied himself onto it.

'Hang on,' Magda was still holding her hand-bag and it clunked loudly against the wall when she jumped up to sit beside him.

'What have you got in there, bricks?'

Instead of answering, Magda took out her remaining bottle of mead and passed it to him. 'Forgot that was in there. Help yourself, Stuart Redman.'

'Don't mind if I do Magda Howard.' He took the cap off the bottle and passed it to her first in a gesture of good will and Magda sipped straight from the bottle and Stuart followed her lead.

'Good stuff.' He said. 'I'm glad you approve. Tell you what, I'll do you a swap.'

Stuart Redman raised his eyebrows. 'What are you after?' He said warily.

'You can borrow my signed copy of The Stand in return for you taking me out on your bike.'

They shook hands and laughed. 'It's a date.' Said Stuart. 'A deal, I mean.'

'Oh yes,' Magda snickered with delight. 'I think I know exactly what you mean.'

'So you're a witch, then?'

Magda nodded. 'And you're the druid from St Mary's parish.' A moment of silence as druid and witch locked eyes, taking the measure of one another.

'Well, that's good.' Magda said simply. 'That's very good indeed.'

'And so is this,' Stuart poured a small measure of mead to the earth. 'Tell me Magda, do you make a habit of keeping bottles of mead in your hand-bag or did you plan on getting me drunk tonight?'

She passed the bottle back to him. 'It's my ritual drink. Bought some stock a while back but I forgot it was in there, to be honest.'

Stuart turned down the second sip. 'I'm on the bike, I'm afraid.' He jumped down from the wall and held out a hand to help Magda climb down. Arm in arm, they walked back to the bonfire and warmed themselves, chatting comfortably for a time before Stuart had to go, the loud revving of his engine sending a roar of cheers through the stragglers who still remained by the fire.

'A good evening, eh, Missis Witch?' Reverend Granger ambled across to stand with her.

'A good evening indeed, Mister Vicar.' Magda replied. 'You sly match-making old scoundrel.'

CHAPTER SIX

'He's such a charmer.' Magda crooned. 'I think I'm already in love.'

'He's gorgeous.' Jasmine said. 'I bet you could cuddle up with him all day and not get bored.'

'I'm not so sure.' Sal shook her head, not denying that he was a gorgeous charmer but she wasn't sure about him and she needed to be sure. She put the little tabby kitten back into his pen and shut the wire door. She'd been along all the rows of cats and kittens in the A wing of the rescue centre and though there were plenty of options, she hadn't found the one. 'Sorry little guy.' She moved away quickly, lest those adorable eyes suck her in. She wasn't sure exactly what she was looking for in a new cat, no creature existed in the world to replace Judy, but she'd know the right moggy when it came along. 'B wing it is.'

Sal sauntered out of the small building and across the courtyard with anticipation, Magda and Jasmine following dutifully behind. 'Here we go, then.' She pushed open the outer door of the second and final cattery building and wrinkled her nose like Samantha from Bewitched.

'Yeah, you wish.' Magda chortled. 'If only it really worked like that.'

'Got to be worth a try.' Sal did it again and quietly muttered a little rhyme. 'Come to me, make friends with me, my perfect new cat and I'll whisk you home at the drop of hat.'

'Oh, that's really sweet, I'm sure we can find you a nice cat to be friends with.' A young woman's voice chirped from the other side of the inner door and Sal felt stupid. 'Come on in.'

'Um, thanks.' The door was pulled open and Sal went in, greeted with a smile from the owner of the voice. A short, slim woman wearing a Cats Protection t-shirt was busy at work with trays of bowls and dishes on a small trolley.

'Hello ladies, which one of you is looking for a cat today?'

The woman looked vaguely familiar but Sal couldn't place her. She locked eyes with the woman and looked away quickly. She realised she'd been caught staring and her face tingled with a flush of colour.

'Me, though the cat would live with all of us.' Sal answered. She focused on her breathing, looking deliberately past the woman with the heart-shaped face to eye up the pens where homeless cats sat dreaming wistfully of a new home.

'She's gone and made us sound weird, now,' Magda laughed. 'I'm Magda Howard, this is my daughter and my granddaughter. Sal's lost her old cat recently, sadly.'

'Oh, sorry to hear that.' The rescue assistant met Magda's eyes and shrugged. 'We get all sorts in here though, you wouldn't believe it if I told you.'

Sal exchanged a glance and mild snicker with her mother and the lady laughed along with them. If only she knew the half of it, Sal patted her gran on the arm, there's no way she would have given me that look. 'I'm looking for a kitten, rather than an adult cat.'

'And you've not seen anyone you like in the other wing?' Sal shook her head and the woman beckoned with a gesture. 'Okay, this way then.' As she passed the pens of older cats, Sal couldn't resist peeking in to look at them and noticed Magda and Jasmine had stopped at to gawp and make cooing noises at one cat in particular. She followed the assistant to the rear of the building where three pens full of fluffy kittens were waiting for her. Butterflies hopped around in her belly and she peered in at the first pen, three black and white fur-balls, all cute enough. Hmm, second pen, two tabbies, two tabby and white ones and an older cat she assumed must be their mother.

'They're all so gorgeous, aren't they? It makes it hard to choose.' The assistant said.

Sal still couldn't quite work out if she'd seen the woman before somewhere or not but when a pair of large, bright green eyes met hers, she forgot all about the woman with the bobbed black hair.

'This one.' She said, pointing to a kitten the colour of ginger nut biscuits. 'Sorry, I mean, can I meet this one, please?'

'Ah, that's Percy.' The lady told her, indicating a slip of paper taped to the Perspex door. 'He's the last one of his litter after his sister was homed this morning, poor lonely boy.'

'What happened to the mother cat?'

'She was adopted last week along with one of her kittens, another boy, it's just been Percy and his sister since then. The babies were already weaned so little Percy here is nine weeks old now.'

As soon as Sal peered in for a closer look, the kitten stopped playing with his mouse toy and jumped at the window, pawed at her face on the other side and then sat down neatly, as if he was waiting. 'Looks like he wants to meet you too. Here we go.'

With the door open, Sal and Percy spent a moment quietly looking at each other. As she reached forward to him, the kitten stood up and sprang toward her playfully, climbing up her arm and mewing sweetly while she started to coo and fuss over him, smoothing his silky fur. This was the one, she could feel it in her bones.

'So you've found one then?' Jasmine asked, coming to see. 'Oh, look at him! He's going to look so pretty in that red collar.'

'He will do when he's grown into it. See how small he is? Who's a friendly little chap, eh?' Magda said with approval, reaching over to fuss him. 'The smile on your face says it all, my girl.'

Half an hour later the paperwork was finished with and Sal hugged the kitten carefully before shutting him into Judy's old cat basket. She squealed happily and kissed Jasmine on the cheek. 'Thank you, Mum.'

Percy miaowed loudly in protest for every single one of the twenty-five minutes it took to drive home, the basket smelled vile with cat urine and as soon as Sal opened the carrier and let him into the lounge, all doors and windows firmly closed, he shat in the middle of the rug. 'Off to a good start, I see.' Magda carefully came through the door, shutting it quickly behind her but not quickly enough. Percy was off like a rocket and bounded through the house, one second nervously miaowing and looking over his shoulder at Sal, the next second bombing upstairs as if he knew his way around. Sal darted ahead of the kitten, shutting the doors to the bedrooms and bathroom, and little Percy made his way back down the stairs, half jumping, half falling as he went. She bent down to scoop him up and he chewed at her hair. 'Those are big, big steps for a little guy like you, aren't they, Percy?'

Sal brought him back into the lounge and flopped down happily. Percy curled up on her knee and was asleep in seconds. 'It's been a long day for him.'

'I must warn you, Sal,' Magda had a stern look on her face as she drank dandelion coffee from a rounded mug designed to look like a cauldron. Sal groaned, wondering what stupid house rules her gran was going to set for the cat but she needn't have worried. 'I can't possibly have a cat called Percy living in this house. You'll have to come up with something more befitting and respectable for a witch's cat.'

'You let me get away with Judy.'

'That was different, you were eleven years old.'

'You let me get away with a lot when I was eleven. Let's think. Titan, Odin, Loki.' Sal plucked pagan sounding names out of the air and they spent a couple of hours happily playing together with the new arrival, cooing over him and dismissing one name after another.

'My friend Agnes had a cat called Loki once,' Magda said. 'He turned out to be a right old vicious brute, I think her present cat is a Malfoy. Ooh, I know, what about Greebo?'

'I don't see what's wrong with Percy,' Jasmine offered. She was about to say more when her mobile phone started ringing. She picked it up from the coffee table and shrugged, not recognising the number. 'Says number unknown. Could be Mr James, I suppose.' She answered it. 'Hello?'

Jasmine's face went white as she listened and Magda moved next to her, suddenly on guard for tears or trouble. 'No, no. I will not.' Jasmine stood up and started to pace the room, phone in one hand, the other one scraping at her hair roughly as her eyes filled with tears and terror. 'Sorry? You're sorry? It's too late, Paul, I'm sick of hearing it. No, I won't. I never want to – no – how dare you? I said no. NO! NO! NO!' Jasmine raged and screamed, dropping the phone and clutching her head with her hands. Her face was bunched up and red with anger and hatred and she paced the room frantically. 'He wants me to go back, Mum. I think he's going to come and get me! I thought I'd be safe here. Oh, help me, oh God! Oh no. Please, no! NO! NO!'

Jasmine fell to the rug, helpless and weak, kneeling on the damp patch where Sal had cleaned up the cat mess. She made cloyingly desperate noises, a wailing mixture of crying and senseless words, her body shaking and jerking. Magda crouched next to her, folding herself over Jasmine and doing her best to give some comfort but feeling inadequate.

Sal left the kitten on the sofa and joined the puddle of women on the damp rug, embracing her mother and rocking her, softly, softly. All three of them screamed when a door burst open loudly somewhere in the house.

*

'Oi! What's going on? Oi!' A deep man's voice that Sal didn't recognise boomed through the house and she stood quickly, standing in front of her mother and her gran protectively. The lounge door started to open from the other side. Sal darted to push it shut and had to struggle. Whoever it was, he was strong.

'Get out! Get out!' Sal screamed and screamed, still pushing hard to keep the door closed. 'Leave her alone, I'll call the police, get out!'

'Okay, okay!' The door stopped moving from the other side and the voice had backed off a little. 'It's all right, it's me, Magda! It's Stuart.'

'Oh bloody hell!' Magda cried out and then she laughed. Sal was confused, Jasmine was hiding behind the sofa with the kitten. Magda moved Sal out of the way and opened the door.

Stuart Redman stood in the hallway, wearing his bulky biker leathers. He filled the doorway. 'I forgot you were coming.' Magda said, resting one hand on her chest as she got over the kerfuffle and panic, breathing a huge gasping breath of sheer relief.

'What's going on? I heard screaming.' Stuart remained in the hallway as he spoke. 'I was just coming to the back door. I was going to knock but it sounded like someone was being murdered.'

'No, we're all okay.' Magda continued, waving for him to come in. 'Jasmine said her abusive husband might be on his way. Gave us all a scare, but that's it.'

'You sure everything is all right?' His eyes searched the room, reminding Sal of an eagle-eyed Action Man, alert for danger. He scanned the hallway, the lounge and the hallway again, finally stopping as his eyes came to rest on Magda. Sal knew then that no matter what happened next, no matter if she never saw him again, she would always be grateful that she had met Stuart Redman. A true hero, she realised, willing to race in and help these women he barely knew for no other reason than he thought helping them would be the right thing to do. She wanted to hug him for it.

'I can't believe I forgot you were coming.' Magda said, leaning forward to rest her hands on her thighs, still recovering. 'Lost track of time, what with the new kitten. Stuart's here to pick me up, he very kindly offered to take me out for a ride on his bike this afternoon, Jasmine.'

'Thank you for coming in to rescue us, Stuart.' Sal said, 'I mean that.' She held out her hand and he gave it a quick shake.

'Any time, I mean that too.' His husky voice boomed through the house, breaking the tension that had hung thickly on the air, somehow seeming to make things right.

'Come on out, Mum.' Sal coaxed her mother out of the corner she was hiding in and guided her to the sofa where they sat close together with their arms around each other, Jasmine leaning her face against the folds of Sal's purple sweater for comfort.

The tall, broad biker looked at each of the women in turn with a stern expression showing through his wild beard. 'He must be a nasty piece of work to scare you like that.' He said, gingerly settling his massive frame down on the arm of the chair nearest to her. He looked slightly out of place with his bulky armoured leathers in Magda's homely lounge, but Sal thought she could very quickly get used to having someone like him around the house from time to time.

'Anything I can do to help?'

'Do you think I should tell the police?' Jasmine whispered quietly, her face ashen. 'He'll get his way, he always does. He'll find out where I am, he'll drag me back.'

'Jasmine, love. He might say that but how would he know where you are?' Magda asked. 'He's never been here with you when you've come to visit. Does he have this address? Does your old boss have this address?'

'Mum, did he actually tell you he was coming?' Sal asked, beginning to wonder if her mother was creating a massive drama for the sake of it. It wouldn't be the first time and knowing her, it wasn't likely to be the last time either. 'What did he really say?'

'That he was sorry, that he missed me and he wants me to come home.' Jasmine shook her head and pulled her sleeve down over her the back of her hand to wipe her eyes, leaving dark smudges of snot and tears on her expensive beige cashmere.

'Yes, but did he say if he was coming to see you or not?' Sal pressed, frustrated. Her mother shook her head.

'If I don't go back, to collect my things if nothing else, then he will, won't he?'

'Please can you be clear about this, Mum.' Sal could feel herself tightening up with the temptation to get angry. Why couldn't she get a straight answer? 'Does he know where Gran lives and is there anyone at work who might tell him?'

'No, he doesn't know.' At last Jasmine started to calm down. Sometimes she needs things explaining to her, Sal realised, because all her life she relied on other people making the big decisions for her. 'He's the only person listed as my next of kin at work. I'm almost certain he wouldn't know where to find me. Damn it, I'm over-reacting to things, aren't I? Again. I think there's something wrong with me.'

'There isn't anything wrong with you, don't say that. It's to be expected that you're scared, after him treating you this way for so long, manipulating you all the time on top of the bruises. No wonder you're frightened. Don't you worry about it.' Magda hugged her daughter and kissed the top of her head. 'He won't come here, all right? We'll keep you safe.'

'My mate Barry owns a security business, I'll get him to sort you out with some alarms, CCTV, decent locks, that sort of thing.'

The three women looked at Stuart with surprise. Thinking of their financial state, Sal said, 'that's very good of you, really, but I'm not sure we can afford...'

Thinking of the protective circle they'd set up, Magda chipped in. 'Oh Stuart, I don't think there's any need for all that, really.'

'How soon can you get it installed?' Jasmine added, thinking of her need to feel secure. 'Cost is not an issue, I want the works.'

'Cost is not an issue?' Sal retorted, straightening up. 'Of course it's an issue, we're both out of work and Gran's...'

'Yes, well.' Jasmine cut her off. She used both hands to wipe her snotty, tear streaked face. 'Those savings I mentioned the other day are not an insignificant amount, let's leave it at that.'

'Please, let me do this for you. I'd like to help.' Stuart insisted. He rose to tower over them all. 'Barry owes me a favour or two, won't cost you ladies a penny. I'll give him a ring this evening and see when he can get his lads over to set things up for you.'

'I suppose a bit of back up would be a good idea, in that case. Thank you very much, Stuart, as long as it's not too much trouble.' Magda patted him on the arm and realised firstly how very kind and generous it was of him considering they hardly knew each other and secondly, that in a situation like this it was comforting to have another person around with a sensible, practical head on their shoulders. Magda had been taking care of things like this by herself for so long and had always been an independent woman, but she wouldn't have come up with the idea of having an alarm system if Stuart hadn't suggested it. She'd never felt the need for it, living in the village. Now the idea had taken root in her mind and she thought it was a good one.

'I'm so sorry.' Jasmine said, 'for all the fuss. And thank you, Stuart, it was good of you to come in here like a hero to save us all.'

'Where did Percy go?' Sal realised she couldn't see the kitten anywhere. They looked behind the sofa, under the loose cushions in every chair, behind the television unit, on the window ledge, every nook and cranny in the lounge was thoroughly delved into but he remained elusive. Sal sighed. 'Look, he'll be here somewhere. Why don't you take Gran off on that bike ride, Stuart, while the sun's still shining and Mum can help me look for Percy, it'll take her mind off things? We'll see you later, Gran.'

Jasmine stood up suddenly, a different look in her eyes from the haunted one she had only moments ago. 'Yes, you should go, Mum.' She said. 'I'll be okay, honest.'

Magda put up a protest but only a half-hearted one; she'd been looking forward to her outing with Stuart for days now.

'Shoo, go on.' Sal flapped her hands at her gran. 'We shall find Percy and settle in for a movie afternoon, we'll see you when you get back.'

'Magda, shall we?' Stuart got up and left the room to collect his helmet. 'Ah, so that's where he got to.' He picked up the helmet carefully and showed it to them. Nestled inside fast asleep was a ball of ginger fur.

'Percy!' Sal giggled and lifted him out. 'He's warmed it up for you.' The kitten opened his sleepy eyes, mewed pathetically, stretched his paws and went back to sleep in her arms.

'See you later on, lock the doors behind me.' Magda headed off outside with Stuart, putting on the spare helmet he'd brought for her and she clapped her hands excitedly.

'Take your – Gran!' Sal shouted to make herself heard through Magda's helmet and mimed the action. 'Take your scarf off – your scarf, Gran!' She had visions of the old crone getting the ends of it caught up in something and being yanked off the back of the bike.

Magda climbed on the back of the bike behind Stuart, wrapped her arms around his waist and with a roaring purr of the engine, they were off. Magda waved an arm in the air madly, her scarf flying in the wind as she let go of it, and whooped with delight, feeling the thrill of an adventure for the first time a long while. It made her feel young and reckless and free and wild and she held on tightly to the leather clad torso of the new man in her life and she was full of joy and delight and happiness.

*

'Cheese on toast?' Sal suggested.

'And a strong coffee.'

'Maybe something stronger.' Sal sighed, she could do with it even it her mother didn't join in. 'Do you think we should tell the police, Mum? Did he threaten you?'

Jasmine shook her head. 'I don't think there's much to tell them, to be honest. You know me, always blowing things out of proportion.'

'All right, Mum. Why don't you get settled? Be back in a minute.'

Sal guided her mother to the sofa with orders to put her feet up, plopped Percy into her lap, and went to busy herself in the kitchen with golden toast and bubbling cheese. She stood at the window, waiting for the kettle to boil, and looked out at the garden to see the green man staring back at her. Sal had always loved a good green man, the leafy face who stood as a symbol of the connections between the world of nature and the world of men. She admired this one in particular as it was carved from apple tree wood which had, many years ago, been part of an apple tree that had stood tall and proud in the village orchard until it was felled by lightning. Roots reaching down to the earth, branches reaching up to the heavens and the trunk in the middle ground, the land of everyday life. The rough-hewn foliate face of the green man, carved into the old tree trunk and now propped up against the tool shed, had been a gift from her dad. He had seen it lying in the orchard on a visit here the year before he died and by the time they went home after their weekend with Gran, he had finished carving the green man. She didn't remember her dad as clearly as she liked but the memories she did have were all good ones. He'd left her mum with a lot of happy memories too and she often wondered if that had some bearing on the way Mum acted now, if her stream of unhappy relationships was unconsciously deliberate. Because when you've had that one, perfect happiness, can you ever hope to replace it, to find it again, knowing that nothing in the world can ever compare or even come close to what once was? Do you even want to replace it?

'Have you got lost in there, Sal?' Jasmine's voice sounded shaky and Sal hurriedly poured hot water over the coffee and shoved everything onto a tray.

'It's all right,' she called. 'I'm coming.' A small sound like the sigh of a cat came from the corner where she kept her laptop and printer tucked out of the way, the place where Judy used to sleep. She looked over and for a split second and thought she saw the shadow shape of a cat but the space was empty and the place of sadness in her heart made itself known again, briefly, lest she forget.

*

'I don't know if I can stay here, Sally.' Jasmine pushed cotton wool padding between Sal's toes and opened a bottle of dark red nail polish. Sal wiggled. 'That doesn't tickle, does it?'

'No, go ahead.' Sal was not surprised at this news. 'I know you're not happy here, Mum, but where would you go? Not back to Manchester, surely?

Jasmine shook her head slowly, dabbing at Sal's toenails. 'Absolutely not,' she said, 'I've been thinking about things a lot, these last few days. It's been different, spending time with you and that crazy old crone, brewing up all the potions and what-not, it hasn't been unpleasant. I think, and don't you dare tell her I said so because she'll only be smug about it, but I think I've actually found it okay, being here. In the village, I mean.'

Sal dramatically raised her eyebrows at grabbed her mum's hand in excitement. 'Don't tell me you've had a revelation? You finally realise after all these years gallivanting around cities where everyone's busy all the time and rushing from one thing to the next, that you're actually starting to enjoy it here? Quiet and sleepy Wilveringham?'

'I know, who'd have thought it?' Jasmine moved onto Sal's other foot, padding her toes with more cotton wool while Sal squirmed and wiggled her toes. 'Behave yourself Sally, I'm trying to be serious.'

'Go on, then.' Sal picked up the coffee pot and refilled her mug, keen to hear what was going on in that poor, battered mind of her mum's. 'I'm listening.'

'You know I went for a walk the other day, along the canal?'

Sal nodded, her mum had being doing a lot of that and she was pleased about it. Walking. It was the sort of activity that could make the soul heal and sing.

'My life is a mess, Sally, I'm just like you and your gran say I am – a rover, never settling in one place for long enough to put down roots. I've been running away, Sally, and I'm not even sure what I'm running from any more. I got into a routine of moving on with the bank. I'm doing so well, I get called in as acting manager all over the place to cover long-term leave or illnesses, and I love it. I like organising things, people and places into a state where it's all running efficiently, I like putting things in order and I'm good at it. But moving all the time isn't nice, it's hard to make friends, which is probably why I've just fallen into bed with the first half-decent seeming bloke who came along.'

'They always turn out to be wrong 'uns, though.' Sal interrupted. 'Let's not forget that.'

'They do, but there was only ever one right 'un, wasn't there?' Jasmine said and Sal knew they were both thinking of her dad. They sat in quietness for a moment then Jasmine finished Sal's toes and put the top back on the nail polish bottle, setting it down on the coffee tray. 'I'd like to find another one eventually, but I was talking to someone the other day while I was out, one of your gran's friends as it happens, and it put things into perspective for me. I need time to focus on looking after myself and getting my confidence back, I'm fine at work, that's different, but I'm not happy. I'm not saying I've changed for ever, but I think living in the village might be good for me for a while.'

'Okay,' Sal said, confused now. 'You said you didn't want to stay here, though. You can't have it both ways.'

'I'm going to have a chat with Stacy and Mark about renting the flat above the grocery. It will be somewhere I can be myself, a place for me to get myself straightened out and rest for a while. I can't do that here, not while there's a chance that he might find me.'

'Gran's friend has said...'

'No, I can't stay here, don't you get it?' Jasmine said, becoming agitated. 'The flat won't be linked to me but there's always going to be a chance he'll find me at the house, I can't risk it. You don't know what it was like, Sally. What he was like.'

'All right, it's okay,' Sal said calmly, 'you can have the alarm set up at the flat. I'm sure Mark and Stacy would be fine with that. But are you sure you'll feel safe on your own?'

'It's a four minute walk from here,' Jasmine seemed determined and once she'd made up her mind and fixed her goals in place, Sal knew there was nothing to be done but to go along with it. 'Besides, Stacy will be downstairs in the shop most of the time and it's on the high street opposite the Black Swan. Plenty of people about in the evenings to deter any unwanted prowlers. I think I'd like it.'

'You've thought this through properly, haven't you?' Sal saw the look of earnest in her mother's face and nodded. She propped her feet up on the coffee table, waiting for the sticky polish to dry. 'What about your job, though? You can't just quit, surely?'

'I'm good with money, Sally.' Jasmine shrugged. 'I've worked in banks since I was sixteen and I will freely admit that I don't know how to run my life but I do know how to look after money. In fact,

I wanted to talk to you about that.' She wiggled her hands into the pocket of her cream coloured trousers and pulled out a folded slip of paper, thrusting it at Sal. 'I want you to have this.'

'What's this for?' Sal frowned, unfolding the slip to discover it was a cheque with a lot of zeros written on it. 'I don't understand.'

'I know you've been hard-up, Sally, and I know how important it's been for me to have a good job, one stable factor in my life.' Jasmine told her. 'You don't have that and you've been out of work for over a month now. I thought this might make things a bit easier for you.'

'Mum, this is a lot of money – are you sure?' Sal looked again at the numbers written on the cheque in her mother's neat print.

'You're not cut out for a conventional job, we all know that. I haven't been there for you, Sally, not like most mums. I'm not trying to buy you, I've given your gran the same so she can have a holiday or get a new boiler or whatever. It's just to tide you over for a bit, take some time off to figure out what you want to do with your life.'

Sal didn't say anything else. She nodded gratefully, tears pricking at her eyes. Why was she always so close to tears lately? She leaned into a hug with her mum, feeling closer than they had been in years and as they sat together, a little paw tapped her face and a fuzzy ginger head poked its way up between them.

Miaowing, Percy decided he wanted cuddles too. Sal laughed and smoothed his velvety fur, playing with his little paws and letting him chase the ends of the scarf she'd borrowed from her gran. 'You gorgeous little boy!' She cooed. 'Who's a gorgeous little lad?'

'Have you got a name for him yet?'

'Yes,' Sal replied, lifting the little kitten up to her face so she could look him the eyes. He batted at her nose and pressed his warm front paws to her face. 'How do you fancy being called Bran from now on?'

The kitten miaowed loudly and raised his paws in the air like a brave hero. 'Bran,' Sal said, enjoying the warmth of his fur, the bright green of his eyes. 'Welcome to the mad house, you pretty little boy.'

'You've really picked a lovely cat, Sally.'

Sal twitched her nose. 'Just call me Samantha.'

CHAPTER SEVEN

'Really?' Sal held her mobile to her ear with one hand and scribbled in her notebook with the other. 'Yes, that's great, I'll look forward to meeting you then, thank you.' She pressed the end-call button and looked back over her scruffy notes. 'I've got a job interview on Thursday,' she said, 'working for a solicitor's office. Not sure I fancy it though.'

'I thought you were desperate.' Magda sat at the dining table in the kitchen, grinding herbs, resins and flowers together with a pestle and mortar. A censor with burning charcoal in the middle of the table puffed with clouds of smoke every few minutes as she tested out pinches of different blends. 'Here, sniff this one. I think this will be more suitable for a Samhain blend.'

Sal bent over and wafted her feather fan over the fumes, inhaling through her nose. 'Not sure, I reckon I preferred that first one. This has got too much sage, smells a bit like sweaty armpits.' She said, absently bending down to stroke the kitten who was mewling up at her from the floor. 'I was desperate, but that money from Mum means I'm not now. I can take a bit more time and hopefully find something I like.'

'And what would that be?' Magda added. 'Want me to lay a few cards out for you?' She picked through the dozens of glass jars and pots laid out on the table, searching for something to add to the incense.

'Yes please, if you don't mind.' Sal said. She put the kettle on for what must have been the fifth time today. It seemed like she did little else nowadays. 'Tea or coffee?'

'Oh tea, please.' Magda reached out a hand. 'Cards are on the shelf behind you.'

'Yes, Gran.' Sal huffed and reached out for them, 'I know where they are.' She put the deck into her gran's out-stretched hand and sat down. Magda cleared a space in front of them and sat with her eyes shut for few seconds. She muttered under her breath, something Sal had noticed her doing a lot lately when laying out her tarot.

'What is that you're saying?'

'My new tarot mantra,' Magda touched her forefinger to her lips, 'a plea to the Gods of fortune telling. But if I told you the rhyme, I'd have to kill you. Kettle's boiled, by the way.'

Sal poured the steaming water into the teapot, giving it a long stir while Magda spread out three cards and made little noises to herself, tapping her fingers lightly over the worn pictures. The Empress, the Chariot, the Magician.

'You've got the start of an idea building up to something new and big. It could bring you what you're looking for if you let go of your past and allow your new dreams to take shape, but you won't be doing it on your own.'

'What are my dreams, though?' Sal shrugged. True enough, she'd had the first few flashes of an idea pop into her head but she didn't know exactly what it actually was yet.

'You'll have to work hard with skills you already have and there'll be new learning too. Something to do with your hands, working with people. It will all come together sooner than you think, I can't quite see the shape of it. It smells like lemongrass, sweet almond oil and something else I can't quite grasp.'

'That'll be your incense, Gran.'

Magda hunched over the cards again, studying the pictures with their glittering colours and ancient symbols at length, before raising her eyes to Sal. 'A red-headed stranger will ask a favour and therein lies your answer. You already know what you want to do, you just don't realise it yet.'

'Oh gosh,' Sal put a hand on her forehead and staggered in fake melodrama. 'So precise – how do you do it?'

'I'll throw these at you in a minute, now stop taking the mickey and get that tea poured.' Magda gathered up her cards, shoved another pinch of loose barks and resins from her pot onto the charcoal and wafted at the cards with Sal's feather fan to cleanse them. A face went past the kitchen window just then and she got up to see to her visitor. 'One of the women's group, what's she after? Put that away and leave us to it for a bit, eh, Sal?'

'No probs, Gran. Thanks for the reading by the way, very enlightening.' Sal picked up the feather fan her gran held out to her and took her mug of tea to disappear into the hall, her footsteps resounding as she climbed up the stairs.

*

Magda invited her visitor inside and settled her at the table with a cup of tea. 'Make yourself comfortable. Milk and sugar, Mrs Owen?' The lady nodded. 'Now, what can I do for you?'

'Bit of a delicate matter, Mrs Howard.' Said Mrs Owen, looking around Magda's kitchen nervously, her nose wrinkling as the last wisps of incense smoke dissipated into the air. 'I trust I can count on your, um, discretion?'

'You wouldn't be here if you thought I'd blab your gossip all over the village, would you?' Said Magda twisting her nose.

'It's about, Dave, actually. I wouldn't normally come to see, well, someone like you. But Mr Owen, you see, he's, ah. Hmm.' Mrs Owen began. She didn't say anything else for now, she just fumbled with her bright pink hand-bag and slurped her tea, putting the mug back down noisily.

'Relax, please!' Magda smiled at her. 'You can't shock me,' she said gently, 'I've heard it all before, trust me.'

Mrs Owen still seemed reluctant to speak freely so Magda asked a few subtle questions, posed a couple of potential scenarios and soon got to the bottom of it all. 'I'll give you some cream for it,' she said, 'I'll have it ready for you tomorrow. Do you want me to drop it off for you or shall you fetch it?'

'I shall be at the church all day; you won't mind bringing it to me there, will you? Discreetly, of course.'

'Of course.' Magda said, keeping a straight face as she ushered Mrs Owen out of the house. She felt proud of being able to keep that straight face, it hadn't been easy. Poor Mr Owen.

Sal knew she was on the verge of working something out in the back of her mind, her gran had been right about that, despite the teasing. She just needed to figure it out properly. She sat in the easy chair by her bedroom window, arranged cushions to support herself and draped a crocheted blanket over her knees. She reached over to the dressing table under the window, lit some incense and chimed a brass bell. The incense was soothing and the bell made a pleasant chime, setting the tone for Sal's inner consciousness to get into the right frame of mind. She closed her eyes, steadied her breathing.

Be calm. Relax.

She felt Bran jump into her lap and moved him gently across to her bed. She closed her eyes again. Calm, relax. She moved the kitten again. Close your eyes, be calm.

My world is a sea of calm and serenity. Picking up the kitten a third time, Sal gave in to his playful demands and reached under the bed, bringing out an old fishing rod toy of Judy's for Bran to play with. He darted about madly, jumping, leaping and knocking things over with as much enthusiasm as he possibly could. She'd have to get a new supply of cat toys and treats for the little guy and made a mental note of it.

'I bet the Dali Lama's cat knows how to meditate properly.' She spent another few minutes playing with her kitten, grinning and laughing as his over-sized paws batted at the toys and at her nose and he chewed strands of her long auburn hair. Sal poked about on her dressing table for a rubber band and tied her hair up out of the way. Glancing out of the window, she could see her gran's visitor leaving. Mrs Owen kept her head down, not wanting to be seen as she walked away from the witch's house. Pathetic, thought Sal, doesn't the woman realise nearly all of her so-called respectable friends have already been to see Gran themselves in the last two months?

As she watched, another visitor appeared. Stuart brought his bike to a stop on the driveway and clambered off. He knocked at the door and Sal rapped on her window to get his attention. He took off his helmet and looked up. She beckoned to him. 'Let yourself in, Stuart, you don't need to knock.'

She picked up Bran and jogged down the stairs to catch up with the biker and then realised perhaps she shouldn't. Wouldn't he and her gran want some alone time? Do people of Gran's age still rush into the bedroom at every possible opportunity? Her mind boggled. Sal decided she was not going to finish that thought.

'Sally, Jasmine, get your backsides in here would you?'

Her gran's voice bellowed from the downstairs hallway and Sal went down the last few steps to see what the fuss was about. She arrived in the kitchen at the same time as her mother came in from the garden where she'd been reading a book with a cup of tea in the last of the late autumn sun.

'You're going to that new yoga class at the village hall on Friday.' Magda announced. 'Stuart and I have plans, so I want you out of the house.'

'Yoga?' Jasmine's eyes flew wide open. 'Why yoga? And why do you need us out of the house?'

'Why do you think? And Agnes's has tickets for the Red Moon Women's Lodge up at Hebden Bridge in a couple of weeks. She was supposed to be going with her sister but she's been asked to step in last-minute to conduct a hand-fasting. You can have their places.'

'A women's lodge? What does that involve?' Jasmine asked suspiciously, already hating the sound of it.

'A weekend of women-only ceremonies, workshops, meditations, crystals, that sort of thing. Agnes went last year and reckoned it was amazing.'

'I'd rather pull my own teeth out, but if you insist. What are you up to, having a party or - oh?' Jasmine couldn't look her mother in the face as understanding began to dawn on her.

'Mum,' Sal rested a hand on Jasmine's shoulder. Having come to the obvious conclusion herself, she didn't want anyone to spell it all out loud and knew that given half the chance her gran would shout it loudly from the rooftops. 'We don't need to talk about the details. It's settled, Gran, we'll go.'

'Stuart and I are having adventures.' Magda pouted and licked her lips suggestively, twisting long waves of grey hair around a finger. Sal groaned out loud and shook her head. 'Sorry, Stuart,' she said, 'but you'd better get used to it, I'm afraid. She's like this all the time.'

He dismissed her apology with the wave of a hand. 'Nah, it's refreshing, being around your gran. More people could do with being honest and saying things how they are. It'd make life less complicated.' He helped himself to a cup of tea, took a drink and then spat it out in the sink. 'That's not tea. What is this?'

'Who knows?' Gran responded, 'I put regular tea in to begin with but I might have added any number things to the pot since then to give it a bit of extra flavour. Think it could be raspberry leaf.'

'Why Yoga?' Jasmine said again with a tinge of panic in her voice. 'I don't have anything to wear for yoga.'

'Did Stacy sort you out a key for the flat yet?' Magda asked, trying to distract her. 'Is she definitely all right with you renting it for a bit?' Sal noticed the odd jerk of Magda's head in the direction of the door and puzzled over it briefly.

'Yes, she said it needs a lick of paint before I can move in. Mark's doing that over the next couple of days. The paint fumes should have gone by early next week so I can move in then.'

'That reminds me,' Stuart chipped in, 'Barry's sorting out an alarm for you, pet. It's a simple system to start with, he needs to order a few bits if you want the full works, but I can install the door and window alarms any time you like.'

'That's great, thank you.' Jasmine said. She took her coat from the rack by the door and reached into a pocket, pulling out a small envelope and passing it to Stuart. 'If you take the key, you can do it when you've got time and you really should let me pay for this, you know.'

'If you're that bothered about it, you could give the money to a charity instead.' Stuart suggested. 'What about the little lad's rescue centre? Be a nice thing to do, eh, boy?' The kitten was in a playful mood and was leaping up at the biker, trying to reach his lap and coming short every time.

While Stuart was engaged with Jasmine, Magda made eye contact with Sal and once more inclined her head towards the door. They do, Sal realised, completing her earlier thought, they definitely do.

'Why don't we take a drive over there now, Mum?' Sal said, picking up on the hints her gran was dropping. Stuart's idea of driving out to the centre to leave a donation in person appealed to her and a small part of her was excited at the prospect of another trip to the cat rescue centre but she didn't know why. 'It's a nice afternoon for a drive. We could drop off a donation, give the staff an update on Bran and maybe pop into Stoke so you can get some yoga gear on the way back.' With that, they left the house and Sal led her bewildered mother to her car.

*

'What are you even supposed to wear for yoga?' Jasmine pondered out loud. 'Is there a dress code? I don't want to be the odd one out.'

'I've got some old leggings and a t-shirt,' Sal said, and then, knowing her mum would want to look the part, she said, 'that'll do for me but you'll want some brand-name label yoga pants and some kind of top with a decent support bra.' She looked around the department store they were visiting at the retail park and found the racks full of slim-fitting sportswear. 'That looks about right, doesn't it?' She picked out a few pairs of leggings and tops in assorted colours, thrusting them at her mum.

'Here, this lot says 'yoga-bear' on the label, go and try things on.'

'What colour is that?' Jasmine held up the label on a pair of ankle length yoga pants. 'Why can't they just call them trousers? Look, it says taupe on the label but that's not taupe.'

'It probably looks like taupe in daylight. If you don't like the colour, pick another pair. Just go and try something on, we haven't got all day.' Sal was already fed up, this was the third shop they'd tried and her mum had turned her nose up at everything. She sat on one of the hard plastic chairs in the changing room and waited, mentally crossing her fingers. After a couple of minutes the thin red curtain opened and Jasmine appeared, dressed in her regular clothes.

'That was quick.' Sal said. 'Any good?'

'Nicely flared toward the lower leg, bit tight around the behind but it'll have to do. I am bored of shopping now and there's a Costa café calling my name. Come on.'

Costa coffee wasn't a patch on the exclusive coffee brands Sal preferred but it would do in a pinch. She ordered a caramel latte and stirred in brown sugar, remembering another time and another cup of coffee.

'That was the same lady, you know.' Jasmine said. 'At the Cat's Protection centre.'

'What about her?' Sal feigned disinterest, she had no idea what her mother was talking about.

'The one with the dark hair,' Jasmine pressed, 'who heard you making up that ridiculous rhyme. I wish you wouldn't do that in public, you're just like your gran. She must have thought you were really weird.'

Sal shrugged. 'I don't care what people think of me.' She stirred her coffee, splodging her finger over some escaped sugar granules to lick them up from the rim of the saucer. Sal had forgotten about the lady at the rescue centre. She'd forgotten the dark hair cut into a neat, short bob that framed a pretty heart-shaped face. She'd forgotten that the woman had seemed familiar, like she remembered her from somewhere. Forgotten that an image came into her mind during their fleeting visit to offer a donation this afternoon, an image of the woman with short dark hair wearing a loose, tattered dress and beckoning with a finger. Where had that come from? Sal thought it might have been the fragment of a dream but it didn't matter, she'd forgotten it.

'Yoga's really good for you,' she changed the subject, 'I went a few times with a couple of girls from my aromatherapy class the year before last. Good for the body, soul and spirit, relaxing, rejuvenating.'

'Supposed to be good for your core, isn't it?' Jasmine asked, scooping up a massive portion of cake onto her fork and cramming it into her mouth. Sal had heard about people making up for lost time before, but never lost cake. She didn't think it would do her mum any harm to put on a few pounds, however, she was barely more than a skeleton. Exactly how much weight had she lost? It angered her that the slug had taken such utter control of her mum's life for so long and despite her work at the women's refuge before it closed, she still couldn't understand how so many women wound up in situations like that, battered and broken. Then, almost as if the thought of him had prompted it, somewhere across the ether, Jasmine's phone buzzed to signal the arrival of another text. They both looked at the screen, on alert like meerkats, and then sighed with relief when they saw that it was a message from Stacy. Undercoat dun, s'b dry tomoz, what colour u want 4 topcoat? Sal hated text speak. She always had to read it twice to figure out what some of it meant.

'Yes, it is,' she focused on her mum. She'd already forgotten about the woman with the pretty cheekbones. 'The class I went to did a ten minute meditation at the end, which was my favourite part of the whole session. Gives you time to breathe and relax properly.' Completely forgotten.

'Maybe so, but I'm not doing it for the spiritual buzz, I've been badgered into it by our Lady and Mistress, remember? The grand matriarch of Howard Mansion.' Jasmine pushed aside her empty cake plate and pulled her coat from the back of her chair, shrugging into it. 'God, that cake was good. Right, let's see if they've wrecked the house in our absence.'

*

There were two motorbikes parked in the driveway when Sal rolled her tired little VW up to the side of the house. Sal and Jasmine looked at each other for a long moment, neither one wanting to say it.

'She hasn't, has she?'

'Surely not? No, she can't have done.'

'I don't think she's even got a licence any more, not for a bike. That does look like a lady's bike though.' Sal noted the pink fluffy dice hanging from one of the wing mirrors and a sticker across the fuel tank, sparkling with pink glitter, which stated: this princess rides a motorbike.

'No licence? She's got to take it back.' Jasmine said, making no moves to get out of the car before she'd had a chance to discuss this properly. 'I don't mind her riding pillion and Stuart is lovely, I think he's good for her, but is this a step too far? I can't have my mother riding about illegally. She'll be arrested. She is sixty-eight, for heaven's sake!'

'Maybe it's not what we think.' Sal wasn't sure though, with Magda, who knew? 'Only one way to find out.'

'Only a mother like mine…' Jasmine whispered as the pair of them dragged their bags of shopping from the car.

'Ah, you've come back in the nick of time.' Magda's voice greeted them as Sal pushed the back door open. The first thing Sal noticed was an unusual, somehow masculine scent hanging in the air. The second thing she noticed was a lady biker at the large table, sitting with Magda who had her cards laid out in a Celtic cross formation. The woman had long, flame red hair and wore a slim fitting navy t-shirt with high cap sleeves, revealing swirling bands of tattoos on each of her upper arms.

'In time for what?' Sal dropped her shoulder bag on top of her laptop in the corner of the kitchen. 'To meet you, I hope? Hello,' she said to the woman. 'I'm Sal.' She nodded politely, waiting for an introduction.

Stuart was also in the kitchen, standing at the Aga and stirring a small pan of something that smelled of sandalwood and cinnamon. 'This is my daughter, Bonnie.'

'Your daughter?' Jasmine didn't know why she sounded surprised. Stuart was around the same age as her mother after all. She went to sit next to the woman at the table, where Magda's cards sprawled over the worn oak surface. 'Well, nice to meet you, Bonnie.'

'Hi, thank you.' Bonnie said. 'Stuart's told me all about his new lady-friend and when I found out Magda reads the tarot cards I bullied him into letting me come for a reading. She's amazing!'

'So that's why you bustled us out of the way.' Sal said to her gran. 'You knew Bonnie was on her way for a reading.'

Magda stared at her innocently, blinking as if she hadn't a clue what Sal could possibly mean. 'Of course,' she said, trying to do a deadpan face but the deep laughter lines around her mouth gave her away. 'What did you think we'd be getting up to?'

'Yes,' Bonnie echoed, looking at her curiously, 'what did you think they'd be – oh.' She shut her mouth, opened it and then shut it again. Her brain grappled with the thought and then she said, 'Stuart, let that be one of the things I never, ever, hear about.'

Stuart and Magda burst into fits of giggles, jostling each other and murmuring as they laughed.

'It's not funny! Stop that, you're acting like a pair of teenagers!' Jasmine pursed her lips together with mild disapproval but only for a second or two, after which her cheeks went bright red and she tried to stop thinking about it.

The normally spacious kitchen seemed to be getting smaller and smaller lately, Sal realised. Any more visitors on a regular basis and they'd have to start thinking about getting a bigger place. If money wasn't such an issue in the long-term then that might not be a bad idea anyway, she mused. The kitchen, big as it was, could get messy far too quickly when potion making was underway and, she glanced across to the cards still spread out on the table without meaning to, a tarot reading was supposed to be private and there was limited room in the house to allow for that.

'You call your dad by his first name?' Jasmine said, now that her mother had stopped giggling. 'Mind if I ask why?'

'Yes of course, funny story actually! So we were at Bloodstock one year, think I was around five or six years old.' Bonnie said. 'I got lost and …'

'First of all, it wasn't Bloodstock, it was the Dragon Rally in Wales and you were not lost, Bonnie,' Stuart interrupted, 'you were only about ten yards away.'

'Yes, but I was tiny and all I could see was a sea of black leather trousers and hairy faces. Everyone looked the same. Anyway, I kept shouting, "Dad, Dad," and within seconds there were a hundred bearded biker dads looking at me, all trying to figure out which one of them was the right dad.'

'So I told her if she ever got lost again, shout Stuart,' he picked up the story, 'lots of blokes get called Dad, but the chances of there being more than one Stuart are pretty low.'

'So it stuck.' Bonnie finished with a big grin on her face, flinging her arm out behind her without looking. Stuart caught it and gave her a squeeze. Sal watched her gran during this little exchange and saw a happy face smiling at her. She smiled back, yes, she agreed silently, this is a good thing.

'Let's just be clear, though,' Jasmine said, 'that is your bike in the driveway, isn't it?'

'Yeah, I'll be out of your hair now,' Bonnie said. 'Thanks for the tea and toast, Mrs Howard, and for the tarot reading. I'll have a think about what you said, it did make a lot of sense.'

'I told you, it's Magda,' Magda stacked her cards together in a neat pile, 'and you're welcome, drop in any time. It's been that good to meet you, Bonnie.'

Bonnie got up and reached for her jacket which was hanging on the coat rack in the corner nearest to the back door. 'Damn, my shoulder still hurts like mad.' She grumbled, shifting the offending joint around to loosen it as she put the jacket on. 'I could do with a decent massage.'

'Oh? What have you done to it?' Sal asked. 'I did a massage and therapy a course a while ago, if you want me to I can have a look at it for you.'

Nodding, Bonnie replied, 'Oh, yes please! I would love that. I think I must have pulled a muscle when I came off the bike last week.'

'I didn't know you'd had a spill, pet.' Stuart sounded full of reprimand and quizzed her.

'It wasn't anything much,' Bonnie went on, 'I was coming off the 537 back from Buxton. Stupid, really, because I'd already bombed round the Cat and Fiddle without any problems.'

Sal looked at her blankly, 'Is this some kind of secret language only bikers can understand?'

'Cat and Fiddle is a notorious black spot for bike accidents.' Stuart explained. 'Well done, lass.' He was clearly proud of her.

'Well, give me a ring and we'll sort something out. Perhaps not here though, it can get a bit busy. My therapy bed is portable so I can drive over to you, just let me know.'

The thrumming of the motorbike engine filled the kitchen even after Magda had shut the door, but Sal barely heard it. She was distracted by that sensation of almost having a cohesive idea once more but this time, she thought, this time it had a shape to it and she thought it was a shape that she could work with. Sal wondered fleetingly about the therapy and counselling courses she'd taken and if they might be put to use as part of her work but the old house simply wasn't large enough for that. She'd have to put some thought into it another time.

Magda resumed her customary position at the Aga, taking the metal spoon from Stuart and resuming control of the stove top. 'We're making man moisturisers and beard oils.' She held out the spoon for Sal to sniff.

'Magda feels bad about spilling cider on my beard.' Stuart ran his fingers proudly through his grizzled facial hair. 'So she says, anyway. Personally I think she's just after any excuse she can get to stroke my beard. Jealous, you see, not having one of her own.'

'It's a very blokey scent,' Sal approved, 'cinnamon, sandalwood,' she sniffed again, 'patchouli?'

'Spot on.' Magda nodded. 'Coconut oil and beeswax in the moisturiser and the oil's got jojoba and sweet almond as the base.'

'What are you calling it? You've got enough of that cream for five or six jars of it at least. I'll run off a sheet of labels.'

'Don't be daft, Sal. I won't be able to sell this.' Magda shook her head. 'Who'd buy it? My doorstep doesn't get many bearded gentleman knocking on it.'

Stuart put his hand over Magda's, she still held the spoon and he breathed in the scent, gazing into her eyes. 'Trust me, love, you can sell this.' He told her. 'Bikers come in packs, you know. I have a lot of friends with big beards.'

'Oh.' Magda hadn't thought of that. 'Hmm, well what about Pan's Paradise? No, Beardy Bikers' Beard Balm. I can't think of anything right now, Sal, you can come up with something when you've time to sort out the labels. How was the shopping trip, anyway?'

'It was all right,' Jasmine said, 'so far as shopping for sportswear goes, I suppose. This isn't taupe, though, is it?' She pulled out her new yoga gear and Magda burst into fits of giggles.

'No, definitely not taupe.'

'Great,' Jasmine stuffed the yoga pants back into the bag. 'I'm going to look like I've, well, you-know-what myself, aren't I?'

'They're not that bad, besides, nobody's going to be looking at you,' Sal told her, 'they'll all be too busy trying to do the downward dog.'

'Are you sure you need us out of the house? And why Friday, and why yoga?' Jasmine protested. 'I'm not sure yoga is really for me, I'm not going to do it. I'll go to my room and read a book or something, I'll be quiet.'

'You may well be quiet, but I might not be.' Magda raised her eyebrows and wiggled them at Stuart who wiggled his in return.

'Very well, I get the point, Friday yoga – go me!' Her phone buzzed and Jasmine delved into her pocket to pull it out. 'I don't believe this, why can't he leave me alone?'

'Get a new phone,' Magda told her daughter, not for the first time. 'You ought to report him to the police.'

'What? For texting me?'

'Love,' Magda carried on, 'this is harassment. You've left him, he needs to get that through his thick skull and you need to sort out what you're doing with your life. You can't sit on your backside rotting in a flat on your own forever.'

'Yes, I know that, thanks very much, Mother. I've already been through this with Sally, this is exactly why I need to move out,' Jasmine said stonily. 'I can't be doing with all this fuss and nonsense, I just want to – I don't know, be on my own for a bit.'

'Oh bugger off upstairs for a lie down then!'

'Gran!' Sal burst out, 'Mum! The pair of you, stop fighting. We're all on your side, Mum, but please just get a new phone for crying out loud, and tell the police what's been going on. No wonder Gran wants you out of the house on Friday. Don't smirk, Gran, I can see you. Stuart is never going to come here again if you carry on like this the whole time, you're both acting like children!'

She scooped Bran up from the inside of Stuart's bike helmet, which was in its now customary place at the bottom of the coat rack, and marched out of the kitchen with him tucked under her arm and muttered on her way out. 'Sorry, Stuart, I think he's peed in it.'

'Why doesn't that surprise me? Never mind,' he called after her, 'I've just got some new beard oil to mask the smell.'

CHAPTER EIGHT

'Good morning, Vicar.' Magda said cheerily, waving. She walked over the road, checking for traffic as she crossed, and stopped to pass the time of day with her friend. 'Lovely day, isn't it, for this time of year?'

'What brings you here, Magda?' Granger asked, eyeing up the wicker basket she carried. A clean white linen cloth laid over the top, the edges neatly tucked in.

'No, it's not cakes, get your beady little eyes of my goodies,' Magda pulled the basket out of his reach, 'this is for Mrs – oh, sorry.' She interrupted her own sentence. 'I promised I'd be discreet.'

'Mum's the word, then.' He held the wooden gate open for her and ushered her into his domain, holding forth with a steady stream of chatter. Ancient yew trees adorned the churchyard and the green grass was still looking bright and fresh, if a little long. That was unusual, Magda noted, the caretaker was usually on top of things like that. She mentioned it to Granger and he took off his hat, holding it in front of his chest and frowning.

'Simon's not very well, I'm afraid.' He told her. 'Been coughing and hacking like the devil himself, must be getting on for three weeks now. He should have gone to the doctor straight away but you know what it's like, trying to get a stubborn man like him to admit there's anything wrong in the first place.'

'Yes,' Magda knew Simon Jackoby well enough to understand. 'Of course,' she continued, 'and Doctor McKenna is a woman, which won't help, I imagine.'

'He's an old man, set in his ways.' Granger shook his head. 'Male doctors and female nurses and woe betide anyone who tells him different.' He shuffled, hummed briefly to himself and looked at her with earnest. 'He might come and see you, though.'

'Me? I'm no doctor and besides, I'm a woman.'

'Yes, but you're our village wise-woman. As much a part of traditional life as anything else, surely? I might try and persuade him, if that's all right with you. If you could palm him off with some placebo herbs of yours…'

'Wash your mouth out!' Magda shrieked indignantly. 'Placebo herbs, my backside! You know very well my remedies have done wonders for a lot of folk hereabouts and it's wrong of you to say any different! Very wrong, in fact.'

'I'm sorry, Magda,' he babbled rapidly, 'bad way of putting it, you know that's not what I meant at all. Simon's cough is bad, Magda. Very bad. I thought if perhaps he got something of yours and found out that didn't work then he might be persuaded to visit Doctor McKenna.'

'I have never once prescribed a placebo,' she said, 'and I don't intend to start now, but I agree with you. I'll see what I can do for him and if it doesn't work, then I'll do my best to direct him to the quack.'

'Good job,' Granger said, happy to have cleared up the matter. 'I shall recommend you to him. Well, must dash, these sermons don't write themselves and with all the noise going on here, I'll do better from home.'

Magda bobbed her head at him and pushed open the heavy door of the church. The cool temperature of the great stone building, with its lofty height and poor heating, made her shudder with cold as she made her way quickly to the rooms at the back. Magda thought she'd arrived early enough to avoid Mrs Beers, who ran a small lunch group twice a week in the hall for the elderly parishioners, but no, there she was. Mrs Beers and several other members of the church congregation were busy setting out tables and chairs and organising crockery for lunch. Mrs Owen was among them but didn't seem to have noticed Magda yet. She hovered near the door, not wanting to bring attention to herself, though with her full-length terracotta dress, ruffled green scarf and dark blue velvet jacket, she wasn't making a very good job of it. Resolute, she remained in the doorway but Mrs Beers wasn't happy about her presence and walked briskly over, fake smile tidily fixed in place.

'Mrs Howard,' she began, 'are you lost or have come to volunteer? We could always use another pair of hands.'

'Sorry to disappoint you, I'm just running an errand.' Magda wondered how she should handle this. Come out and tell the truth or fudge around it? No, discretion had been asked for so she'd do her best under the circumstances. She rose her voice slightly, hoping Mrs Owen would overhear and notice that she'd arrived. 'A small delivery for one of the volunteers, I'll wait here until she has a free moment.'

'Oh, I can take that for you,' Mrs Beers said in a sickly-sweet voice, 'who's it for, dear?' The nosy woman grabbed for the basket and Magda swung it quickly out of reach. She didn't want to make a scene but Mrs Beers wasn't making things easy. The insufferable woman reached out again, this time hooking her pudgy fingers onto the handle and yanking it away from her.

Magda tried not to raise her voice while she wrestled for control of the basket. 'I'll hand it over myself, thanks all the same.' By this time a few of the greylings, the inherently nosy well-to-do women of Wilveringham, had stopped what they were doing and were watching to see what happened next. Magda tugged, Mrs Beers tugged harder and the inevitable happened. The basket spilled and a small round jar of white cream went flying to the floor. Magda darted quickly and managed to grab it just before Mrs Beers did. Magda brushed dust off her dress and stood up, trying to look respectable in her elegant dress and ruffles while Mrs Beers struggled to her feet clumsily in plain brown trousers and a frumpy flowered blouse. Yes, Magda beamed inwardly, knowing she had come out on top of that little scuffle and she fully appreciated the fact that everyone watching would see Mrs Beers having to fasten up a blouse button which had come undone.

Mrs Beers narrowed her eyes into thin little slits, desperate to regain the upper hand, but Magda wasn't giving in.

'People are watching.' Magda said the one thing that was bound get Mrs Beers into a flap. She shifted her eyes several times to look behind Mrs Beers and the woman followed her glance. Mrs

Beers took a pile of plates from a nearby table and started barking out orders to her hapless volunteers.

Magda remained by the door, fixed her own smile into place, and was relieved when Mrs Owen finally caught her eye. She nodded her head towards the hallway and left the room, deciding that if anywhere in the church would be considered private after that, it would probably be the nave itself. She sat on one of the hard wooden pews in the quiet church, patiently waiting for Mrs Owen. What a disaster, the poor woman might be in for a grilling from Mrs Beers over this, and the cause of it all was not the sort of thing that should gossiped about. At last Mrs Owen appeared and Magda handed over the pot of cream, which was looking quite professional, she thought, with one of Sal's new labels.

'Thank you for this,' Mrs Owen said quietly. 'How long should it take before he can, well, you know?'

'A week or two at the most, I expect. Tell Mr Owen he should be more careful in future,' Magda told her. 'Sorry about that, by the way, that moment in there. I thought you'd be looking out for me.'

'Don't apologise, Mrs Howard.' Mrs Owen looked distracted and slightly sad and Magda thought she might be about to cry. 'I should have seen you but my head was elsewhere, it's just that, well. I shouldn't be telling you this, but I know you won't repeat it ...'

'Then let me stop you right there,' Magda interrupted her. 'If you shouldn't be telling me, then don't. I can't be doing with rumours and hearsay and keeping other people's secrets for them. I always say, if you don't want a secret to get out, don't be the one from whom it escapes.'

Mrs Owen took a moment to make sense of this. 'You're right.' She said. 'Thank you.'

The woman took the cream gratefully and dipped into her trouser pocket to pull out an envelope. Magda couldn't open it now, that would be rude, so no way of telling what it held. She stuffed it in her own pocket until later. She thanked Mrs Owen and left the greyling women to finish their lunch preparations with no further incidents.

She stepped out of the church into the bright light and fresh air. That little incident could have been worse, she thought, not discreet at all but she smiled at the possibility of Mrs Beers having a bruised behind and at least nobody else had seen what was written on the jar. Poor Mr Owen, she shouldn't laugh but she did anyway.

Magda called in to see Stacy on her way home to pick up some eggs and a few veggies. 'Good to see you, love.' They exchanged a quick hug and Stacy told her how the flat was coming along. Magda had to agree the pale mushroom colour walls and minimal furniture would suit Jasmine down to the ground.

'It'll be nice to have someone in it,' Stacy said. 'It must be six months since our last tenant moved out. Ooh, is that your biker friend?'

The throbbing roar of an engine and a flash of black and chrome passed along the high street. Magda and Stacy rubber-necked to watch the bike disappear from view.

'No,' Magda grunted. 'Some other beardy bloke.'

'They don't all have beards, Magda.' Stacy chided. 'Any more gossip, then? Has Sal found herself another job yet?'

'No. I was a bit worried about her to be honest,' Magda admitted, 'but I've done a reading and if she plays her cards right, she'll be rushed off her feet with work soon enough.'

'That's something, I suppose. Ask her to give me a call, though, if you wouldn't mind. Mark's been doing a lot of overtime and then we've been working on the painting upstairs, so he could do with getting his back sorted out before it goes again. He had a rough time with it a few months ago.'

Magda promised to mention it to Sal and strolled out along the high street with her basket full of groceries. She looked at her watch and shrieked with alarm to see she only had half an hour to nip home and change into something more appropriate to wear on the bike for her date with Stuart. She was spending the afternoon at the garage he ran repairing motorbikes in the hopes that her beard oils would go down well with his customers. And after that, with Jasmine and Sal out of the house for the evening – well, she giggled like a little schoolgirl, who knows what will happen?

*

'I can't believe I got roped into this. Do they really do ten minutes of meditation at the end?' Jasmine whispered. Struggling into tight fitting yoga pants in a miniscule toilet cubicle in the village hall was not her idea of a fun thing to do on a Friday evening. Especially not when a dozen yummy mummy types brazenly used the communal changing area and paraded around with their toned stomachs and muscular limbs as if they were a bunch of supermodels getting ready for the catwalk.

'This is nothing,' Sal told her, 'just wait for the Red Moon lodge, more meditation than you can shake your wand at.'

'Jamieson is writing in upper case letters now.'

'I'm sure baby Pansy-May is ready for potty training already.'

'Daniel and I had a date night last weekend and the sitter said Hestia didn't cry at all.'

'Do these women realise their children are going to grow up hating them with those kind of names?' Jasmine hissed.

'Mother, be quiet!' Sal hissed back through the adjacent cubicle door.

'I told you this wasn't taupe!' Jasmine complained, 'I'm coming out.'

'One second,' Sal squeezed out of the adjacent loo and they looked at each other. 'Oh.'

'What do you mean, oh?' Jasmine said. The gaggle of yummy mummies looked awkwardly at her and as if called by a silent bell, they filed out of the cramped changing room and disappeared to the main hall, all of them carrying neatly rolled towels. A couple of them had their own mats and foam yoga blocks and Jasmine felt like an ugly duckling in a world of precocious swans.

'No, that's not taupe.' Sal admitted, eyeing up the suspiciously dark yoga pants. The top was fine, an all-in-one sports bra with a

95

longer, looser cream coloured top over it. But aren't yoga pants meant to have a bit of room for movement? They belled out towards the lower legs and ankles but the backside area? Sal would have been worried too, had it been her own behind at risk of imminent exposure but it was too late to do anything about it now.

'We'll just have to hope they don't make us do a downward dog.' She pulled her mum out of the changing room and they traipsed after the yummy mummy brigade to the main hall where pastel coloured mats were laid out in symmetrical rows.

The yummy mummies, with their pristine messy-bun hair dos and lithe, toned figures were warming up, stretching gracefully and arranging themselves across the mats. There were only a few places spare.

Of course, Jasmine thought, of course she would end up in the middle of the front row where everyone could see her. She and Sal took up their positions and copied the pose of the other women, sitting cross legged, hands on knees, as the instructor walked in. He was a tiny man with a thin grey ponytail and bright yellow leisure wear. He smiled at them, said hello, and started to direct the class through a series of yoga poses. A gentle atmosphere settled through the room, guided by his voice, smooth, silky and relaxing. Jasmine stretched her arms in time and glanced over her shoulder to Sal, who was holding her pose beautifully.

'I think I'm going to fall over.' Jasmine whispered, her legs starting to wobble.

'Just ease into the pose, feel your core centred over the earth. Breathe.' The instructor said, holding a hand out for her to balance with. Jasmine breathed and tried to sink into a state of relaxation but her legs didn't hold and she toppled over.

'It's your first time,' said the instructor gently, 'yoga is a gradual process from one state to the next, a flow of energy. So you must feel the energy flow within you.'

Jasmine nodded, 'I'll try.' Her Mum had been trying to teach her about the flow and ebb of the subtle energy he was talking about since she was a child, but it had never felt natural to her. The only thing she felt inside herself lately was emptiness.

Sal, on the other hand, was doing much better. She was as graceful as the rest of the women in the group and she looked so serene. She moved easily through the salute to the sun while Jasmine tottered unsteadily. She righted herself and copied everyone else as the instructor took them through different positions, movements and poses. And then came the moment she had dreaded.

'And to finish,' the instructor's voice held not a hint of worry though his words made Jasmine nervous, 'downward dog, then ten minutes to meditate.'

Sal whispered across, leaning over. 'I think you should sit this one out.'

'Don't be ridiculous, Sally.' She hissed back, checking behind her to see what the yummy mummies were doing. They were already starting to limber up for downward dog. 'I can't back out, what would they think?'

'Suit yourself.' Sal started to follow the instructor's movements and Jasmine nervously did likewise.

She stood tall, stretched her arms and started to lean forward, pressing her palms against the mat. She pushed her backside into the air and grimaced. The yoga pants tightened up, she could feel it. The instructor, who had been gliding through the hall to correct a pose here or offer a hand for balance there, stood beside her to give her some encouragement.

He patted her back lightly. 'Keep this straight.' Jasmine felt a rumble in her stomach while she leaned over. 'Push your head and neck downwards, straighten your legs.'

Then three things happened at the same time. The seam on the yoga pants stretched beyond capacity and with loud ripping sound the stitching across her bottom tore open. That was the first thing. The second thing that happened was that the instructor, that kind man with the aura of a saint who was only trying to help her and didn't deserve what happened next, he moved his hand to her lower back and therefore was in the direct line of fire when the third thing happened. Jasmine trumped. A loud, rip-roaring, yoga-pants tearing, earthquake inducing fart.

The room fell completely silent, the instructor swiftly moved away, Sal gasped out loud and the yummy mummies burst into fits of horrified laughter.

Jasmine stood up, screamed, thrust her hands over the offending gape of material and ran to the nearest door. It was locked. Damn, wrong door.

Her face was hot and red and all these horrible people with their stupidly named babies and perfect messy buns, they were staring and laughing at her. She wailed again, ran to the other end of room and burst through the door into the corridor. She raced into the changing rooms, grabbed her clothes and was already in the cubicle wrestling off the catastrophic yoga pants when Sal caught up with her.

'Mum,' Sal rapped lightly on the cubicle door, 'are you all right?'

'What flipping colour is this anyway?' Jasmine said, throwing the offending item over the door. Sal put them into her duffle bag, changed back into her own clothes and waited patiently for her mum to stop ranting. After a few minutes Jasmine ran out of steam and opened the door. 'I have never been so embarrassed, Sally, I hate yoga.'

Sal held her arm out and they walked out of the village hall, leaving the yummy mummies and the yoga pants firmly in the past.

'I mean I really hate yoga. It's so stupid.'

'Yes, Mum. Yoga is stupid.' Sal didn't laugh.

'Don't tell your gran, will you?'

'Of course not.' Sal said, still not laughing. Her face was starting to hurt with the strain of it, but she did not laugh. 'I won't tell a soul.'

'I really, really, hate yoga.'

*

98

Magda felt her skin tingle with anticipation as she and Stuart got ready for their night-time escapade. It would be the first time in a long while she'd done this and she hoped they would be finished and back indoors by the time her little tribe came back from yoga.

'And your garden is definitely not overlooked?' Stuart wanted to double-check.

'No, not even a footpath going near it. Last house in the village, so no reason for anyone to come past it on the road either, except by car. Most of the garden is surrounded by trees, we shall be totally alone.'

'Then let's get ready to rumble.' Stuart said, raising his eyebrows a couple of times.

Magda grinned. 'Oh, we're going to rumble are we?'

'Absolutely.'

She picked up her besom and led the way up the stepping stones through the garden to the circle of lawn with the bird-bath altar. 'I know you're leading this ritual, Stuart, but I can still use my besom to sweep round and cleanse the circle, can't I?'

Stuart nodded and she started sweeping, calling out into the circle as she did, cleansing away what did not need to be there and invoking her sacred space. When the circle was complete, she lay down her broom and faced Stuart. 'What now?'

He gently took hold of her hands, kissed her lightly and lifted the hood of her cloak from her face. They were both wearing their everyday clothes beneath the voluminous cloaks for extra warmth in the late autumn night and Magda felt a rising atmosphere of anticipation as they went through this, their first ritual together. And that's all it will be, Magda said to herself, at least for now. She was happy with her decision to be close to Stuart but they were still getting to know each other and it was important to them both to deepen their friendship and romance before anything else. Working rituals together was something they had talked about as a way of deepening that connection and Magda knew he was as excited about it as she was.

Stuart led her to the east of the circle where he called out his druidic invocations to the elements. At the east he called in the air, direction of the rising sun for inspiration, dreams and communication. In the south he called to the element of fire, the heat of midday that represented success, achievement and passion. In the west, the elemental direction for water, he spoke of the ebb and flow of the tides, the twilight hours of emotions, tears of sorrow but also of joy. Finally, in the north he called on the element of earth, the firm foundation and nature itself that gives life to all things and is eternal and never ending. A cycle of seasons, emotions and life in continuation forever, a cycle of birth, death and rebirth.

Deep peace of the running wave to you, deep peace of the flowing air to you, deep peace of the quiet earth to you, deep peace of the shining stars to you.

She listened to his deep voice carefully, getting the feel of the words, so unlike the ones she might use for an invocation but yet, so similar in tone and meaning. She had circled with a druid grove years ago, once upon a time when her husband Sam had been alive, so Stuart's ritual tonight wasn't completely alien to her. Besides, her witchcraft and Stuart's druidry had the same roots and the same sense of reverence in nature, honouring the sacred celebrations of the wheel of the year. This ritual was a good way of seeing how much they harmonised with each other in the circle and Magda copied him now, raising her hands to the sky, to the crescent new moon.

She let his voice soothe her and then, when he went silent, she made her own plea to the Gods and the Ancestors, asking that Sal would soon figure things out and that Jasmine's heart would be healed.

Stuart finished the ritual at the altar with the words of the druid oath.

We swear by peace and love to stand, heart to heart and hand in hand, mark o' spirit and hear us now, confirming this, our sacred vow.

They fed each other from the chalice and plate. A sip of

mead, a morsel of cake and the circle is open, yet ever unbroken. Magda felt completely at peace, at one with nature and deeply connected to the earth, the stars and the ancestors who had come before her and had trodden this pagan path for centuries, paving the way for those to come.

'That was wonderful,' she said. 'Thank you, really, that felt good.' It was nice to have someone else leading the ritual for a change. 'Next time, we'll do it my way and after that we can combine our forces.'

'Sounds good to me.'

Reaching behind her to pull up the hood of her cloak, Magda shuddered with cold. 'Let's get back inside, the wind is picking up.' She looked over to Stuart and saw the way his clothes were hanging under the cloak and realised with a blush that the wind was not the only thing which was picking up. 'Put that away,' she said, 'nothing going on tonight, we agreed.'

Stuart made a half-hearted protest and then he trotted across the circle to pick up the chalice which had fallen off the altar, noticing something on the ground near the hedges as he did so. 'Hello, what's this, then?'

'Oh, that's where we put poor Judy, Sal's old cat.' Magda saw he was looking at the seashells and pebbles and the photograph wrapped in plastic.

'No, that's not what I mean,' he had a serious expression on his face, 'you'd better come and see for yourself.'

Magda walked over and crouched down near the mounded earth. Behind it, nestled at the bottom of the shrubberies that surrounded the garden, was a charred scrap of something. She pulled it out and put a hand to her face.

'Oh no, she hasn't.' Magda held a small, partly burned doll. 'Oh please tell me she didn't.'

Chapter Nine

Sal called out loudly before walking into the room, just in case.

'I don't believe it, look at this.' Jasmine dumped her bag of yoga gear on the couch and discovered an abandoned tea-tray with half-eaten slices of carrot cake on the coffee table in the lounge. 'Do you think they're upstairs? Surely they can't be… well, you know.'

'No, we are not. We heard you come in just now, we've been in the garden.' Magda entered the room, Stuart standing behind her. They were still both wearing their ritual robes over their clothes and Magda had a serious look in her eye that Sal didn't like the look of. 'Doing a ritual.' Magda added, to remove all doubts.

'I'll get my things and see myself out, Magda.' Stuart awkwardly leaned over and muttered in Magda's ear as he left. 'Go easy on her, pet, she's had a rough time.' He pecked her on the cheek. 'See you soon.'

Magda chose not to sit down. Instead, she hovered and looked agitated. 'How was yoga?'

'I hate yoga, can we leave it at that?' Jasmine spat out quickly, piercing Sal with a meaningful look.

'It wasn't quite what Mum was expecting.' Sal said, trying to be helpful. 'Perhaps a regular cinema trip might be a better option – all right, what's wrong?' She knew there was something on her gran's mind. Better to get it out now than to store it up until the pressure built up and she erupted.

'We found this.' Magda held out the charred remains of the little fabric doll and put it on the coffee table. 'I understand why you did it Jasmine, I can only hope you were thinking the right things when you did it.'

'Mum, I'm sorry, but I had to do something.' Jasmine's eyes watered and Sal put a hand on her shoulder, not sure what else she could do.

'I thought you knew better than to mix with things like this when you're feeling hurt and angry. Magic is supposed to protect, to heal, to help.'

'And I need protecting and healing!' Jasmine stood up and wailed. 'Do you honestly think a few thorns and a bit of salt water is going to stop him coming after me? He is texting me nearly every day, I can't bear it.'

'I wish you'd asked me,' Magda sat down, hunched forward, leaning her head into her hands. 'I could have helped you.'

'You told me not to! Look, I know you think I've done something wrong, but when I got to the altar, I remembered what you've always said, about being in the right frame of mind, not doing anything with hatred or rage. I calmed myself down and then I did this, to stop him from hurting me, yes, but not to harm him in the process. I said that out loud.'

'You swear it?'

Jasmine nodded, reaching out her hand. She was crying and she was hurt and in the end, Magda understood. She couldn't fault her daughter for doing whatever she could to keep herself safe. She would give Stuart a ring tomorrow and explain it to him. Magda was getting quite fond the gnarly looking gentle druid and didn't want didn't want him getting the wrong impression of her little tribe.

*

Sal fixed the legs of her portable massage couch into place and turned the nuts to secure them. She arranged fluffy white towels over the top, rolled one up to place at the end of the table and invited Bonnie to lie down.

'I'm going to use sweet almond oil with rosemary and comfrey oils,' Sal warmed the oil in her hands and began to massage Bonnie's back and shoulders, enjoying the scent of the essential oils and the warm atmosphere provided by the vanilla candles she'd brought with her. As she and Bonnie exchanged the odd comment and she got into the flow of energy, Sal wondered why she didn't do this more often. It virtually guaranteed customer satisfaction and she enjoyed making people feel better, emotionally as well as physically.

'You've got quite a lot of tension just here.' Sal kneaded and smoothed Bonnie's shoulder muscles with her hands, working at the knots in the tissue. 'Not painful is it?'

'Oh no, that's good.' Bonnie said quietly, her voice serene and peaceful. 'Ooh yes, just there – mmm.'

Bonnie was a lot like Stuart, Sal noted, easy to get on with, the sort of person who everybody likes. It was nice to be making friends with Bonnie, Sal needed more friends in her life and doing something nice like this made her feel useful. She thought briefly about the advert she'd seen in the paper for a shop to rent but that was out of the question, she couldn't see making that work on a therapist's income and the thought of actually running her own business would be more than she could handle. Though it would be nice to supplement her income a bit by doing this sort of thing more often for friends and family, she would still have to look out for a more reliable full-time job in the long-term.

'This is so nice,' Bonnie murmured. She sounded half-asleep and Sal smiled, pleased she was doing something that made people feel so good. 'Can I give your number to my friends? Everyone should have massages like this every week.'

'I'm that good, eh?'

'Yes.' Bonnie moaned softly. 'This is heaven.'

'Thank you, and yes, of course you can.' She went through to Bonnie's kitchen and switched on the kettle, giving Bonnie a few minutes to raise herself from the couch and make herself comfortable. 'Lovely house, by the way.'

'Let me guess, not what you expected for a biker?' Bonnie's house was a plain, modern semi-detached on the outskirts of Barlaston. The décor had alternative touches here and there but with an overall theme of cream and white and pink and velvet. Although it had been a bit of trek to get here, Sal was pleased to be out of her own house for bit. With Gran's discovery of the doll in the garden, the atmosphere was uneasy.

'I'm not sure that I expected anything in particular.' Sal

brought mugs of chamomile tea into the lounge for herself and
Bonnie.

'People see me on the bike and think I'm living some mad,
way out life. Truth is,' Bonnie put her feet, complete with fluffy pink
slippers, onto her cream sofa, 'I grew up surrounded by bikers but my
mum's still quite girly, and I've got a sister and lots of female cousins,
I suppose all the femininity soaked into me.'

'So that's why your bike has got the glitter on it.'

'I love bikes and engines and the throbbing of the tank
between your legs, the rush of the speed, it's exhilarating.' The way
Bonnie explained it, Sal could see the attraction. 'And I'm fairly
alternative in most things but I still like to have a few girly touches
around me.'

'I think it suits you.' Sal said, putting down her mug. 'Well, I'd
better pack up my things and get off.'

'I'll give you a hand if you like,' Bonnie offered, but Sal waved
her off.

'No, you sit there and relax. Nobody wants to be lifting and
shifting things after a massage, keep your feet up.'

By the time she'd put the towels and oils into her bag and
wrestled the couch back into its cover, Bonnie looked like she'd fallen
asleep so Sal headed to her car as quietly as she could. She had to
struggle to get the bulky couch in the small boot and as she jiggered it
about, she heard a tapping on the window. Bonnie beckoned her back
to the house.

'Did I forget something?'

'No, I did,' Bonnie held out a cheque, 'you should have
reminded me. I didn't know how much you charge, though, is that all
right? That's what I used to pay a while ago to a lady who doesn't do
it anymore.'

Sal looked at the cheque. 'Forty pounds.' She said, feeling
stunned. 'Are you sure? That's great, thanks Bonnie. See you around.'

'Thank you so much, it was brilliant.'

Driving home, Sal wasn't sure what to think. She'd offered

Bonnie a massage because she wanted to help her, she hadn't intended to ask for anything in return, let alone that much. Still, she wondered again about this massage business and where, if anywhere, it might lead her to. If she had the space for it at home, a room she could use solely as a therapy room, it might be workable, especially at that kind of price. She didn't want to rip people off, but Bonnie had come up with her own price, Sal hadn't asked for it. If she could do it for say, twenty-five or thirty a time… Sal wasn't good with figures and she struggled to work out how many clients she would need each week to make up a full-time salary. And that's exactly why it would never work, even if there was an extra room in the house she could use, Sal just didn't have the right kind of mind to do the plotting and planning behind running a small business.

Working in offices for someone else was one thing, doing it for yourself was a different world altogether. How did you even go about finding premises, securing a bank loan, touting for clients and not only that but doing it on your own from scratch? If she was going to be a therapist, then that's what she would want to focus on, leaving the administration of it to someone else, someone who enjoyed that kind of thing. For Sal, working in admin had only ever been a means to an end. She would have to do some serious thinking about her future and start making decisions before it was too late and she got sucked back into the world of working nine-to-five in another dull and mindless office with colleagues she couldn't relate to and worse, a nasty world of bad quality office coffee.

*

Jasmine and Magda faced each other across the spacious kitchen table, the air between them feeling thick and stale with the dried sludge of last night's discovery. A pot of coffee was going cold on the counter behind them. Neither of them was in a mood for conversation and that suited Jasmine for now. The Archers was playing on the radio, Sal was upstairs soaking in the bath and Bran the kitten curled up on top of Sal's printer, his loud purr threatening to out-do The Archers. Jasmine was reading a magazine and Magda, knitting away with her feet up on the chair next to her while she listened to the programme, wondering why on earth the woman didn't pick up a decent book from time to time.

A tiny tinkle rang out and Magda looked up over her shoulder to see the kitten still fast asleep. And the collar Jasmine had given Sal for him was still far too big.

'Hello Judy,' Magda said, 'we haven't forgotten you.'

Jasmine put her magazine down. 'That's starting to get a bit creepy, isn't it?'

'Creepy? Don't be absurd.'

'I found my vase knocked over yesterday, it was empty but still…'

'Probably the wind. Was it on that window sill on the left-hand side of your room? Always been a bit of draught through there.'

'I suppose so.' Jasmine picked up her magazine again, turning the page. Her phone buzzed. She looked over at her mother and with calculated ease, placed the magazine over the top of her mobile. 'I don't want to know.' She said bravely. 'I've phoned work to let Mr James know I definitely won't be back and I've turned down the transfer to Hastings. I'm moving on, from everything.'

Magda turned her attention away from the goings-on in Ambridge but didn't reply. She carried on knitting, something she'd learned to do with her fingers while her mind was focused elsewhere. She was making a baggy cabled jumper with a pentagram on the front for Sal as a gift for Yule and wanted to race on with it, not sure if she'd have time to finish it.

'So I'm going to get a new phone number and I'm moving into the flat on the high street. I'm not sure what to do about all of the things I've still got in Manchester, though.'

'Paul will want to get rid of it after a while, won't he?' Magda said. 'But leave that to me to arrange, I have a biker boyfriend now. Should you want anyone to go over and collect anything for you, I can get him to rustle up some muscle.'

'Rustle up some muscle?' Jasmine put a hand to her mouth

and laughed. 'You're turning into a dirty old woman, aren't you?'

'Oi!' Magda paused in her knitting to point a finger. 'Less of the old, if you don't mind. By muscle, I meant big burly and intimidating bikers to collect your things from the slug. And take that grin off your face, little madam!'

It was Magda's turn for a phone call now, her mobile ringing loudly and making the table vibrate. 'Hello?' She answered and felt her heart do a little leap when she heard her lusty Pan's voice respond. 'Ooh, really? Yes, sounds great. Half an hour, see you then.'

'Going on another date?'

'Pagan pub moot.' Magda said excitedly. 'Haven't been to one for a couple of years but Stuart's just heard about this new one and it sounds like something we might enjoy together. Oh bugger, now I don't know what to wear.'

'Start with the scarf first and see what matches it.' Jasmine suggested helpfully as her mother flew out of the room and darted upstairs. Magda rapped on the door of the bathroom and loudly informed Sal where she was going.

Four different outfits later, her hair pinned up in what she hoped was an elegant mess of soft grey curls with a bright purple flower wedged on one side, and Magda was ready. She swept her hand over the bannister rail as she came down, letting her fingers run over her numerous, colourful scarves until one caught. She snared it and looked. Bright yellow, that wouldn't do at all, a dreadful clash with the red floaty top and the dark green ruffled skirt she was wearing. She put it on anyway, her horror-show of colours was a talking point, after all.

'Just pass me that knitting please, love.' Magda poked her head through the kitchen door.

'Oh dear, I bet bumble bees love you, don't they? You look like a flower. Several flowers actually.' Jasmine remarked at the purple, red, yellow and green ensemble. The doorbell rang. 'You can't take your knitting, Mother.'

'I shall be sat on my backside all night,' Magda said, 'I could be half way through another sleeve by the time we leave.'

'And you can't wear that skirt on the back of the bike.'

'Ah, dammit.' Magda dashed off for another change of clothes. 'Let him in for me, won't be a sec.'

She returned in a thin sweater with a pentagram on the front, jeans, boots and a thick jacket, only to find Stuart without his leathers. 'I've come in the car,' he told her, 'weren't you listening?'

Magda nearly insisted on changing again but Stuart firmly guided her to the door. 'Nobody's going to be judging you on your clothes when you're sitting next to a handsome face like this all night.'

Jasmine groaned and slammed the door shut behind them. 'Worse than a pair of teenagers.' She said out loud. A loud mewling noise drew her attention away and she played with Bran the kitten for a while before settling down in the lounge with the television for the night.

*

The Green Man was an appropriately named venue for a pagan pub moot and as it was mid-week, the pub had a few regulars and one or two couples spotted around the bar but it would be a stretch to say it was busy. Stuart ordered drinks while Magda had a good nosy about, seeing straight away the small gathering of pagans. She could have spotted them a mile away, with the slightly louder than necessary conversation and guffaws of laughter. Broad grins perched on every face and the crowd was a mixture of all ages and all styles of dress from token gothic to ultra-smart. To an outsider, it may be an odd collection of people but Magda had found that no matter how diverse the pagan scene looked, there was a thread of commonality among them all. She thought she recognised a couple of faces from other pagan events in the area. She and Stuart squeezed themselves into some spare seats and Magda, bold as ever, introduced them and the conversation carried on, taking them into the flow with ease.

Magda reached into her bag for her knitting and sat happily cabling and purling away as she chatted to Caz, Mel, Amethyst, Ian and Pete.

'I've got a friend called Pete,' Magda said, 'he's a vicar, though.' That revelation brought on an interesting conversation about the differences and the similarities between paganism and other religions and Magda took the opportunity to do a little bragging about her stint at the interfaith event.

A Dave turned up to join them. Nobody present had met this particular Dave before but he fit in well with the group straight away. An odd thought struck Magda then. There was always a Dave at things like this. It was virtually an unwritten rule that stated out of every gathering with more than six or seven people, one of them had to be a Dave. Dave was a druid and though he and Stuart hadn't met, they knew of each other through mutual friends. Magda was loosely connected to Mel via her friend Agnes's sister, Willow, and Amethyst had gone to the same college as Sal when she'd left school though she couldn't remember if she knew Sal or not.

'What are you knitting, Magda? I wish I'd brought mine, now.'

'Baggy jumper for my granddaughter, I'm trying to replicate the pattern on this one.' She answered, indicating the sweater she had on with the pentagram on the front. She showed Mel the intricate pattern on her needles. 'I'll bring you the pattern next time.'

The evening wore on, the conversation and the laughter came readily and after a while, Magda took a break for the loo and a fag. She stood outside in the cold with Dave and Amethyst, the other smokers in the group.

'Bloody freezing out here.'

'Ah, but look at the Lady.' Magda puffed on her electric vapour stick and pointed at the moon. The silver crescent was starting to thicken and bulge towards being gibbous. 'How lovely is that? Samhain and the full moon are nearly here already. The year's gone by so fast.'

'Every year seems to fly past more quickly than the last.' Dave agreed. Amethyst wasn't old enough to appreciate how valuable time was, Magda thought. But us oldies, us silver haired foxes and vixens, we know just how little of it we have left.

'Always seems like a shame to see Samhain arrive,' Dave said, 'knowing that's it just darkness and grey until the snowdrops come around at Imbolc.'

'I like winter,' Amethyst piped up as the trio headed back inside. 'I like to think of all the animals hibernating underground, cosy and warm in their little burrows.'

'Are you sure you didn't meet my Sal at college? That's just the sort of thing she would say.' Magda took up her place beside Stuart and gave him a warm smile and a peck on the cheek.

'Have we missed anything good?' She whispered, picking up her knitting.

'We were just wondering if you'd like to come to our Samhain ritual.' Said Mel.

'Oh? Have you got something planned?'

'This is, what? Our third meeting now and we talked last time about a ritual for Samhain, up at Spinney woods near Ashton, weather permitting of course.'

'I know where that is,' Magda said, 'there's an old clootie tree, isn't there? Are you sure we'd be welcome?'

'I can't see why not.' Mel replied. 'We haven't got a ritual per se, just thought we could take turns to do the quarters and share our memories of the Ancestors, that sort of thing.'

'That sounds nice,' Magda said, making a note of the details Mel gave her. 'I'll let you know if I can make it.' Under the table she tapped her foot against Stuart's leg, willing him to keep his mouth shut. She'd already been thinking about her own ritual for Samhain, the witch's end of year celebration to honour the departed souls of the beloved dead, and wasn't sure if she wanted to share the festival or stick with her own plans. But then she realised she hadn't talked to Stuart about it and felt bad about making sure he didn't say they would go. He might well want to accept the invitation and it was none of her business if he did. She'd apologise for her assumption later.

'I still think I've seen you somewhere before, Magda,' Pete told her, changing the subject. 'Were you at a talk on mediumship at the Stoke conference a couple of years ago?'

'I don't think so, no, but I know what you mean,' she answered, losing her grip and dropping her small cable needle under the table. 'The pagan community being what it is, no doubt we've all been to some of the same events over the years.'

She leaned under the table for her short needle but it had rolled and she had to reach over Stuart's lap to retrieve it, sniffing his beard on the way back up. 'You're wearing it!' She said happily. 'It does smell good, doesn't it?'

Stuart stroked his beard and held his chin out proudly. 'Beard oil made especially for me by the lady's fair hand.'

'I could do with some of that for my beardly beloved,' Mel honed in for a smell and made appreciative noises. 'I don't suppose you sell it, do you?'

'As it happens,' Stuart spoke up before Magda could beat him to it, 'there's one bottle left, if you want it. Forgot to tell you, the samples you left at the garage went like hotcakes, remind me to give you the money for it later.'

'I don't suppose you've got it with you?' Mel said, picking her bag up from the floor and taking out her purse. Stuart went to fetch the remaining bottle of beard oil from the car and Magda was surprised to find out he'd been charging a tenner for it.

'Hope you don't mind but I could do with getting off, I've got to be at the garage early tomorrow to open up, it's Ben's day off.'

'It's been lovely to meet you all, thanks for being so welcoming.' Magda kissed and hugged everyone goodbye and promised to keep in touch.

'What a pleasant evening, Stuart.' She took his arm as they walked to his car. 'Thanks for inviting me, I've really enjoyed it.'

Stuart drove back to Wilveringham, not saying very much to her all the way and she wondered if something was on his mind. When he pulled up outside the old house he got out of the car to open her door for her.

'You've been very quiet, Mr Redman.' She eyed him up and

waited for him to respond. When he did, it wasn't with words and she felt herself melting under his randy yet respectful touch. No, she had promised herself and him that it would be some time before she went down that route. They were waiting, they'd made the decision together and she'd stick by that.

'Miss Goldsmith,' he began, 'would you – oh for heaven's sake.' Magda had exploded into fits of giggles at the joke and she couldn't stop. A light came on in the window above the back porch, Sal's room, so they ducked quickly out of sight, Magda stuffing her hand into her mouth to stifle her guffaws.

'Let's go for a walk,' Stuart suggested, 'if you'd like to, that is.'

Magda said that she would like to, very much, and arm in arm they braced the chill of the October air with no destination in mind. Witch and druid ambled along and found themselves, without realising it, staring up at the imposing stone edifice of St Anne's, beautifully majestic in the darkness and quiet.

'I am sorry, by the way, I shouldn't have assumed you'd want to spend Samhain with me.'

'Of course I'd like to spend it with you,' he said, 'I have been thinking about things, though.'

Magda turned her head away and let go of his arm, stuffing her hands into her jacket pockets, wondering if there was a tissue in there, just in case she needed it.

'Don't beat about the bush, Stuart.' She said, not looking at him. 'Be honest with me, please.'

He surprised her by saying, 'I'm not sure how long I can manage with this waiting business.'

'Oh, I see.' Magda's stomach did somersaults. 'You randy old goat.'

They walked along a little more, down a side street behind the church where it was quiet and unwatched and private and before long, they were leaning up against the stone wall between the orchard and the graveyard and things were stirring in the bushes. Magda was thrilled right through to her bones and then things really started to stir in the bushes.

'There's someone here.' She whispered. A rustling noise in the nearby shrubbery sounded far too loud to be rabbits or a fox.

'Are you sure?' He hushed her with his lips.

'Really, I can hear someone.' Magda broke off their kiss and whispered. 'Listen.'

More loud rustling in the bushes and then, silence.

'Who's there?' Stuart called out, quickly darting over the wall to see but by the time he got to the spot the sound had been coming from, whoever it was had gone.

'I can't believe it!' Magda was indignant. 'Someone was watching us! How horrible.'

'They'll be disappointed though,' Stuart clambered back to the orchard side of the wall and like a gentleman, he walked Magda back to her house, 'it's not like they were interrupting us further down the garden path.'

'No, not quite.' But Magda still had to adjust her clothing. She felt ruffled and out of sorts. 'Dirty little peeping Tom.'

'There'll be another time.' He gave her a kiss goodnight and handed over the money he'd taken for the beard oils and then he left for the night.

'I hope so.' She said out loud after he'd gone. 'I certainly hope so.'

She felt a very happy kind of warmth as she went to sleep, her head full of giggling excitement.

CHAPTER TEN

'What do you think, Mum?' Jasmine asked nervously, dumping her hand-bag down on the sofa. 'Stacy's had the plumber in to do a gas check and it's got smoke alarms, we tested those yesterday.'

'It's…' Magda looked around the small flat, not quite sure what to say. It was nicely decorated and roomy enough for a single person, she supposed. There was a separate lounge and kitchen, bedroom and bath and an inner hallway with room for a coat stand. The pale mushroom walls and plain furniture suited Jasmine's pristine taste but it wasn't what she would call homely. The front windows opened out over the high street and the sounds of people talking and walking by drifted up into the flat. The Black Swan was immediately opposite and with the shop below, which was currently open, Magda thought the noise would drive her mad. Still, she wasn't the one who was going to be living here. She hoped Jasmine wouldn't be lonely. 'It's going to be very different for you, isn't it, after being at home where it's so quiet? I don't think I could stand all the noise. I'm sure you'll settle in quickly, though.'

'I love it,' Jasmine walked through the flat, opening all the windows and letting in the fresh air. 'And I don't think it's noisy at all, I'm used to living in cities. I like being able to see what's going on outside. I think it's perfect, a blank canvas.'

Jasmine was feeling some degree of apprehension at the thought of living on her own now that it was finally time to move in, but she wasn't going to admit that out loud and certainly not to her mum, who would fuss and cluck and would never be out of her hair, given half the chance. She put the bunch of flowers her mum had given her into a vase, one that Stacy had provided, and placed them on the small white wooden cube that Jasmine assumed was a coffee table. 'Thank you, they're lovely.' Pink carnations, stocks and white roses. She breathed in the floral scent and smiled, fanning the flowers out prettily in the vase.

'Stuart,' Magda shouted down to the street below where he

was unloading boxes from Jasmine's car and her own. Two bikes were parked in the bays on the street as well as the cars and Stuart and one of his mechanics, complete with leather jacket and gigantic boots, were hauling boxes through the narrow alley that led to the back of the shop where the outdoor stairwell for the flat was situated. 'Do you need a hand?'

'No thanks, pet, we're coming up now.'

'It's so good of him, Mum, you've snagged yourself a good 'un.'

'I like to think so, it's early days, so I'm not counting my chickens yet but things are heating up. He's funny, he's kind, he's intelligent, he's a druid and, sorry to be so blunt, but he's also a bit bloody sexy, isn't he?'

'Oh God, he's a pensioner!'

'So am I. He's only partly retired, he still does some work himself at the garage most days.' Magda started to dance around the lounge, shaking her hips and flaunting her larger than average chest. 'Everything still works you know, not that we've put it to the test yet, but still, give us time.' She started singing Shania Twain's I Feel Like A Woman.

'Stop prancing around, people will see you!' Jasmine couldn't believe her mother's brazen attitude. On reflection, she shouldn't be surprised at all, the daft old hag had always been like this. It was embarrassing. She was relieved to be spared further conversation on the topic of her mother's impending sex life when Stuart and his mate came in with the first of the boxes. Some of those held Jasmine's few belongings, mainly clothes and a few books, CDs and trinkets she'd had stored at the family house for years, the rest contained the equipment Stuart's friend Barry had provided for the alarm system. Magda and Jasmine started to open boxes and organise the flat while Stuart and his mate, Phil, got to work with the alarm sensors and fitted high quality locks to the main door and windows.

The two men worked quickly and while Stuart's mechanic tidied up and packed his tools away, Stuart guided Jasmine through the alarm system. The flat had an external door opening directly onto the stairwell and just inside was a second, inner door coming straight into the hall. Next to the inner door, they had installed the alarm's small black box. There was a digital display and an array of buttons beneath it.

'What's your new phone number?' Stuart asked. 'If I programme it in here, you can connect the alarm to your mobile. It gives you alerts while you're out.'

'I haven't got a new one yet,' Jasmine confessed, 'I decided I didn't want the hassle of changing my number, would have to give to everybody, and it is just so time consuming.'

'Oh Jasmine,' Magda exclaimed, disappointed, 'what are you thinking? I thought you were moving on.'

'I am.' She should have known this would not go down well. 'But I can't be bothered to spend four hours texting all my contacts, letting the bank know, you know what it's like. I'll just ignore him, I'll be fine.'

'You're being foolish.' Magda's voice was like granite and her face was not far off it either. 'How can this be a clean slate if you're letting that moron keep in touch with you? It's like handing him a free pass to keep control of you. You'll be cringing with fear every time the damn thing beeps at you.'

'I'll be all right.' Jasmine said, though she was reassuring herself of that just as much as her mother. She would be all right, wouldn't she? Suddenly she wasn't so sure but it was too late for that now, Stuart had put in the alarm and she'd paid Stacy and Mark a month in advance. No backing out now. 'Stop fussing.'

By the time her visitors had packed up and left, she was finally on her own in a new and nearly bare environment, surrounded by furniture and kitchen utensils that didn't belong to her, Jasmine caught herself locking all of the windows and doors. She sat with a cup of coffee trying to read a magazine until the coffee had gone cold and she lost count of the number of times she had gone to check if the light on the alarm was still green. Oh try and relax, you pathetic woman, she scolded herself.

And then her phone lit up with Paul's number.

She read the text. 'I hate you, Paul.' She said the words aloud but her voice was small and quiet and bounded off the bare walls.

She cried for a few minutes and then she read the message again.

Where R U? Burning UR stuff if u don't come back 2moz.

Jasmine deleted the text and cried again. 'You can't do that!' She said it quietly, knowing her voice might carry to the shop on the ground floor and for the first time in her life, her habit of talking to herself out loud didn't seem normal anymore. The thought of going back to the house in Manchester, which fortunately she had no financial interest in, sank over her like molten lava. Did she even want her things back? Clothes she'd worn when they'd been together, the diamond earrings he'd given her to make up for the second black eye, the photograph of her award ceremony from work, taken on a day when she'd been so happy for the recognition but had lied about staying for drinks afterwards so she could avoid coming home for another hour? No, she didn't miss, want or need any of it.

'Go ahead, burn the lot.' Jasmine said into the lonely lounge where only she could hear it. 'I hope you die choking in the smoke.'

She thought of how little she had really achieved in her life, how little she had given to Sally and her mum over the years and slow, stinging tears fell over her cheeks. The noise of the street kept her company. That and the steady green light of the alarm system that was designed to protect her from harm. It wouldn't keep anyone out, she thought, it was only a deterrent, an early warning system and it couldn't enter her mind to keep her self-saboteur at bay. Jasmine was her own worst enemy, dwelling over and over again on the hurtful things other people had said to her in the past, things said so long ago they should be forgotten and buried but she dragged them all out and flogged herself with them every week, every day, every hour.

Jasmine thought the noise of the high street would be soothing, an indication that the world outside carried on as always, but it wasn't soothing and she wondered how long it would be before she came close to feeling normal again. She stood at the window for a time, arms around her shoulders, watching the people below. From up here, it seemed the whole village was on display just for her, the pub, the butchers, the old war monument surrounded by iron railings, and next to that was the church of St Anne's. Jasmine stared at the old stone building, the gargoyles and stained glass, and the priest, her mother's friend Reverend Peter Granger. She could see him now pottering in the churchyard, dressed in dark trousers and a burgundy sweater. He had so many volunteers running events inside the church, it seemed a shame to see him doing the gardening by himself. She had felt a bit better after speaking to him a few days ago and resolved that as soon as this awful women's weekend was over, she would pay him a visit and offer to help.

*

Feeling wretched at leaving Jasmine on her own and regretting her sharp tongue getting the better of her, Magda took her wicker basket out of the car, deciding she would walk home. Stuart and his friend had already zoomed off on their bikes, back to the garage to work with oily engines. She was only minutes away from home and the walk would do her good, she could come back later for her car or get Sal to fetch it for her. She nipped into the shop on the ground floor and felt reassured when Stacy promised to check in on Jasmine before she locked up the shop for the day.

Magda walked slowly, passing the bakery and eyeing up the display of tarts and sausage rolls in the windows. She made better than that herself at home. Mrs Beers' young assistant was behind the counter, reading a magazine and scoffing a flaky pastry. Magda often wondered how Mrs Beers justified calling herself a baker when she spent most of her time fawning over the village community groups, leaving her minions to staff the shop and do most of the actual baking.

Mr Owen appeared by her side, pushing open the bakery door, shopping list in hand. The man nodded at Magda and mumbled hello. She was pleased to see him up and about but resisted the urge to ask how he was doing. Better not to embarrasses the unfortunate chap in public, he'd suffered enough.

Magda stopped at the butchers for sausages and sliced ham. 'Two-fifty please, Mrs Howard.' The butcher's wife, a sweet woman in her early thirties whose name Magda always struggled to remember, handed her a package of chilled meats wrapped in white plastic. It was much larger and heavier than a few sausages and cold cuts ought to be and she wondered if she'd have room in the freezer for the extra. As she handed over a fiver and took her change, Magda notice the woman's slightly rounded belly.

'Any news, then?' She asked, nosy as ever.

'Well, we haven't told anyone yet, but yes.' A grin the size of the crescent moon lit up her face. Lucy, Magda remembered now. 'I'm twelve weeks pregnant and everything seems okay this time. Keep your fingers crossed for us, won't you?'

'Congratulations, I wish you all the best.' She said, noting the change was wrong. She'd got three quid back but didn't mention it. Sometimes that was how things were still done, out here in the middle of nowhere in a sleepy little village separated from civilisation by only fifteen or twenty minutes.

Magda remembered Mrs Owen's white envelope at last and took it out of her pocket, her wicker basket hanging from her arm. A lottery ticket with two entries on it. Whoopee doo. She didn't mean to be ungrateful, but a ten pound note would have been a more useful and fair exchange of resources. A few extra sausages, a bit of loose change, a lottery ticket, which now she looked at it properly, had last week's date on it, and the odd fiver shoved through the letter box in the middle of the night with nothing to identify its source. She sighed, shoving the envelope in her basket and covering everything with her white linen cloth.

Magda decided to stroll along the canal bank on her way back home, loving the scent of the last wildflowers on the breezy air and the sound of ducks quacking at each other as they swam lazily about, pecking at the bank for worms and grubs. Is it ungrateful of me, she thought, to want a bit of hard cash in return for my hard efforts? Without her regular tarot clients, she'd be really struggling and as always when her thoughts turned to finances, she thanked her lucky stars, and Odin and Freya and Artemis and Apollo, that she owned the house outright. That was the one thing her husband Sam had made sure he finalised before he abandoned life on earth for the Summerlands. She didn't think of him as often these days, ten years after his death from cancer, but when she did it was always with gratitude. He'd been the one who was good with money, which must be where Jasmine got it from. Even without a mortgage, there were still bills to pay and she rarely earned enough from her tarot clients to be able to put anything aside. Sal's rent and board and her own small pension had been keeping them afloat for a few years now and with Jasmine's recent arrival and a healthy sized cheque to make a few repairs around the house, things were good financially, at least for a little while. Last week Stuart had talked about holiday plans and she was tickled pink at the idea of a saucy trip abroad now that she could afford it. She fancied somewhere romantic. Paris, Venice, Prague – hell, even the Lake District would make for a nice change. She was grateful to Jasmine for making it possible and wished she hadn't been so hard on her daughter. Sometimes, Magda Howard, you should keep your big mouth closed. She would go and pick her car up herself tonight, maybe she would make a casserole for Jasmine as an apology.

Magda sat by the side of the canal for a while, watching the slow and peaceful journey of a brightly painted narrow boat making its way gently downstream. She waved to the middle-aged couple aboard and they waved back, exchanging pleasantries while the ducks quacked noisily and swam alongside. What grated at her, she reflected once the noise of the boat's engine was out of ear-shot and she could think again, was that people didn't really value what she did. An hour's worth of her time for a consultation in her own home, another hour or more brewing up some concoction on top of the cost of the ingredients she used, and all she got was a few extra sausages in her weekly order and a used lottery ticket. Pathetic. Perhaps she should jack it all in and open a café. She'd always fancied having a café but not enough to think about it properly, she wouldn't want to work that hard anyway, not at her age, which made itself known a little bit more with every passing winter. She marvelled at her daughter's cleverness with money. When the rest of the woman's life was in tatters, her job was a security blanket that must have been more highly paid than anyone realised and very wisely, it seemed that Jasmine had squirrelled away and invested a significant amount.

Good for you, my girl. She was proud of her. 'Oi, bugger off!' She pulled the ruffled hem of her skirt away from the ducks who'd started pecking around her for food.

Magda went home, put away her few bits of shopping and got out her gilded tarot cards, shuffling them well and smudging them with her feather fan. Both Sal and Jasmine were unsettled and she felt it keenly in their auras as they wandered aimlessly about the house over the last few weeks since Jasmine had been back. Sal had been busy gardening, helping Magda prepare creams and oils and coming up with a range of labels for them; Jasmine was scouring the papers and the internet every day, looking for work. But they were both so introspective and quiet and she was usually able to coax them out of their shells. It felt like the quiet before a storm, Magda could sense the tempest on its way and she was determined to get to the bottom of it if she could, before it smacked her on the backside and knocked her for six without warning.

'Lady of fate and destiny, let me see what there is to see, show me this in honesty, as I will it, so shall it be.'

She held her hands over the cards, breathing deeply to ground and centre herself. She laid out the first of a simple three card spread. Her immediate obstacle was the death card, the hooded figure who grinned at her with skeletal glee, scythe raised to harvest the souls of the Beloved Dead.

'Well, that's a bloody cheery start.' Her fingers teetered over the next card, reluctant to discover more bad news when there was a short, sharp knock at her back door. 'This had better be some good news.' She placed the card back into the deck and shoved the pack up on her spice rack, out of the way.

'Reverend Granger, do come in.' Magda was pleased to see him when she opened the door. She switched on the kettle and then rummaged in her cupboard, wondering what flavour of tea might be fun today. 'Regular tea, or as I like to call it regulari-tea, or something more interesting?'

'Coffee please. I don't always trust your tea,' he said, 'not when you've got that mischievous look in your eyes.'

'I don't know what you mean.' Magda smiled, all innocence. Bran wound his tail around her legs. She picked the kitten up and handed him to the vicar who petted the little creature happily. 'You have grass on your shoes, by the way.'

'Sorry about the mess, been gardening.' Granger helped himself to a home baked biscuit from a plate on the table. 'I've spoken to Simon Jackoby, by the way, said he'll come and see you if he doesn't improve soon.'

'Well, we can't drag him here against his will.' Magda shrugged. Some folk wouldn't jump in the river if they caught fire. 'I'm sure that isn't what really brought to you my doorstep.'

'Yes, bit delicate, I'm afraid. One wonders,' Granger cleared his throat, 'if perhaps you may have gone a little bit too far this time, my dear.'

'Who have I upset this time?' Magda wondered, 'I knew there was something on your mind, your face has gone bright red and I know it's not the communion wine causing it this time.'

'Now, hold on a second,' Granger held up a waggling finger. 'That wasn't communion wine, I had food poisoning, as you well know, and the font needed a good scrub anyway. Now,' he said, still petting little Bran, 'I'm sure I don't need to remind you that the church and its grounds are hallowed, you know, sanctified. Not suitable for – shall we say – certain behaviours?'

'Certain behave – oh.' Magda's face changed as she realised

what the vicar was implying.

'Yes, oh.'

'I knew there was someone in those bushes! So, which dirty sod was it? Not that there was all that much to see.'

'Well, it wouldn't be fair of me to say, but suffice to say, you might want to make your own bread for a while.'

'That little snoop!' Magda jumped up out of her seat, spilling her mug all over the vicar's lap as she did so.

'Ow, that's hot!'

'Sorry!'

'No retaliation, Magda.' Granger grabbed a napkin and started dabbing at his trousers. 'I don't want there to be any trouble, all right?'

'Oh fair enough,' Magda sulked, 'have it your way. I won't say anything, but ask yourself this, Mister Vicar. What was she doing in the rose bushes at that time of night, eh?'

'Other than snooping on your good self, you mean? Your new acquaintance is ruffling a few feathers in the village, in case you hadn't noticed. That bike of his is a talking point, people are curious, that's all.' Granger stood up and brushed at his coffee-stained trousers and helped himself to another biscuit. 'Off the record, Missis Witch, I can't see the Good Lord frowning on any activity involving genuine love but perhaps in this little village He would prefer it not to take place in the churchyard.'

'We were in the orchard, if you must know. Very well, discretion is my new watch word, eh?'

'There was something else, if you've got time?'

'Always,' she patted his hand and sank back in her chair, nursing her mug of re-filled coffee.

'I'm sorry to ask you, Magda, I wondered if everything's all right with Jasmine.'

Magda had plenty of good friends, people she could trust and count on, and of them all, Peter Granger was the one she most respected. Talking to him always made her feel better and over the years, she had done the same for him, lending him a sympathetic ear when he'd gone through his divorce and later, when his eldest son had turned his back on the church.

It was natural, then, that she poured her heart out to him now, expressing her concerns and putting into words the jumbled thoughts and feelings that had been swirling in her mind. She laid it all out at his feet, right down to the bare bones. He listened to her and when she was done, she let him dry her tears with the sleeve of his jumper.

'So there we are, she's a troubled woman and yes, I'm worried about her.' she said after a long pause, pulling herself together. 'Why do you ask?'

'We bumped into each other walking along the canal bank and, well, we had a bit of a talk. She told me some of her problems and I did my best to give her some comfort, words of wisdom, that sort of thing.' He told her, and Magda nodded agreeably, pleased that he been there for Jasmine. 'And then I saw her again a few days ago. She was sitting in one my pews when I was leaving the church for the day. I wasn't terribly surprised to see her there, even you drop in now and then, after all. But I was surprised to see that she was praying.'

'Praying?' Magda wasn't sure what to make of that. 'Was she upset?'

'On the contrary, it looked as if she had been crying but had got it out of her system; she was quite calm, in fact.'

'Did you speak to her?'

'Prayers are a private matter, Magda, I didn't ask her about it. She told me anyway, though. Jasmine said she was asking forgiveness for something she'd done. You know I wouldn't normally say anything about it, what people choose to tell a priest is sacred, as it is when they confide in you, but she did say you knew all about it. Something to do with a doll?'

'Yes, I know about the doll.' Magda stood up and sighed, leant against the edge of the sink and looked out on the garden where all of the greenery was starting to change and wilt and die off in readiness for winter. 'We've talked about it; she had her head in the right place at the time, and that I do believe. I'm glad she had you to talk, thank you Peter.'

He stood up and thanked her for the coffee and biscuits. 'Things will get better, Magda, they always do.'

She turned back to him and smiled gratefully.

Granger tugged open the heavy back door and was immediately surrounded by a halo of golden light streaming in through the door. He looked positively radiant, Magda thought, it was sickening.

As he walked away and disappeared from view, the same sunshine which had him glowing with divine light struck Magda in the face and she blinked fiercely, leaving sun-trails in her vision and she probably looked like a wrinkled old prune, the way it made her eyes squint. Typical, she thought to herself as she returned to the kitchen and fished her mop and bucket out of the cupboard to clean the floor, even the bloody sunshine conspires to make that man look saintly!

CHAPTER ELEVEN

Three and a half hours of driving, alternately speeding on the motorway and being stuck in relentless queues, accompanied by arguments over whose turn it was to buy refreshments at the service station and what radio station to listen to, the options being radio four or one. By the time they arrived Jasmine was fed up.

'That was a little slice of hell on earth. Two extra hours to get here. Why can't they do road works at night?' Jasmine grumbled crossly, pulling her overnight case from the boot of Sal's car. 'At least your dinosaur managed to get us here in one piece. You must get the heater sorted out, Sally, I'm frozen solid. Get Stuart to look at it for you, he's a mechanic.'

'Yes, Mum, a bike mechanic.' Sal shut the boot and picked up her own bag, excited now they'd arrived. Her gran had regularly attended pagan camps and weekend retreats and always came back rejuvenated and filled with a renewed enthusiasm and zest for life. She hoped she would have a similar uplifting experience but the chances were slim, she was here with her mother, after all.

The Grange was a large country house with a gravel parking area and little more than fields surrounding it. There was a covered porch over the door which had thin pillars on either side. Sal knocked and they were warmly welcomed by a Magda replica; an older woman with long waves of grey hair, floaty layers and ruffles, and silk flowers in her hair. The woman told them the house was part of an organic farm with expansive lawns, poly-tunnels and rooms galore in the house itself.

'You're in here,' the woman, who introduced herself as Birch, showed them into a spacious and comfortable looking twin room with a tiny en-suite, 'if we do get any rain, there's a bucket in the en-suite to go under the damp spot in the corner. Dinner's almost done so pop down when you're ready and make yourselves at home, everyone is super-friendly.'

'Thank you, Birch, we'll be fine.' Sal said, shutting the door and breathing a sigh of relief.

'Unless it rains, of course.' Jasmine chose the bed on the opposite side to the damp spot. 'What is a red moon lodge anyway? We're not going to be talking about our periods, are we? I don't think I can do that.'

Sal laughed and put her clothes in the dresser. 'Come on, I'm starving.'

The food was all vegan and there was plenty of it. Sal tucked in heartily but Jasmine picked at the rubbery, badly cooked tofu and felt out of her depth when the dinner table conversation turned into detailed discussions about how to become an empowered Ultimate Woman by unleashing your chi, balancing the chakras and connecting to your womb.

'I am who I am and I want what is best for the inner me, do you see?' A woman named Rosie spoke at length about her own womb and her connection to it, revealing how much it had helped her recover from self-harming.

'Yes, I see.' Nodding politely but not seeing at all, Jasmine decided it would be best if she just listened from now on. Bottles of red wine accompanied the assortment of vegan curries and tofu dishes, the couscous and rice and pasta, and Sal and Jasmine had their glasses filled several times without realising it.

After dinner, Jasmine and Sal joined the rest of the women for introductions and an opening blessing. This took place in the orangery, which was laid out with over-sized floor cushions, rugs and dozens of brightly coloured fleeces, furs and crocheted blankets to keep off the cold of the late October night. Birch and two other women, identically dressed with crescent moons in their hair and long white dresses, blessed everyone with spring water. They handed out pieces of moon stone so that every moon sister would have a memento of the weekend to take back with her.

Birch led them in a long and silent meditation before speaking softly, inviting each woman to introduce herself.

'I shall start.' Sal noted that as she spoke, Birch seemed to draw something into herself as she breathed, some kind of essence that came out in her mannerisms. She looks regal, Sal thought, beautiful. Her gran exuded a similar state of being when she held ceremonies, she realised, a commanding, loving presence that was hard to describe but impossible to ignore. 'My name is Birch, I'm here because I want to provide an experience which helps my moon sisters find out where their hearts and their destinies lie.'

'My name is Bethany, I'm thirty-eight, I'm here to connect to my ancestors and develop my spiritual practice.'

'Hello,' Sal didn't know where to begin. 'I'm Sally, Sal, actually. Hmm, I'm not really sure what I want. I suppose that sums it up. I want to discover what I should be doing with my life.' She shrugged and turned to her mother who sat beside her with a crocheted blanket over her knees.

'My name's Jasmine, I'm forty-four. I'm Sally's mum. I'm here because my life is a mess and my own mum thought this would help me.'

There was pair work next, everyone taking turns to share and explore the feelings and events that had brought them to this place, this moment, and although she thought she knew everything there was to know about her daughter, Jasmine was surprised to learn that she didn't know so very much after all. Huge areas of Sally's life were new discoveries to her and despite feeling closer to her, through the tears and confessions, she was left feeling as if there was still some deep secret Sally wouldn't share with her.

'I'm so tired of running,' she told Sally, when it was her turn to speak. 'I just want to hide under the duvet until I wake up feeling strong and capable without having to go through all of the hard bits in between.'

'How are we getting on over here?' Birch flitted around the room, an elegant vision in her white gown that draped over everything she touched. 'Super, good work.' She was carrying a large silver bell and rang it three times.

The collective of women traipsed off to various rooms and

Jasmine noticed a few of the younger, more hardy looking women, sloping off outside to the extensive lawns where a couple of large yurts and several smaller nylon tents were pitched. She was pleased they had been allocated a bedroom in the house and not a tent in the grounds, but as they undressed for bed and took turns to use the musty smelling en-suite, her head a little muzzy from drinking wine she wasn't used to, it began to rain and sleeping in a waterproof tent didn't seem like a bad idea after all. She put the bucket under the damp patch in the ceiling and lay awake listening to the drip, drip, drip.

In the morning, she and Sal had a cooked breakfast of toast and beans with scrambled tofu and Birch led a workshop on crystal healing and Reiki. Sal seemed to know what she was talking about but still brought out her biro and took several pages of notes.

'What about you, Jasmine?' Birch gestured to the empty therapy couch and reluctantly, Jasmine clambered onto it. She lay without moving, uncomfortable because her knickers had moved about when she'd climbed up, and twelve strange women crowded over her in turns with crystal pendulums and chunks of rose quartz, drawing strange symbols on her forehead with consecrated salt water. She closed her eyes, not feeling anything but tired.

'I can feel a pull, here.' Rosie said, waving her pendulum above Jasmine's chest. 'Heart chakra, lots of hurt in there.'

'Yes,' Birch confirmed, 'I can feel it too, so painful.' She helped Jasmine off the couch and sat next to her. 'Rosie's right, isn't she? We are all here to support you, we can help, Jasmine. You need to let go of the pain, open up to the love which is all around you.'

'I don't – I don't know,' Jasmine blurted out, 'I've made a lot of mistakes, I suppose. I get myself into such a mess and then – I'm sorry, I can't talk about it.' She didn't know these women who were suddenly calling her sister and putting their warm, sweaty hands all over her shoulders as if that would somehow make it all better.

'We're here for you, sister,' Birch said, 'whenever you're ready. I'll make sure you've got my number before you leave.'

'Great, thank you.' Jasmine smiled nervously and waited for the ground to swallow her up but it didn't do so she leaned into Sally, who was sitting next to her. Sally put an arm around her shoulders and this seemed to satisfy Birch who dragged up another victim for the therapy couch.

There was more tofu for lunch and Jasmine picked at it, wondering if anyone would notice if she nipped out for a kebab. Unfortunately the Grange wasn't in Hebden Bridge itself but on the outskirts, surrounded by trees and fields for miles around. The afternoon was taken up with a shamanic journey led by a lady named Dawn who had ribbons and crow feathers stuck in her hair. One of the yurts outside was the designated venue and after a sleepless night, Jasmine hoped she wouldn't snore too loudly if she fell asleep among the multitude of cushions and blankets and rugs that were laid out for her and fifteen other women to lie on.

I'm having words with that mother of mine when I get back, she said to herself, having the sense not to say it out loud.

*

Sal made herself comfortable on the sheepskin rugs, drew a blanket over her feet and legs, and listened to the beat of the frame drum that resounded and reverberated through the ground beneath her. She breathed softly and moved her head on the velvet cushions, making sure she was completely at ease. She relaxed into the sound of the drum, soft, like a beating heart, her senses and thoughts becoming slow and rhythmic.

The drumming stopped and was replaced by a shushing rattle and Dawn began to speak softly and slowly, her voice like golden honey. It reminded Sal of bees, gently buzzing.

She led the group into a deep and dream-like state, the rattle softly pattering and whispering, resembling the susurration of trees in the wind, lulling Sal into a peaceful steadiness of breathing. A woman coughed lightly on the other side of the yurt but it didn't disturb her, she felt so light and relaxed she was almost floating away, the material world no longer concerned her. Dawn's voice led her on a journey

131

through trees and over rocks, along the edge of a gorge surrounded by the flitting of butterflies and bees and filled with the sound of a waterfall around the corner. The scene unfolded around her in all dimensions. In her mind, she was completely at peace.

'In front of you,' Dawn whispered, 'is a stairway carved into the rock, a rope to guide you down or up, and the choice is yours. When you take that first step, notice how you feel and focus on your questions, knowing that when you arrive, you will find the answer. The stairway is slippery in places, following the course of the waterfall, the rope keeps you safe and the rocks weave you on your way. Climbing, up or down, the steps lead you to the place where your answers await.' Dawn paused, her rattle silent.

'And what happens next is what happens next.'

Sal faced the steps carved into the rocks, up or down, she didn't know. In the unknown realm of journey she closed her eyes, opened them and looked at the path again. Down, she decided, reaching for the thick cord of rope to aid her descent on the moss covered steps. No other footfalls had been there before her to wear away the layer of damp greenery growing on the steps. She was the first to pass this way and it felt sacred. The rock face curved to the left and the rushing talk of the waterfall became louder, louder, thunderous now as she reached the last step. She looked up at the waterfall, a beautiful cascade, a torrent of white spray with rainbows of light dancing in patches of amber sunshine that beamed its rays through the trees high above.

A bird called out with a single cracking note and Sal followed the sound. A solitary jay with its tell-tale flash of vivid blue called to her again. He was sitting on the branch of a yew tree growing tall from the base of the waterfall, unlikely in the material world, but not here, not in the land of the unseen. Red berries among the branches of needles seemed to swell and grow and fall before her eyes and she watched them drop to the water covered rocks. A darkness behind the tree drew her attention and she moved towards it. Drawing closer, she saw it. There was the entrance to a cave and she walked carefully over the stepping stone rocks to reach it. Into the cave she went, all else forgotten and unimportant, into the pitch blackness of the earth that closed around her. A sense of anticipation filled her body, a light rash of goose bumps, wide eyes in the dark, a pinch of light coming towards her. A speck at first, the light moved closer and she saw it was a candle flame and the candle was held by a woman who must surely be the very Goddess herself.

Walking, gliding, effortlessly moving to stand in front of Sal, so close that their bodies were almost as one and they shared each other's warmth, breathed one another's breath and: behold! For I am She who resides in the heart of all that is living and all that is not. I am She who gives birth to courage, delight and love. I am the stars, I am the moon, I am the truth within.

Sal's eyes pricked with tears of love, she bowed her head with reverence as she stood in the presence of majesty. The candle light grew to illuminate the cavern with soft tones of amber and russet, the colours of a sunrise on a midsummer's day.

A hand came forward to raise her head and Sal knew she was supposed to say something. She didn't know the words but started to speak, regardless. 'My Lady, my Goddess, I came here to seek answers.'

'As do all of my children,' with a voice that sent shivers through her belly, the Goddess spoke. 'All you need to do is listen to your heart, which is where the answers lie.'

'I don't understand,' Sal replied, feeling inadequate in this world of mystery and journey. 'My life is on hold, I've fallen off my path and I can't see where it should be going next.'

'Your path is in your hands, your touch, your healing words. It's right in front of you, Sal, you need only to open your eyes.'

Sal didn't know she'd had them closed. She opened them now and saw herself in place of the Goddess. She was beautiful and serene and she was looking back at herself through the eyes of wisdom and she knew where her path was leading to because the key to unlocking it all was right there, in front of her. Why hadn't she seen it? She reached out to take her own hand and as the hands made contact Sal opened her eyes again and stared into the eyes of the Goddess once more.

'Call for me as Demeter in this journey world of the unreal and the unknown and whenever you stray again from the path, from the destiny that lies ahead, there will be signs and the signs are these.'

The Goddess Demeter touched Sal's forehead and she saw the signs that had been there all along and then the glowing light was fading and the warm, comforting, silken presence of the Goddess was retreating, drawing away from her. Sal was bereft. Demeter was still with her, though, Sal touched the spot on her forehead where her third eye was located and she could feel that sense of majesty and awe and knew she would never be without it again for it lay within her own heart.

'Thank you,' she said and she lay down a white rose where the Goddess had been.

The cave wall was gaping open, the yew tree outside dropped its scarlet berries to the ground and the weight of water cascading over ancient rocks was roaring, wild and tumultuous and it drowned out all other noise. Sal took hold of the rope and ascended the rocky steps at the side of the waterfall, the moss now gleaming a brighter green, the sky a purer shade of blue and the jay calling to her a final time and Dawn began to speak.

'Come back through the trees, to where your journey began.' The rush of water gave way to the pulse of the shaman's drum as Dawn spoke. Sal reached the middle of the stairwell, promising herself that next time, she would go up. She followed the sound of the voice and with every step she became more solid, more firmly rooted in her body and she could feel the rugs beneath her, hear the rustles of the women around her, shuffling as they returned from their own visions and journeys.

'And we find ourselves back in the here and now,' Dawn spoke more loudly now, 'and in our own time, when we are ready, we open our eyes and we come together again.'

Sal rubbed her eyes and yawned and stretched and slowly sat up, knowing from her experiences with meditation that it would make her feel light-headed if she rushed.

'And if you want to, you can share your experience with the people around you.'

Sal leaned over to see her mum starting to sit up. She wondered how much she should tell, if anything at all, but the question was moot when Jasmine opened her eyes, sat up and yawned loudly, stretching out her arms.

'I take it I wasn't the only one who fell asleep?'

'I think you were, Mum, but never mind.' Sal resigned herself to the fact that the pagan path wasn't right for her mother and never would be. She'd tell her gran about her meeting with the Goddess though, and in the meantime, she ignored her mum and scribbled in her notebook before she forgot the details.

*

Jasmine and Sal had time to themselves after dinner was served, another round of quinoa, rice, curried tofu, nuts and lentils and far too much wine. They spent their free time wandering the organic gardens of the old farm, linking arms as they walked.

'Do you believe in all of this, Sally? Crystals and chakras and shamanic journeys and the great presence of a Goddess?'

Sal thought about it for a moment. 'Yes I do,' she said. 'Not just because I grew up with Gran, though. It's hard to explain. I can feel it in my soul, like I'm part of everything. Someone watching over me, a great force of nature and energy. So yes, I believe in the Goddess, this source of knowledge, power and life.'

'I think I can understand that. A bigger power, you mean, something that is more than we are? That makes sense.'

They came to a slatted wooden fence at the edge of the gardens and turned back so they were looking over towards the lawn. Five robed woman with their arms outstretched were chanting and dancing in a circle. As Jasmine and Sal neared, they were drawn into the singing circle and started waving and swaying with the other

135

women, picking up the words to the chants.

'We all come from the Goddess, and to her we shall return!'

'We are at one with the earth, the earth, the earth. We are at one with the earth.'

The women chanted as one, joining with their empowered moon sisters and feeling the rush of the wind in their hair and the harmony of the voices resounding out to the rest of the gathering and the chant went on as more women joined them. It was magical and mystical, a great joining of one woman with the next, empowering and freeing. But it was also freezing cold, hands were clutching too tightly and the chanting was slow, tuneless and monotone and Jasmine didn't feel much like an empowered woman after all.

They left the circle of chanting women and sat in their room drinking and talking. They shared and they bonded and they drank a bottle of red wine.

'We are – at one – with the earth.' Jasmine intoned slowly. 'Do you feel empowered? Can you feel your womb, Sally?'

'Only when I'm cramping up with period pains.'

'Oh, my moon sister, I can feel your pain.'

'They're not that bad, you're being mean.'

'They are Sally, and they've all got armpit hair.'

'So have you.'

'Yes, but I shave mine off and I use deodorant. What do you think your gran's up to, by the way?'

'I bet Stuart is feeling empowered, you know what they say about druids.' Sal said. Jasmine shrugged, she didn't know.

'They have big staffs.'

'A wizard's staff has a knob on the end...' Jasmine cackled out loud and they fell about laughing and singing.

'What are we going to do with our lives, Mum?' Sal wondered out loud. 'We're both a bit of a mess, aren't we?'

'Well, you've got your big idea brewing,' Jasmine said, swigging the last of the wine and Sal knew then for certain that alcohol was the catalyst for her mum's supressed psychic ability. 'The answer is right in front of you. What kind of a name is Birch, anyway? I wonder what her family call her.'

A sudden rapping on the door interrupted them.

'It is close to midnight, ladies.' A stern voice came through the door and they shut up, Sal stuffing her hand over her mum's mouth to stifle the laughter. 'Perhaps we can hold off on the chit-chat.'

'Sorry,' Sal called back, 'didn't realise we were being so loud.'

'It's not the volume of conversation we are objecting to, Sally, it's the content.'

'Yes,' another voice piped up, 'we don't appreciate our love and harmony being made fun of when we've done everything we can to make you feel at home here.'

'Oh, for crying out loud!' Jasmine couldn't help herself. Sal shot her a horrified look and the door opened to reveal several women in fleece onesies staring stonily at them. 'Don't get your knickers in a twist love, we'll bugger off at first light, all right?'

'Mum!' Sal objected, trying desperately to keep a straight face. Then she looked at the faces peering in at her and she felt ashamed. 'I'm sorry.'

The woman nearest the door pulled it closed and the house fell into a stony silence. Sal crept into bed, ignoring her mum's hissing whispers.

'A wizard's staff…'

'Don't start us off again, Mother. Good night.'

She pulled the covers up to her face and her head whizzed through a kaleidoscope of emotions and ideas. Unable to sleep, Sal wrote some of her thoughts down in her notebook and set an alarm for six. It seemed like only minutes before it went off and she found herself packing up and skulking out of the house quietly with Jasmine close at her heels.

'Did you leave a note?' Jasmine asked.

Sal nodded. 'A heart-felt apology and letter of thanks combined.'

Jasmine put on a pair of designer sunglasses that covered nearly her entire face. 'This is precisely why I don't drink. Words come out of my mouth.'

'Never mind, Mum.' Sal said. 'Come on, let's get back and see if she's been up to mischief while we've been gone.'

'Do you remember when you were ten and your dad and I took you to visit your gran for the weekend thinking she'd be lonely because your grandad was away for a month, only when we got there the house was empty because she'd been arrested?'

'Do not tempt fate.' Sal remembered it all too well. That was the first time her gran's photo had ended up in the local newspaper. Magda had been spotted getting into the back of a police car, waving like a lunatic as it pulled up outside the house to cart her off for questioning.

One of the farms on the edge of the county was trialling a field of genetically modified sugar beet and Magda had taken part in a televised protest. The protest was peaceful and uneventful, if Sal recalled correctly from the archive footage she'd seen; there were hundreds of people wearing colourful hippy clothes, all holding placards and singing protest songs to the tune of badly played drums. On the march from the meeting point to the site, the police had to lead the way because none of the protesters knew the exact location of the specific trial field on the farm. A few days later, the police came to regret pointing out the beet field because although the protest had gone without a hitch, they were called in to investigate the complete destruction of the crop. Every single plant in the field had been dug up, thrown into a bonfire and burnt in the middle of the night. The police hadn't found any evidence to point the finger of blame at any one person or organisation but Magda and her friend Agnes had been among the loudest in the peaceful protest so they made up two of the six prime suspects. Nobody was ever charged but Sal had often wondered about the glint in her gran's eye in that hazy, black and white photograph.

'Do you think it was her, Sal? Dad was working away at the

time so she didn't have an alibi.'

'She's never admitted it,' Sal replied, 'not to me anyway. But you wouldn't admit to something like that, would you?'

They put their bags in the car and drove home but this time they didn't argue about the radio. Instead, they sang songs from the Fiddler on the Roof, indulging Jasmine's penchant for classic musicals. They stopped at a service station for coffee. Jasmine ordered drinks and waited for them, letting Sally find them a seat.

Jasmine watched her beautiful daughter wending her way towards an empty table and she pulled her sunglasses down as a very good looking man, about Sally's age, stopped to talk to her. Sally brushed him off without a second look and Jasmine shook her head in disbelief. What was wrong with her? The boy was drop dead gorgeous. Wearing tight jeans with a backside like that ought to be illegal. At her age, I would have been in there like a shot, Jasmine sighed wistfully, managing to keep the words from escaping her lips. Maybe that was the problem: seeing her mother going through heartbreak again and again had clearly put the poor girl completely off the idea of dating. In fact, now that she thought about it, Jasmine couldn't recall Sally ever having a boyfriend. Mind you, Sally was definitely holding back something yesterday, so maybe there had been boyfriends she didn't want to talk about. She shrugged, Jasmine had enough trouble sorting out her own affairs. She's only twenty-three, there's still plenty of time for serious boyfriends.

Chapter Twelve

When Sally dropped Jasmine back at her little flat on the high street, it was still only half-past seven and the streets were deserted. Apart from the newsagent, the village shops stayed closed on a Sunday and she marveled at how very quiet it seemed after the busy service station on the way home, where even at this early hour, hundreds of weary drivers and passengers queued like zombies for their morning fix of bacon rolls and sweet tea.

The weekend had been a disaster. Sally had made her promise she'd write and apologise to Birch for ruining the retreat. She was truly ashamed of her behavior.

Jasmine saw her mobile phone on her bedside table, where it had been all weekend. She had not wanted to spoil things with any more texts from Paul. She checked her messages. Nothing. Not a single text from him. Thank God for that. He must be too busy dragging all of her things out of the house and burning them in the garden.

She ran a hot bath, dropped in some fizzy bath bombs and spent an hour soaking, shaving legs and underarms and feeling guilty for taking the mickey out of the moon sisters. The more she thought about it and tried to blame it on the wine, the more she remembered other times when her words had been sarcastic, mean or thoughtless over the last few weeks. In all honesty, she thought, hating to believe it of herself, I've been downright rude and nasty at times.

Jasmine had upset both Sally and her mum more than once since she'd come back to the village and pangs of guilt stabbed at her, a headache building up behind her eyes. She wasn't ordinarily such an insensitive person; Paul's nasty temperament had left its mark on her. She rubbed her temples and sank into the warm water and raspberry scented bubbles, wishing she could hide in them forever. Instead, she resolved to apologise and start doing more to help herself. If she didn't pick herself up, nobody else would do it for her, especially if she kept taking her anger and hurt out on the very people who were trying to help her the most. The first thing she would do, she decided, was follow up on her thoughts about offering to help Peter take care of the churchyard while Mr. Jackoby was off.

*

Gran's car was absent when Sal pulled into the drive and the house was empty, except for Bran, who was working hard on his beauty sleep. He purred muzzily when she petted him, breaking his sleep only for food.

She spent most of the morning doing house work before she rang Stacy to arrange a time for Mark's massage one evening after he finished work.

'Brill, thanks Sal,' Stacy said, 'fancy coming with me to the Black Swan later? I could do with getting out of the house for a bit.' Sal agreed, looking forward to it.

Sal pulled out her notebook and flicked through it, trying to make sense of the thoughts and ideas she had scribbled in there. Her mobile rang, an unknown number.

'Hello?' She answered. 'Yes, this is Sal.' She listened carefully, 'yes, I'll be happy to, what's the address?'

When she hung up, Sal jotted down the details of Bonnie's friend who wanted to book Sal for a mobile massage session. The words of the Goddess Demeter came back to her.

Your path is in your hands, your touch, your healing words. It's right in front of you, Sal, you only need to open your eyes.

Neurons firing in her brain like a volcano she could no longer ignore, Sal went to fix herself a pot of coffee before going up to her room to figure it all out. She reached up to the top shelf for her small range of filter coffees, choosing one at random. A few minutes later, Gran's tarot deck fell off the spice rack from the shelf below the coffee packets, the loose cards scattering on the floor. Kneeling to pick them up, ignoring Bran who was now in one of his playful moods, she noticed three of the cards had landed face up. The Empress, the Chariot, the Magician. The same cards her gran had read for her recently. Had she disturbed the deck while reaching

141

for her coffee or was this one of the signs she'd been told about in her shamanic journey? It had been a real experience to her and Sal marveled that her mum could cast off so lightly the spirituality they had both been brought up with.

She clutched the cards and her notebook in one hand, Bran in the other and went up to her room where she would be most comfortable, and resolved to figure it out. She played with the ginger-nut fuzz ball until he curled up to sleep and then she could focus.

She lit her incense, a blend she'd made herself with patchouli and lemongrass, and rang the brass bell on her dresser to put her brain into relaxation mode. She spread the three cards on the patchwork bedspread and silently asked for the meanings to become clear. The empress – feminine intuition and spirituality, communication and connections, fertility, birth, abundance. The chariot – strength, determination and will power, a journey of success and victory. The magician – action, power, resourcefulness and skill, taking control of one's destiny.

She wrote down her thoughts on the cards in her notebook, drawing rough sketches in the margins to accompany the descriptions. Writing down her thoughts and flicking back through the last few pages, Sal started to piece together the burgeoning idea that had been slowly blossoming. She thought about her job, or rather her lack of one, and realised it wasn't a job she needed, as much as a reliable income. She wanted to do something worthwhile to get it and if she made a living doing something she enjoyed, like massage, it would relate to the empress, the fertility and abundance of a new venture.

Bonnie's praise of her massage skills gave her the confidence to think she could do it professionally. She'd only taken the evening course in alternative therapies for fun and hadn't intended to make it pay but she didn't want to return to admin work. If she could make a living doing aromatherapy and finish her counselling course as well, she could help people that way too. She related that to the chariot, the driving force, her will power and determination to forge her own future.

All well and good, but what put her off the idea of being a therapist was seeing her gran struggling for money. Magda gave a lot of her products away for free or in exchange for goods and services instead of hard payments. No, Sal didn't want to live that way, never knowing if she'd be paid at the end of the month. She'd had enough of that as an admin temp and in any case, the house just wasn't set up well enough to facilitate its use as a therapy centre, no matter how small. Sal sat up suddenly as she realised this venture was going to be bigger than she first thought. She couldn't do it all herself, massage, counselling, creating labels for her gran on the side and the admin and finances – it would be too much for her. Her gran had said she wouldn't be doing things by herself. The magician meant taking action, taking control of the resources she had at her finger tips, and her resources were not only the things she could do herself, but the people around her who could help her make it work.

In addition to her aromatherapy, Sal knew how to make salves, tinctures, herbal teas, moisturisers and incense and she'd often been asked to do candle magic or make charm bags for the women on her therapy course. Combining her skills and knowledge with her gran's hedge witchery practice would provide a holistic service that would really help people and doing it on a professional basis would make it attractive to paying clients. If she could persuade her mum to run the business side of things, it would leave Gran and Sal free to focus on the clients and she thought, she really thought, that together they would be able to make it work. Aromatherapy, herbal medicines, counselling and tarot readings – she could see it now, a small reception area with a couple of private rooms to use for therapies and readings or counselling. They could display a range of teas, herbal creams, bath sachets, charm bags, incenses and hand-made scented candles in the reception area.

Sal's skin was buzzing at the prospect. Not only would a family-run business give them all a new purpose in life, satisfying Sal's need to do something worthwhile, it would go down well with gran's current clients. No more skulking to the witch's house at the break of dawn in fear of being seen, a therapy centre would be respectable and above board.

Sal warmed to the idea and the action and drive of the chariot spurred her on as she made page after page of notes, pinning down her ideas and inspirations before they ran away. After an hour of writing, wracking her brains for yet more snippets and clues to her future business success, Sal needed a break.

She rolled over and reached out to switch her radio on, lit another charcoal disc for her incense and picked up her book. She was reading The Stand by Stephen King, after the third time of her gran explaining it, she still didn't get the Frannie Goldsmith joke and was determined to find out why it was funny. 'Maybe you have to be a Stephen King nerd to get it.' She said to the kitten who yawned at her, showing off his needle-sharp tiger teeth.

Propped up on her pillows, Sal started to doze and woke up with a start when the book, a mammoth volume, fell out of her hand and tumbled to the floor with a thud. She sat up sleepily, rubbed her face and tugged her hair out of its rubber band, shaking out the strands. A fleeting shadow crossed her field of vision and she whizzed her head round in time to see, from the corner of her eye, a glimpse of nothing, the shadow of something that wasn't there, moving across her dressing table. A bottle of deodorant spray fell over and rolled to the floor.

'Judy!' Sal gasped, cautiously rising from the bed and setting the bottle back on the dresser. 'Oh my poor lost moggy, I do miss you so much.'

Bran nuzzled against her leg, striking his razor needle kitten claws in to her skin as he climbed up to lie on her chest. 'Don't worry, boy.' She lifted him up to her face and rubbed her nose against his. 'I love you too.'

*

Magda arrived home, disrupting Sal's afternoon nap with a flurry of animated chatter.

'A day out in Matlock Bath takes on a whole new dimension

when you go with your biker boyfriend,' she said, waving her mobile phone in front of Sal's face. 'Look at that! Who'd have thought it? Little old me rocking it with the leather trouser crew.'

'Gran, that's so cool!' Sal pinched the phone and scrolled the photographs Magda was showing off.

'I did a selfie! Get me, getting down with technology.'

Magda and Stuart standing in their leathers next to the bike. Magda and Stuart with fish and chips standing next to the bike. Magda and Stuart on the back of the bike...

'Since when did you own leather trousers?'

'Since yesterday.' Magda declared. 'I went shopping. Got my own helmet too. They're still at Stuart's though, I had to change before I came back here.'

'Never tell me,' Sal wanted to make it plain, 'why you have left your clothes there.'

'Don't be so crude! I'm a pensioner, you know.' Magda grinned. 'Not that age is enough to stop us, far from it, in fact.' She giggled and pulled out her phone again.

'You haven't taken a selfie of that, surely?' Sal's eyes nearly popped out of her head.

'Don't you want to see?' Magda thrust the phone in her face and Sal put a hand out to stop her. 'I'm joking!'

Sal gave her gran a high-five, 'thank heaven for small mercies. Nobody needs to hear about it, much less see it.'

'I told you, I'm joking. Chance would be a fine thing, we keep getting interrupted. No, I had to nip in to see Simon Jackoby on the way back, he rang and said he's finally had enough of his cough and I couldn't very well turn up at the poor chap's house in my motorbike gear. Tell me, how was the red moon lodge?'

'Ah, well,' Sal didn't know what to say.

Magda shook her head. 'I should have known something would go wrong. I hope she didn't upset anyone.'

'How do you know it was Mum?' Sal cringed, trying to dodge the bullet. 'We left early, we left an apology, let's leave it at that. I'm sick of eating tofu but I enjoyed the journey work. It was so deep, Gran, so real.'

Magda leaned over the kitchen table, listening intently with the occasional nod or comment. 'Demeter, eh?' Magda hummed and nodded her head. 'Interesting, have seen you seen any of the signs she gave you?'

'Weirdly, yes,' Sal had vague memories of recent dreams, 'and she was right, the answers I'm looking for have been right in front of me the whole time. I don't know why I haven't seen it before. I have an idea, Gran, and I want to see what you think about it.'

By the time they'd finished talking about Sal's plans, it was dark outside and her stomach was rumbling. 'I'm meeting Stacy at the pub later, I might get something to eat there. Fancy coming along?'

'Still full of fish and chips, pet,' her gran said, and Sal smiled at her use of Stuart's word. 'But I'll join you for a drink or two.'

'I was thinking I might make some Demeter incense Gran, and maybe a mojo bag for prosperity and success.'

'We could make one for your mum while we're at it. Shouldn't take long, we can drop it off for her and see if she wants to come with us to meet Stacy when we nip out later. If you want a hand, that is.'

'I was hoping you'd offer,' Sal said happily, not because she needed any help as she wound her magic into the charms and herbs to put in her bag for good luck, but because she enjoyed her gran's company, even if the crazy lady was always on the verge of saying something crude.

*

Sal couldn't help feeling a little bit sorry for the Black Swan, with 1990's wall paper and a shabby carpet that was permanently sticky in places, it was the sort of village pub that could have been a quaint little tourist attraction for the dozens of hikers who passed through the area en route to Cannock Chase or the Peak District. Unfortunately for landlord Stevie Green, the regulars were all locals and there was no budget to refurbish the pub to draw the hikers in.

'Over here, Sal.' Stacy had already arrived and was sitting with her friend Jules, who worked at the newsagent and sometimes helped out Stacy in the shop.

Sal waved, got herself a lime and tonic and joined them. 'Gran should be here in a sec, she's just gone over the road to see if Mum's coming out to play.'

'Play?' Jules scoffed, nearly spitting out the cherry she'd plucked off the end of her cocktail stick. 'I'd like the chance, around here.'

'I know what you mean,' Stacy said, 'it's so quiet here.'

Sal looked over her shoulder to the other customers. There were only a handful of regulars in this evening. 'We shall have to make some noise,' she said, 'we are the life and soul in here tonight, the life and soul, I tell you.'

'With a lime and tonic?' Jules sipped her own drink which was dark pink with a cherry on a stick in the glass. 'Here, try this.'

Sal did so and grimaced. 'Gross, what is in that?'

Jules leaned over, lowering her voice. 'I've no idea, I think it's got grapefruit in it. I asked for a sex on the beach.'

'Ooh, I fancy having sex on the beach!' Magda screeched, strolling up to the table with Jasmine in tow. 'I reckon me and Stuart could manage that. Mind you, it'd take ages to get the sand out of all your parts. There's a cocktail called the full Monty now, I might have that instead.'

'Introducing my mother,' Jasmine clapped her hands, 'setting the tone since 1914.'

'Seriously, Magda?' Jules, who wasn't known for her academic prowess, looked at Magda with scrutiny. 'You do not look that old!'

'I make my own moisturiser with calendula oil.' Magda said, stroking her face. 'Feel that skin, smooth as a baby's backside.'

'Can I buy some off you?' Jules said, 'you look great for a hundred and whatever it is.'

'I'm only sixty-eight, you cheeky mare!'

'Right, but still,' Jules said, 'can I have some?'

The evening went on much as it had started until Sal dug into her bag and instead of her purse, her hand fasted on the silk-wrapped tarot cards. She slipped them back in her bag quickly but not before Magda noticed.

'I'm really sorry, Gran.' Sal said, 'I shoved them in there earlier, I meant to put them back.'

'Let's have a reading, then Sal.' Stacy cleared a space, shifting everybody's empty glasses to an empty table.

Sal shook her head. 'I'm not sure, that's more my gran's forte than mine.'

'Go on,' Jules encouraged her, 'do Stacy's then mine. How much do you charge?'

'Twenty-five, normally.' Magda piped up quickly, 'but seeing as you're friends, we'll make it fifteen.'

'Gran!' Sal widened her eyes at the crone. 'Can I talk to you for a moment, please? In the loos?'

'I'll get the drinks in,' Stacy called as Sal and Magda left the table, 'don't dip out on us, will you?'

'Gran, I'm not sure about this, I don't normally read tarot for other people.' Sal washed her hands at the bathroom sink and faced the old battle-axe. She hated that expression on her gran's face, the one she wore right now. It was the kind of face that said: you will never know what I am really thinking.

'Seriously, I don't think I can do it.' She put up a protest but Magda's expression didn't change. 'I could do with some guinea-pigs first, it doesn't feel right charging people a proper fee. Oh, take that look off your face.'

'It's about time you started using your gifts, besides,' Magda said, reasonably enough, 'you're not charging a proper fee. Stacy and Jules are paying apprentice rates.'

'So I should get my backside back in there before…'

'I kick it there for you? Yes, I think that sums it up, love.'

'What did Mum say when you gave her the mojo bag, by the way?'

'Give you two guesses.' Magda huffed, folding her arms over her chest. She was wearing a ghastly bright green top with yellow flowers inappropriately placed to draw the eye over her breasts. 'It's still in my hand-bag. Stop looking at my flowers, woman!'

'Sorry, hard to concentrate on anything else.'

'That's what Stuart said when he was trying to eat his fish and chips.'

'I bet that blouse looked great with your leather trousers.'

By the end of the night, Sal left the pub with an extra sixty pounds in her purse and sense of glee at the results of her tarot readings.

She had moved to the adjacent table to spread the cards out at Jules's insistence. 'That way it won't matter if any sex escapes from my beach!' A round of guffaws and innuendo kept the other women occupied while Sal got herself ready. She'd felt her nerves rising but breathed deeply and thought about how her gran would handle it.

In her mind, she repeated a little phrase she'd overheard at the red moon lodge. By all the power of moon and sun, let me be guided and let it be done. Probably not as elegant as the mantra her gran kept secret but she hoped it would do. And then she laid five cards out carefully on the table between her and Stacy and she started to speak, answering Stacy's questions with the information laid out in front of her. One card was for the past, one for the present, one for the future, one for emotions and one for the outcome. Stacy listened far more than she spoke and Sal decided to take that as encouragement.

When she had finished, Stacy thrust some money at her and insisted that the reading was worth it. Sal found her feet a little more when she sat with Jules and when that second reading came to an end, two of the pub's regular customers had joined the rest of Sal's group and were waiting for a turn at what had been dubbed, while Sal had her focus on the cards, as the tarot table.

'It's a pity your mother didn't stay till you'd finished.' Magda linked her arm with Sal as they walked home together. 'I think she would have been pleased for you.'

'Thanks, Gran.' Sal looked up at the sky, the moon was high and the stars were bright and the cold in the air reminded her that Samhain was upon them. 'I would never have found my tarot feet if you hadn't led me there. I reckon you've been preparing me for it all of my life, haven't you?'

'Who, me?' Magda laughed. 'It's nice to have someone I can pass it along to. The recipes, the magic and the what-not.'

'I'm sorry it skipped a generation, though,' Sal looked back along the high street, noticing absence of light coming from the windows of the flat above the grocery. 'I know you would have liked Mum to follow in your footsteps.'

'What was it you once said? She and I are like sugar and spice?' They reached the house and Magda unlocked the front door, nearly tripping over Bran as the kitten came to greet them. 'I'm pleased you seem to be picking it up, though.'

'It's hard not to, I've been studying herbalism and magic with you since I was tiny.' Sal gave Bran a treat stick and poured herself a glass of orange juice. 'You still haven't found me a cure for a hangover yet, though.'

'I'll keep working on it, but you know the real answer to that problem.'

'Don't get drunk in the first place. Why are you so keen all of sudden for me to start doing tarot? You've never pushed me into it before tonight.'

'Well, as it happens, I think your idea of a healing centre could be a good way forward. For all of us.' Magda sighed heavily and went through to the hall, hanging her burgundy scarf over the bannister post. 'And besides, somebody will have to take over from me one day. I won't be around forever.'

'Are you kidding?' Sal called after her, rinsing her glass at the kitchen sink. 'You're virtually immortal. Look how soft your skin is, nobody would believe you were born in 1914.'

Chapter Thirteen

Samhain, the pagan celebration of life, death and rebirth, had always been important to Magda and she liked to spend it with the people she felt closest to. Normally Magda decorated the house for trick-or-treaters with huge, carved pumpkins and spider webs, donning traditional witch's garb for the evening, complete with a pointy hat. Her friend Agnes and one or two others came round with contributions for a meal and after the local kids had called round to the witches house for their sweets, they held a midnight ritual in the garden with a feast in the house to finish.

As much as she enjoyed doing the celebration with a small group of close friends, she had another invitation to consider and wondered if it was about time she broke free of her routine to spend the festival with new friends. It would be a nice way to mark a new phase in her life, the start of her first romantic interlude in years. At least she thought it was romantic. She joked about her rampant sex life in front of her tribe, but the truth was, she enjoyed the gentle druid's company and his sense of humour but they had never got further than a bit of fumbling and kissing in the orchard. Destiny was keeping them at a distance and Magda didn't mind, she was getting older every year and while she would never admit she was past it, she wasn't and hoped she never would be, she did admit that her hips were becoming arthritic.

Riding pillion was a blast but after their long ride to Matlock Bath, Magda hadn't been at all comfortable. She'd confessed it to Stuart and he agreed that shorter trips or taking the car would be fine with him. She adored him with all of her heart and wanted nothing more from him than a beautiful friendship full of innuendo and laughter. In time, if there was more than that, she would welcome it, but for now, she was happy.

Samhain, then, she mused, still undecided. Jasmine had already said she wasn't coming, regardless, so that would leave herself, Sal, Stuart and Agnes. Stuart's daughter Bonnie had said she might be interested in coming, along with a friend of hers and one of Stuart's druid friends, another biker might be coming. That made a total of seven, not so small a gathering after all. She decided to phone Mel, her new friend from the Green Man pub moot, to go over their ideas.

'To be quite frank, Magda,' Mel had explained, 'we haven't planned anything further than what I said last week. We thought we would do a bit of invoking and then everybody can say something about their loved ones who've passed over. I think Ian and Pete were thinking more about the pub afterwards than anything else.'

Magda had a plan and she'd told Mel who agreed to it eagerly. 'Join forces? I think it's an excellent idea, you're sure you've got room for us all?' Mel agreed to let her friends know the change of venue and Magda spread the news at her end, ringing Agnes and then Stuart.

On the morning of Samhain itself, never one to put off a ritual until the closest weekend, especially not this year, when it coincided with a full moon, Magda pestered Sal into working the printer for her, churning out a ritual that should be easy enough for everyone to follow, no matter what their path or experience.

'It will make a nice change to spend Samhain with a larger group.' Sal sat at her laptop in the kitchen and typed up Magda's notes for the ritual and printed out a dozen copies. 'Will that be enough?'

'People can always share.'

Bran the kitten jumped with fright when the printer started up and Sal picked him up, cooing and shushing him. 'I'll have to shut you upstairs, little guy,' she told him, 'to make sure you're safe because you're still so tiny. But I'll save you some treats.'

They spent the rest of the day preparing a feast of pumpkin soup, butternut tarts, cheese scones and rosemary breads to lay out for everyone to tuck into after the ritual. Sal hung Halloween bunting in the trees and fences to the front of the house and filled several large bowls with sweets and pieces of fruit, copper coins, plastic spiders, fake severed fingers and fortune cookies. She made sure there were plenty of treats and sweets that were suitable for anyone with allergies too, thinking of one little boy whose mum ordered gluten-free cakes and biscuits especially for him from Stacy's shop.

Magda blew dust off her guising mask and then whizzed through the house, collecting glass jars and putting tea-lights into them. At noon Stuart arrived with Bonnie and her friend, Sarah. Sal helped them carry their haul of bright orange pumpkins into the house.

'I don't know if we've ever had this many before.'

'Are you any good at carving them?'

With five of them working together on getting the pumpkins, the bunting, fake cobwebs and bowls of salads and breads and soups ready for the evening, time flew past and the early dark of winter set in for the night. Magda controlled her kitchen and directed people with the skill of an orchestral conductor. The only thing missing, she thought, was Jasmine.

'We could use those big garden candles we've got in the cupboard under the stairs.'

'Sal, where's my black velvet cloak, the one with the celtic edging?'

'In the lounge. While you're there, see if you can find my athame.'

At half past six, Agnes arrived, carrying a huge pot of casserole and two large chocolate cakes. 'I'm not sure this casserole has survived the car journey, darling.' Agnes said, plonking her contributions to the feast on the kitchen table. The dish was wrapped in cling-film and dark brown liquid had escaped the lid and trickled inside the flimsy plastic.

'It's only five minute drive, you loopy hag, look at the mess you've made.' Magda unwrapped the sticky mess and licked her fingers. 'Ooh, I do like that, Aggie, well done.'

Sal finished getting Bran settled in her room upstairs with everything a kitten might need and got changed into a gothic dress, predictably black, with corset lacing up the front over a red centre panel. She topped it with a witch's hat and trotted down to answer the door. A trio of children in fancy dress gratefully took sweets and stood looking at her in awe. The youngest, a girl with ringlets of blonde hair wearing a witch's costume looked her up and down.

'Are you a real witch?' The little girl asked, standing very close to the older boys who judging by the similar looks were most likely her brothers. Sal bent down and smiled. 'Yes I am. But don't worry, I'm a good witch. I only cast nice spells to help people. Here, would you like a chocolate skeleton?'

The girl took the sweet and raced off with her brothers, skipping along the road back towards the village. More children followed, some of them coming inside to look around the display of witchy items Magda and Sal had dotted throughout the hallway and rooms downstairs and more guests arrived for the Samhain ritual, milling around in the kitchen. There was a fair amount of hysterical giggling coming from Mel, Agnes and Magda, and within minutes they were dubbed the cackling crones. Before long, the trick-or-treaters stopped calling and Sal stood back and watched as her gran started to get that look in her eye. The look that said, 'magic is about to happen.'

With the weather now firmly changing from late autumn to early winter and a definite coldness in the air, Magda and Sal dragged out their assortment of cloaks and handed them around for their guests to wear over the everyday clothes they'd travelled in and Magda donned her mask. The path through the garden was marked with glass jars of tea-lights, and solar lamps and over-sized garden candles lit up the altar and the circle. Sal had laid out a low table in front of the altar with decorative flowers, ritual tools, apples and nuts. A photograph of Judy and one of Magda's husband, Sam, were set out, along with photographs and memorial trinkets the others had laid out. There were fourteen of them standing together, pagans, druids and witches, all with one common aim, to celebrate their ancestors and the turning of the wheel.

Illuminated by dozens of golden flames and the silvery light of the full moon, Magda swept the perimeter of the circle with her besom and the ritual began with chanted invocations to the elements, to the Horned God and the Goddess of birth, death and rebirth.

Reading a ritual from paper, especially by wavering torch and candle light, felt unnatural to Magda so she put her own copy of the words on the ground behind her and relied on her memory, her intuition and her long years of experience instead.

'We gather now on Samhain night, to receive and offer love and light, to all of those who have left our lives, while we celebrate them here, tonight.' She wasn't much of a poet and her words felt a little clunky but it didn't matter. With rituals, it was your intention that was the key, not so much the words themselves.

The rest of the participants read out loud from their sheets of paper to honour the Old Ones and spoke freely of their own family, friends and pets who passed over this year, proudly showing off their photographs or sharing a story. There were tears, inevitably for Samhain, and there was laughter too as the Beloved Dead were honoured.

Magda hoped that Stuart wouldn't be offended when she picked up her photo of Sam and spoke about him. After this long, there were no more tears, just happy memories that she never wanted to forget and she smiled when a strong arm came round her shoulders, hugging her and she knew she needn't have worried, Stuart understood.

Mel and Caz handed round a bag of ribbons, thin cords and cotton strips and the clooties were tied to Magda's wishing tree on the other side of the garden where they hung in a jumble of colours, red, green, blue, yellow, white and silver, like a cheerleader's pom-pom jostling in the branches.

Ian and Pete had brought mead to share and a plate of Mel's shortbread was passed around to each person with a kiss and the traditional blessing phrase, May you never hunger, may you never thirst.

With a hail thee well and a merry meet again, the circle was closed and the gathering traipsed one by one back to the house, some taking longer than others, some sitting by their photographs and whispering their own, private prayers and good wishes.

After this was the feast with dozens of dishes of pumpkins, butternut squash, home-made cakes and breads and apple strudels and to Sal's horror, somebody had brought a tofu curry. 'I've had enough tofu to last me a life time, but thank you anyway.'

Amethyst and Sal didn't remember each other from college but Amethyst recalled another friend of hers. 'You used to hang out with Jules Brennan, didn't you?'

'Yes, and Sarah Chase – she was pagan too, you know.'

'Really? I'd got no idea.' Amethyst replied, 'I wish we'd known each other then, I could have been so much further on my path. I didn't really start looking into it until last year.'

'Ah, the impatience of the young,' another guest, Stuart's druid friend Mike teased, 'I didn't stumble into this until I was in my forties.'

Agnes's casserole dish came crashing to the floor, narrowly missing bare feet and Sal cleaned it up, glad that she'd had the foresight to shut the kitten up in her bedroom to keep him safe and out of trouble. The drinking and eating went on until the early hours and by the time everyone had left, the kitchen was nothing but piles of dirty pots and left-overs. Sal and Magda wrapped the food to store in the fridge and rinsed any dishes that would be hard to clean in the morning.

'I thought Stuart might have been staying over.' Sal said, a cheeky grin on her face.

'He's working tomorrow and besides, he offered to drive Bonnie so she could have a glass of wine.'

'I think Bonnie had quite a few more than that.' Sal grinned. 'It's been a really good night, Gran, we should do it again. Felt wrong not having Mum here though, not when she's only just down the road.'

'We'll call in and see her tomorrow, see how she's settling into the flat.' Magda said, hanging up a cloak that had been left over the back of a chair. She yawned loudly. 'I do love having people over and

I don't even mind the washing up the next day but I also love it when they leave and I can get to my bed. I'm so tired. Good night, love.'

*

Jasmine woke up early to the sound of a delivery van pulling up in the street below her window. She rolled over in bed and checked her phone. Half past six, it read, along with an alert bar which she ignored. She grunted, manoeuvred her pillow into a more comfortable position and sank into it. Then she looked at her phone again, unable to settle until she'd read the alert. She had a missed call from an unrecognised number, left in the middle of the night. She noticed there was a message too. She cringed and tried to settle but couldn't. It had to be him, using a new phone or borrowing one to trick her into answering.

'Well tough luck, Paul.' She said, more confident now about speaking out loud in the flat. 'I never want to speak to you again, you sleaze.'

She tossed and turned for another few minutes before grumbling and shoving the duvet back. 'Hope you're happy, you little turd, now I can't sleep.' Jasmine pottered around the kitchen making herself tea and toast and watching breakfast television on her iPad at the little breakfast bar near the side window of the flat. Still tired and yawning, she decided that as the weather was starting to look pleasant outside, at least for the time of year, she would get herself ready for the day and within an hour she ambled along the high street to the church.

There was no sign of Reverend Granger in the grounds or in the church itself and feeling as if she ought to do something while she was here, Jasmine lit a votive candle and then sat in the nave for a while, waiting and wondering. Should she pray, she wondered? She had been here about a week ago, needing somewhere quiet and solitary to spend some time on her own to think and it had felt like the right thing to do. But she was all too aware that last night had been the feast of the dead, the Samhain ritual she'd been brought up with. She had never been completely at ease with her mother's paganism, even as a child, but she still wanted to honour her relatives who had passed over. Was it right to do that in a church when her upbringing had been so firmly rooted in such an alternative religion?

It was her thoughts about Samhain that had brought back memories of her dad and now here she was in a church lighting a candle for him. She got up and went over to blow it out and had another mooch about to see if anyone was around yet. Surely somebody must be here? After a few minutes of aimless wandering through the empty church she ended up back at her lonely pew and decided she had better pray after all. She pulled the hassock out from under the seat and knelt down quietly. She screeched in surprised, jumped and hit her head on the pew in front of her when a heavy hand laid itself on her shoulder.

'Sorry, sorry!' The vicar said, holding his hands out apologetically. 'I didn't mean to startle you.'

'Ow, I'm okay, never mind.' Jasmine rose to her feet, rubbing her head. 'It's not too bad.'

'I should have let you know I was here,' he said, 'you looked so peaceful.'

'I was just…' she fumbled for the words, knowing how close the old man was to her mother.

'Praying?' He smiled at her. 'Or waiting?'

'A bit of both.' Jasmine shrugged and looked at her feet, feeling awkward. 'I was looking for you, actually, Mister Granger, Reverend, I mean.'

'Peter is better.' He told her. 'Is there something I can help you with, Jasmine?'

'I thought I might be able to help you for a change. I saw you gardening the other day and it seemed such a shame you've got all of those simpering, bored house-wives falling over themselves to make cakes and tea for the events you put on but when it comes to the hard work, they're nowhere to be seen. I thought you might like a hand with it.'

Granger smiled and nodded and gestured for her to follow

him. 'Good timing.' He looked up and held his hands together briefly before leading Jasmine out of the church and toward the rear of the churchyard. 'I've been asking the powers that be to send some help, come on. Tool shed's this way.'

He led her to a neglected corner of the churchyard, the grave stones here were moss covered, eroded and barely legible. A stony path led through thick weeds of bramble, willow herb and nettles and Jasmine was stung, even through the denim of her jeans. A dilapidated gate in the crumbling stone wall led in to the orchard and the contrast between the well-kept grounds of the orchard and the sad, sorry state of the churchyard was stark. Along the wall, away from the churchyard, Granger unlocked the small barn where Mr Jackoby kept his tools and handed out a strimmer, secateurs, wheelbarrow and other assorted gardening tools.

Jasmine was left to her own devices; after an hour when the old vicar excused himself on grounds of being tired and needing to rest before returning to his church duties she carried on working, soon getting the hang of the strimmer and seeing to the overgrowth of weeds. What seemed like an hour turned into an entire morning and she was startled to see the reverend return with a tray of tea and biscuits.

'What a transformation,' he said, clearly delighted and touched by the work she'd done. 'I can't believe how much better it looks. You're hired. Thank you.' He chuckled.

'Any time.' She wiped her forehead and leaned up against the wall of the church. 'I think it's done me good, a bit of manual labour for a change. I'm not used to it.'

'Gives you time to think, doesn't it?'

'I think it had the opposite effect on me,' Jasmine smiled, taking another chocolate digestive, 'it gave me time to not think, if that makes sense. My body was occupied but my mind was free, somehow, just drifting into space. I needed that, time to let my brain stop working for a while instead of churning every little issue over and over. It's been good.'

They put the tools back in the barn together and when Jasmine left, Granger walked with her as far as the wooden gate with the archway above it which led out onto the high street. He paused to pull something out of his pocket before saying goodbye to her. She noticed he seemed hesitant and pressed him on it.

'Oh, this?' Granger grimaced. 'Wasn't sure if I should mention it or not. Not sure if it's right for you, but well, here you are. Read it in your own time and let me know what you think.'

Jasmine took the paper from him, a tri-fold advertising leaflet. She looked at it suspiciously, Granger shrugged. She thanked him and took the leaflet home with her anyway and when she got there, after a shower and change of clothes, found herself once more at a loose end in a flat that didn't feel quite like hers. She mooched for a while and then hoovered the flat, feeling more out of sorts with every long minute that passed.

In the back of her mind was the message she hadn't listened to. Eventually, she gave up, knowing she wouldn't be able to relax until she heard whatever it was he had to say but when she picked up her mobile, she noticed that the same unknown number had called another three times while she'd been out.

She was surprised when the voice on the answerphone was one she hadn't heard for a long while. Jasmine, it's Margaret. Paul's sister. Phone me back as soon as you get this, it's important. Please. Ring me.

*

Magda stared out of her kitchen window, eyeing up a magpie who was sitting in the hedge. As she watched, the white and black bird with its blueish sheen flapped its wings, cawed at her and flew off. One for sorrow, or so the saying went. 'Good morning, Mister Magpie, how's your wife?' Magda said the rhyme automatically, hoping there was a second bird nearby to ward against the bad luck that a solitary magpie was supposed to bring. A few moments later she saw Jasmine coming to the back door.

'Hello, love, nice to see you. Sal and I went round to you

160

earlier but you were out.'

'Yeah, I was – busy.' Jasmine tried to dodge around it but decided not to in the end. 'I was helping your vicar friend with some gardening.'

'Oh, I see.' Magda wasn't overly surprised that Jasmine had been talking to Granger again. 'Gardening, though? Have all my years of wisdom finally rubbed off on you?'

'I saw him struggling the other day so I offered to help, that's all. What do you mean?'

'A cheap and productive form of therapy, gardening. Just you wait, you'll have hands like mine before long.'

'Ha! Is that supposed to be encouraging? I'll stick to wearing gloves, all the same.'

'Hey, there's nothing wrong with my hands. For a woman of my age who's been a gardener all her life, they're good hands. Bit stained and my finger tips are getting hard and gnarly, but you feel the skin on the back of my hands here, like a baby's behind.'

'Is Sally in?'

'Nope, she's gone shopping for supplies. Candle waxes, oils, bulk bags of herbs, jars and bottles, that sort of stuff.'

Supplies? That was an odd way of putting it, Jasmine thought. There was an excited look in her mother's eye and she shuddered to think what she was up to this time. 'Can I talk to you, Mum?' Jasmine said, 'I've had a message from Paul's sister asking to phone her and I – I don't know if I should.'

A cold spot touched the back of Magda's neck, sending a jolt through her head to creep around to the front where it sat nagging at her and in her mind's eye she could see and hear the magpie, cawing at her from its leafy perch. 'I can't make that decision for you, love,' she said cautiously, 'but I wouldn't advise it. You don't want to get sucked back into – anything.'

'Yes, you're right. Thanks.' Jasmine breathed deeply and took down a packet of Sal's filter coffee from its spot on the top shelf of the kitchen dresser. 'Shall I make enough for you as well?'

'Don't mind if I do,' Magda said, 'but you'd best get her a new pack to make up for it. You know what she's like with her coffees.'

The coffee percolator bubbled and popped and Magda listened to The Archers on catch-up while Jasmine remained silent and looked out of the window to the rear garden, the green man's leafy face watching her. It reminded her of things she didn't necessarily want to think about right now and she looked away, determined to say what needed to be said.

'There was something else, I wanted to talk to you about, Mum. I want to apologise.'

'Apologise?' Magda was taken aback. 'Whatever for?'

'I've been so horrible to everybody since I left Paul, I've taken my anger out on you and I'm so sorry, Sally too. I want to make it up to you, both of you.'

'Oh, Jasmine, love, you never need to say sorry to me,' Magda pressed her wrinkled hand to her daughter's face and held it there for a moment, looking into Jasmine's eyes while her own filled with tears. 'You've been under a lot of stress, it's bound to show itself in some way and there are reasons why we always blow off steam with the people who love us, it's because we know they won't turn their backs on us, no matter what. I will always love you, you could never do anything to change that. Never.'

'I know but, I just…'

'Shush.' Magda shook her head. 'I may not have been happy with some of the choices you've made in the past, but I can't judge you. After all, you don't get to my age without having made a few mistakes of your own.'

'I've made another one,' Jasmine confessed. 'The flat, I thought I'd manage but it's horrible, the slightest noise and I'm nearly jumping out of my skin. When I came back here there was always someone around and now…' She trailed off, unsure of how to phrase it. She was damaged and she needed people around her.

Magda nodded, she'd been half-expecting it. 'Stacy and Mark will understand, and now they've spruced the place up a bit, it won't take long to get a new tenant in. If you move back here, you'll need to pull your weight, though, no more lying around moping all day. I need help. And so does your daughter.'

'I'll do my share of the washing up. And don't panic, I'm looking for work. Not another bank, though. After almost thirty years of mortgages and loans, I could do with a change.'

'Oh?' Magda hid her smile for now. 'What do you fancy?'

'Maybe accounts I suppose. A small business or – what are you up to? I can see your little brain plotting away. Out with it, Mother'

Magda outlined Sal's idea for a family-run therapy centre and Jasmine pulled a face. 'You want me to be a glorified receptionist?'

'Oh no, Jasmine, you'd have to be much more than that. You could be…'

Jasmine stared at her hand-bag. Her phone was ringing and she looked blankly at the number for a moment. 'If it's Margaret, I'll see what she's got to say. If it isn't, I'll hang up.'

'Jasmine? Is that you? Thank God.'

'Margaret, I don't know what he's told you but I've left him for good, I'm not p-'

'No, Jasmine, listen, please.'

And then she did listen because she heard an urgent, desperate edge to her sister-in-law's voice. She listened without saying another word and when she hung up the call, Jasmine stood up and dropped it. Colour drained from her face and she stared at Magda with a blank expression.

'It's Paul.' Her voice was stilted and slow, she struggled for every word. 'There's been an accident.'

Jasmine stood still, the world around her a blur of movement and dull colours and silence and she reeled dizzily on her feet, felt herself drifting and then her mother's hands caught her shoulders and she was guided to a chair where she sat, unthinking, unblinking.

'It's my fault,' Jasmine whispered, her voice barely more than a breath, 'I wished him dead.'

'Jasmine, what happened?'

Jasmine felt limp and hollow and cold. 'He's – oh God! Mum, he was killed in a car crash last night.'

CHAPTER FOURTEEN

'Of course it's not your fault.' Magda said for what must have been the ninetieth time. She scoffed at Jasmine then scoffed a bite of her scone. 'It was an accident, Jasmine. You had nothing to do with it.'

Time had slowed down over the last three days and Sal, washing-up at the sink, had learned to tune out the repetitive conversation. It was like living in a ground-hog day that she was doomed to live through, day after depressing day in a never-ending cycle of repeating sequences. First of all, she woke up to the sound of crying. Then she showered and came downstairs to make breakfast and listened to her mum's guilty confessions, which amounted to nothing more than wishful thinking and if that was a crime, everyone in the world would be behind bars. After that, Sal tried to make a start on her plans for her business idea; she needed to sort out exactly which of the many governing bodies and associations she needed to belong to for accreditation and licences to practice her therapies as well as figuring out if she would qualify for business loans and grants to finance it. She was also preparing a batch of scented candles and had moulds, coloured dyes, fragrances and flower petals littered all over the kitchen counter. Sal never seemed to make much progress on any of it, however, because by mid-afternoon her mum had dragged herself out of her fog and seemed a little brighter and would insist on the three of them watching something on the TV together to cheer her up further. So far Sal had had to endure Harry Enfield, cringe her way through Mr Bean and put up with a few Monty Python re-runs. She didn't mind Monty Python, but she did mind her gran's annoying whistling and singing about the bright side of life for the rest of the afternoon. At this point in the day, Sal had been ground down by the heaviness of the atmosphere in the house and today, faced with the very grim and horrifying prospect of watching Benidorm, she was at breaking point.

'You're right,' Jasmine said now, tucking her hair behind her ears. 'I need to accept it and move on.'

'That's the spirit, eh, love?' Magda was so patient, Sal thought. She admired her gran for that as she didn't know how much longer she could keep it up herself. She was becoming increasingly frustrated with the cycle and had a desperate desire to do something that didn't involve opening up the floodgates of waterworks her mother seemed to switch on and off like a tap.

She dried and put away the dishes and looked up again to see the trees blowing in the wind that had picked up outside, shaking the multi-coloured clooties still hanging in the gnarly wishing tree, some of them hanging there from the recent Samhain ritual and others, older ones, from times gone by. The weather was getting colder with each passing week but today it looked bright and she wanted to be out of doors, feeling something light and real and fresh and she longed for the wind on her face to blow the dust off and shake her back into life.

'I'm going for a walk.' Sal announced. She knew what came next in the concentric circles her mother was living in, these repetitive, endless days of sorrow and grief that were tinged with a heavy dose of relief. After the comedy hour there would be another slump to the bottom of the emotional rollercoaster. Her mum would sink into her fog again, churning all of her guilty thoughts up to the surface to be picked through as if they were real. 'Why don't you join me? We could all do with some fresh air.'

'I'm not sure I – ' Jasmine didn't get the chance to finish her objection because Magda jumped up cheerily, said what a grand day it was for a walk and reminded them to put on a coat and scarf because the weather was turning.

The canal bank was not overly busy this afternoon but there were ducks, a pair of swan and a solitary coot in the water. They passed a few dog-walkers and hikers as they walked, heading right out to the foot bridge where a path forked away from the canal and circled through fields and scrubby heathland for several miles before branching off again toward the other end of the village, ending at an open lane near the orchard.

'Have you made up your mind about the funeral?' Magda asked, turning over a piece of smooth heamatite in her pocket, willing it to ground her.

Jasmine nodded. 'I've got to do what's right for me, so no,' she said with finality. 'I won't be going. I can't stand the thought of everyone saying what a good person he was and how much they'll miss him. His sister, Margaret, she's the only one of his family who knew what I was going through with him. She knew exactly what her brother was like, she'll understand why I'm not there. I was never close to any of his friends or the rest of the family though, so let them think what they like. I don't care.'

'What about the house and all your things, though? Will there be anything you need to do?' Magda hoped not. 'Will there be a will? Or an inquest into the accident?'

'Margaret rang yesterday, apparently there were two small boxes in the house with my name written on them and the remains of a bonfire in the garden so it looks like he did burn most of my things. His kids from his first wife are getting the house and everything else. Four years of crap and I've been written off but to be quite honest, Mum, I'm just glad I don't have to spend the rest of my life looking over my shoulder the whole time.'

'I know it's a horrible thing to say, Mum,' Sal joined in, 'but I'm glad too. That you don't have to worry about him anymore, I mean.'

Magda nodded at that, Jasmine sniffed and shook her head briefly, and the three of them linked arms as they carried on walking along the lane to the bend where, after going past the orchard, it opened out onto the far end of the high street adjacent to the church. Magda blushed as they passed the stone wall where she and Stuart had been rumbled. She couldn't help looking over the wall.

'Hang on, what's that?' She pointed to some flimsy red fabric hanging onto a rose bush and Sal vaulted over the wall into the churchyard to get it. 'Looks like a pair of ladies knickers.'

'Eeww, gross!' Sal held the offending article of underwear by the tips of her fingers until Magda rooted through her hand-bag and dragged out a disposable carrier bag. 'Is there anything you don't have in that bag?'

'Put them in here and we can throw them in the bin on the street.' Magda said, wondering how on earth the knickers had got there. They were definitely not hers and besides, her own lingerie had not had the chance to end up in the roses. By the look of it, the garment had been fluttering in the wind-swept bushes for about the right length of time – tattered but still intact. She cast her mind back to the night in question, thinking Mrs Beers might have been up to mischief of her own when she stumbled upon Magda and Stuart on the orchard side of the wall. But Mrs Beers was not the sort to go around with underwear like this, surely? She shrugged, it would have to be a mystery for another day.

'And weirdly,' Jasmine continued, breaking her mum's train of thought as her own headed into happier territory, 'It's made me feel proud of myself for leaving him. You know, plucking up the courage to walk away from it. Imagine if I was still living with him now, I'd have to play the part of the grieving widow when all I really want to do is spit on his grave.'

'Good morning, ladies.' Reverend Granger greeted them, tipping his hat as he came down the steps of the churchyard and met them on the high street. Jasmine covered her mouth with a hand in embarrassment. 'I'm sorry, Peter. I didn't mean any offence, I was – '

'Sorry? I didn't catch what you said.' He said it with a straight face and she believed him. Sal believed him too, but Magda knew the old man better than that and she'd already clocked his initial reaction to what Jasmine had said. Realising she was still holding a bag with another woman's dirty pants in it, she stuffed it quickly out of sight in her hand-bag. She winked at him and, after they passed the time of day and Granger dished out his condolences for the hundredth time, he winked back at her.

Stacy was in the street cleaning her shop-front window and

she waved to the trio, calling them over the road for a chat. 'I'm so sorry, Jasmine. But it must be a relief, in some ways, I suppose.'

'In some ways.' Jasmine agreed. 'I wanted to talk to you actually, about the flat.'

Sal excused herself, wanting to get on with her candle making experiments but Magda stayed with Jasmine for support. Stacy ushered the pair of them into the back room of her little shop where deliveries were kept and a small kitchen was laid out with tea things. Files and papers sprawled messily over counter tops, and shelves weighed heavily with folders and envelopes. Mark, sitting at a desk in one corner, grunted a quick hello to them and made himself scarce. 'Don't mind me,' he said, 'I've had enough of this for now anyway.'

'He's been going through the accounts,' Stacy explained when he'd gone out to take over the window-washing duty, 'and it's an absolute minefield. Neither of us have the time to keep the books up to date. Every now and then we go through the back-log of bank statements, invoices and receipts and do a big stock-take but by the time we do, there's so much that it turns into a giant headache.'

'Oh? If you want a hand with it anytime, let me know. I'm good with numbers.'

'We had thought about hiring someone to do it for us regularly, actually. Maybe just one day a week, if you're serious. We'd pay you, of course.'

'That sounds great, I'd love to help out. It'll keep me out of trouble. I'm not a chartered accountant, but…'

'No, that's fine,' Stacy said, thinking it over, 'you'd save us so much trouble. We get Andrew from Barn's and Co. to do the end of year stuff in March but if you can keep on top of the rest, it'd be a god-send. Anyway, you wanted to talk about the flat?'

'You've been so good, getting it painted for me and the flat is lovely…'

'But you're letting it go?' Stacy predicted. 'You do whatever you need to, Jasmine. We'll find a new tenant soon enough, don't worry about it. The shop's doing really well so the rent is a bonus at the moment, not a necessity.'

'Thanks, Stacy.' Magda said, patting Jasmine's arm. 'Did you want to nip up there now, love? Collect a few bits to take back and we can pick the rest of it up tomorrow?'

'Is that all right, Stacy?'

'Of course.' She said. 'There's no hurry.'

Magda led the way to the alley and the metal stairs leading up to the second floor flat and Jasmine let them in. After being empty for several days now, the flat was cold and quiet and as she helped Jasmine pack a few things into a couple of strong bags, mainly items of clothing and some toiletries and make-up, of which Jasmine had enough to set up her own counter in Boots, Magda kept up a steady stream of chatter to cover the silence.

'What about this jersey?' She held up a pale salmon cashmere piece with a soft turtle-neck and puffed sleeves. If I had to wear that, Magda thought, I'd be depressed too, even without the deceased ex-husband.

'Nobody says jersey anymore. It's a sweater and yes please, the green one too.'

'I know you're not making this decision lightly, love,' Magda said, finding an identical top in forest-green and folding it neatly, 'but I hope you've put some thought into living at the house. I know we've got the three bedrooms but the kitchen is already more of a workshop than anything else and if Sal's serious about her business idea, which I think she is, we might have to put our heads together and come up with a solution.'

'That won't be for a while, though, surely? If she wants to run a holistic centre, she'll need funding, business loans, a sound proposal. I know she's got a lot of experience doing admin for other people, but it will take her a while to sort all of that out.'

'It's a bit much for one person, isn't it?' Magda opened her eyes deliberately wide and blinked them, with a sly grin, right in her daughter's face.

'Oh for heaven's sake, all right! All right! I give in, I'll be your glorified receptionist and help Sal with the business side of things, at least till she gets things up and running smoothly.' Jasmine conceded. 'After that, we'll see how it goes.'

'Good girl. Right, here's two bags each to lug back, anything else while we're here?'

'There should be a few magazines on the coffee table, Mum.'

Magda picked up several battered and well-thumbed copies of Cosmopolitan and Hello and underneath them all she saw a tri-fold leaflet that could only have come from one place. 'I see you've been talking to Peter Granger a fair bit.'

'How do you – oh, yes. That.' Jasmine took the leaflet and opened it out, looking at it properly for the first time. It was an introductory break-down of the church's Alpha course, a guide to the teachings of the bible through a series of discussions and talks. She folded it up again and stuffed it into one of the carrier bags, looking slightly embarrassed. 'I told you I'd seen him last week, struggling to keep on top of the gardening along with everything else he does.'

'And?'

'I gave him a hand with the weeding, pruning and chopping things back, that sort of thing, like I said. Anyway, we talked while we worked and I had that thrust at me. No biggie.'

'Are you going, though?'

'I don't think so.' Jasmine shrugged, as if it really was like she'd said, no big deal. Magda saw a deep thought process going on in her daughter's mind. According to the leaflet, Granger's next intake was starting soon and as much as she had always wanted Jasmine to feel at home with the paganism and witchery she'd been brought up with, if it ended up being the church that made her happy, then so be it.

*

'Stuart, come in.' Sal opened the back door when he arrived. 'I keep telling you, you don't need to knock. I'm surprised Gran hasn't given you a key by now.'

'She has, seemed rude to just walk in though. Is the kettle on?'

'Ha! You should be so lucky, I've got to keep watching this pan so the wax mixes properly.'

'She in the lounge?' Stuart asked.

'Yes, watching another naff comedy with Mum.' Sal said, carefully adding several drops of pink dye to her batch of molten wax to achieve the shade of candle she was looking for. 'Before you go, smell this for me, please.' She picked up the small pan and wafted it around.

Stuart wrinkled his nose. 'Like a tart's boudoir.'

'That's what I thought too, I've over-done the geranium essence.'

'You're turning into her, you know.' Stuart told her. 'A little mini-Magda.'

'How delightful for me,' Sal said. She put the pan on the counter, standing it on a heat resistant mat. 'Go on then, scram. Gran will appreciate a reprieve from Mum's melancholy.'

She looked at the moulds she had carefully laid out on the kitchen table only to find half of them had been knocked over as a bike helmet and enormous leather gloves took over the space. 'Seriously?'

'Sorry.' He set the moulds back upright. 'I didn't want the cat sleeping in it again. Took me ages to get rid of the smell last time.'

'Is that biker here again?' Magda's voice rang out from the hallway. 'Better get yourself in here, Mister Biker, there's a pair of lips with your name on 'em waiting for you!'

'Oh, take it out of the kitchen, you two.'

Magda and Stuart retreated to the garden, sitting side by side on the willow arbour, overlooked by Sal in the kitchen. After a few minutes of saying hello with their lips, Magda chuckled when she saw the blind in the kitchen window had been pulled part-way down.

'I've raised a prude. Two of them, I think.'

'You've done a good job, they're both smashing, really.'

'As is your Bonnie. Oh, she's got Sal another three aromatherapy clients, by the way.'

'Good.' Stuart said simply. He looked around the garden and found a rose bush to focus on and then ran his left hand through his long and bushy beard. Magda knew him well enough by now that she could read him like a book. She could either hurry it up or wait patiently for him to say whatever was on his mind. As she debated this, a bumble bee droned past her nose and settled in the straggly honeysuckle that traipsed over the arbour. A solitary bee so late in the year, she took it as sign.

'I don't know what you're thinking,' she began, 'but I hope it's something good.'

Stuart stood up, put his hands in his pockets and turned away. He walked a few steps and then walked back, taking up his place next to her again.

'You've obviously been thinking about something serious and now you're wondering how to bring the matter up without saying the wrong thing.'

Stuart didn't reply. 'But here's the thing. I don't care what it is.' Magda sensed something big was coming up and she thought about all the times their blossoming romance had been interrupted, the deep ache in her hips she'd told him she suffered with after riding pillion on the longer rides they'd had. Her life and his were so different, were they really compatible? She thought so but perhaps he did not. Magda took one of his large hands in hers and felt the warmth and strength coming off him in waves, filling herself up with how good it felt, just in case the conversation went the wrong way and she didn't get the chance to feel it again. 'I'm glad I've met you, Stuart Redman. No matter what you've decided, I'm glad. Because you brought me back to life.'

He opened his mouth but Magda put her finger over his lips and shushed him. 'No, please. Let me finish. I had become stagnant.' She said. 'Filling my days with village gossip, making cough syrups and lavender sachets for local dim-wits who don't appreciate it, filling my nights with cups of coffee and reading too many books. You've done me the world of good. I've woken up and realised how much there is left to enjoy and I will always thank you for it. So it's all right, you see, you can say it.'

And then he did and Magda was so surprised she jumped up with a start and fell off the arbour onto the lawn where she sat getting a soggy backside with her feet in the air. Her mouth bobbed open twice before she managed to say another word. Stuart laughed loudly and offered her a hand up which Magda took gratefully.

'I think I need a hearing aid. What did you say?'

She struggled back onto the willow covered seat and listened to Stuart as the sun began to slowly sink and the day drew to an early end. Magda nodded in all the right places and let Stuart finish his speech. She chortled to herself, he must have been practicing it for days, poor man. Then her laughter got the better of her and she let it out loudly, filled with glee. She clapped her hands and grabbed hold of his scruffy white beard and kissed him. Stuart looked at her with a puzzled expression.

'I haven't got a clue,' he said helplessly, 'what you're thinking.'

'Well, maybe I'll keep you guessing then!' She screeched again with giggles and forced herself to take a deep breath and act sensibly for a minute. 'I thought you were calling it off, oh you poor thing. I've driven you mad, haven't I? Of course,' she said, 'yes, absolutely. I think it's a bloody fantastic idea.'

'You're like a cauldron, you witch.' He smiled at her and the bumble bee made its round once more, landing in his hair. Magda brushed it away and the sleepy bee droned away. 'There's always something bubbling under the surface and I've no idea if you're going to steam or simmer. Just don't explode on me, will you?'

'On the contrary, I hope we explode together,' she grinned and stood up, inclining her head at what she hoped was a saucy angle, 'but perhaps not just yet? I know we're both up for it, but things do seem to get in our way and oddly, I quite like the way it's building up a bit of tension. If I'm honest, my hips are getting worse, Stuart.'

'There's no hurry for that,' Stuart pulled her close and gave her a long, deep kiss. 'I'm not going anywhere.'

'Come with me, biker boyfriend,' she trotted back with a sudden spurt of energy, fired up by the revelation and invitation. 'We're telling the tribe.'

She clutched Stuart's hand tightly, never wanting to let go, and they sat side by side on the brown leather sofa in the lounge, waiting for Sal to join them.

'I was watching that, you know.' Jasmine was disturbed by her mother's invasion of her comedy programme and the sudden, dramatic need for what the batty woman had described as a family conference. 'Have you been drinking? You've got that weird, glazed-over look on your face.'

'I'm completely sober, you cheeky bugger!' Magda said indignantly, sticking her tongue out. 'So there. Get a move on, number one grandchild!'

'I'm your only grandchild.' Sal came in, still drying her hands on a tea-towel. Her long hair had spatters of melted wax in it and some of the geranium essential oil fragranced wax had spilled on her t-shirt.

'Good job too, can't be doing with any more of them. You're enough of a handful.'

'Thanks, Gran. Love you too.' Sal on the arm of a chair next to Jasmine. 'What's this about? You've been up to mischief, I can smell it like a sixth sense.'

'That would be one of the regular five senses, Sally.' Jasmine teased. Her comedy hour had worked its magic and her melancholy mood was lifted, at least temporarily.

'Hush, now, the pair of you.' Magda rapped her knuckles briefly on the coffee table. 'I call this meeting to order! We've been talking about things and decided that Stuart will be moving in.'

'If that's okay with you two, pet.' He added.

Jasmine and Sal stared at them both with surprise and neither of them spoke for moment. Magda looked from one face to the next and in her mind's eye, she had her fingers crossed. On both hands. Stuart held her hand firmly, her anchor, her rock.

'In that case,' Sal waved at him with a pointed finger, 'it's about time you learned how to put the kettle on yourself.'

'You know,' said Stuart, 'that would be a lot more intimidating if your finger wasn't covered in bright pink wax.'

'Stuart, you just heard my daughter,' Jasmine chided, 'we are very happy to have you join the family, but honestly,' she hutched forward in her armchair and prodded her empty mug with her toe, 'I'm gasping.'

'Are you sure you want to do this, Stuart?' Magda asked, wiggling her eyebrows at him. 'A house full of women, only one bathroom, a kitchen that smells like a cross between a brothel and an incense factory and a deranged kitten who pees in your helmet.'

'There's worse things in life than that.' Stuart said. Now that the question was settled, he relaxed and sat back, resting his arms behind his head.

'Milk and two sugars, please.' Jasmine reminded him.

'Mine's a black coffee,' Sal chimed in, 'with a splash of caramel syrup, please.'

'And we shall have a gin and tonic.' Magda said. 'After all, you're not driving home tonight, are you?'

'Oh no!' Jasmine put on a mock horrified look and put her hands over her ears. 'You'd better keep the noise down. I do not want to wake up in the middle of the night.'

Magda followed Stuart to the kitchen and gave him a gentle squeeze. She was glad they had both seemed to be happy with the idea and it was good to see Jasmine more relaxed and at ease than she had been for days. Now it was about to really happen though, Magda suddenly wondered how on earth they would all manage – four of them living in such a small house. It had not seemed all that spacious with just her and Sal but now?

Stuart's idea of them living together had been sprung upon her like a bolt out of the blue and while she was just crazy with happiness at the thought of it, Magda knew they couldn't all survive in the house for long without getting under each other's feet and as

Stuart's current home was rented – well, she wasn't giving up her home of thirty years only to start renting at her age.

'Well,' she decided, 'we'll just have to avoid treading on each other's toes for now and then see what can be done about an extension I suppose.'

'You didn't have to say yes.' Stuart reminded her. 'I'm a big bloke, I can handle it.'

'You are indeed.' Magda's eyes boggled at him. 'I hadn't given it much thought, if I'm honest, but I do like the idea of having you around. As for the space, we'll work it out.'

'Yeah,' he grinned, leaning up against the Aga at what had become his customary position in the kitchen, 'extension, motorbike shed…'

'Motorbike shed? Where the bloody hell is that going to go?'

'We'll work it out,' he said and took his cup of tea from Magda.

A sudden, sharp bang shook them both, the mug crashed to the floor and they whizzed round at the sound of laughter. Sal and Jasmine stood in the doorway holding party poppers and a bottle of wine.

They called out together loudly. 'Welcome home, Stuart Redman!'

CHAPTER FIFTEEN

The next few days were a flurry of movement for Magda and Jasmine, both of them unpacking boxes and finding nooks and crannies around the house to put things in. Stuart kept a lot of his things in heavy duty boxes and stored these at the back of his little office in the garage he ran and Jasmine managed to empty the flat with no more than she had left with. Stuart was out of the house a lot, either working on motorbikes at his garage, working on his own bike in the driveway or off on bike rides with a couple of his friends. Even so, the old house was starting to feel cramped, especially as Magda's tarot clients and the locals wanting potions and lotions hadn't slowed down and there were still at least one or two people calling in every day. With all of the residents and guests, there didn't seem to be enough room to breathe some days and consequently, Sal spent a lot of her time outside in the garden or upstairs in her room, reading or meditating. But most of what she did was to start putting her thoughts into order and planning how she could make a business work.

She'd had several attempts at creating some kind of business proposal, outlining some of the practical things a centre could offer, finding out which of the governing bodies of therapists she and her gran would need to join, luckily there were several and Sal's course was already accredited with one of those, and trying to pin down exactly what the centre's building would need to be in terms of looking for a place with enough room for it. She'd gone back over the paper from a few weeks ago to look for the advert she remembered seeing for retail or business space to rent. The advert didn't give much away so Sal gave the agent a phone call to find out the property had already been let and when she cheekily asked how much the monthly rent would have been she thanked them politely then hung up the phone and swore out loud.

'All right,' Magda said, hands on her hips as she stood in the kitchen by the Aga. The warm and comforting aroma of baking bread filled the kitchen with a hungry anticipation and Sal wondered how much longer she'd have to wait. 'How much were they asking for?'

'Two and half thousand a month.' Sal dropped her head in her hands and made a mournful noise. 'How on earth do small business owners manage to make a living with outgoings like that?'

'Where there's a witch, there's a way.' Magda sounded confident and she raised her lips in a little smile. 'Fancy stirring things up a bit?'

'Oh dear.' Sal pointed a finger at her gran. 'I know what you're thinking and yes, I agree that a little bit of magic to ease the way might not be a bad thing. But choose your words carefully, Grandmother, I don't want a repeat of what happened the last time you wanted to stir things up a bit.'

'Don't worry,' Magda prised herself away from the stove and opened the heavy door of the oven, using her thick, worn mitt to pull out the pans of steaming hot bread, 'I learned my lesson. It was worth it though, the look on your mother's face was priceless when she saw the queue of people lining up outside the front door. They were all wearing one. Bright pink, as I recall. Even the radio presenter had one.'

'That was the second time you ruined my week at school with your photo in the paper. Remind me exactly how you managed it?'

'Ah, well.' Magda was on a roll and Sal was beginning to wish she hadn't asked but there was no stopping her now. 'Granger put on a church fete, raising money for charity, but it was just after Hallowe'en so I couldn't resist turning up with a pointed hat. The newsagent still had a few costume hats left over and Hilary donated an unopened box.'

'I remember now.' Sal groaned. 'There were...'

'I'm telling the story.' Magda insisted. 'The whole lot of them were bright pink and misshapen. Actually, they looked like giant phallic symbols. The reporter thought it would be hilarious if the Wilveringham Women's Group posed with them. He found it highly amusing that the local vicar was friends with a witch and you know what Granger's like. He went along with it and before you could say boo to a goose the whole parade was wearing one.'

'And why did they all come to the house?'

'Posing at Chez Howard? So the photographer could get an authentic witches cottage in the shot, of course. I posed with my broomstick and the greylings went along with it all because they were so desperate to steal my limelight.'

'I bet Mrs Beers had a field day.'

'She did do when I put one of the pink willy hats through the bakery door for her while she was serving a customer. I told her she didn't want to miss out on all the fun and she threw a cream cake at me. She still talks about it now, you know, every time anyone new shows up in the village. She points me out to them if I walk past her shop.'

'That's horrible of her.' Sal sympathised.

'Ah, but what she doesn't realise is that every single one of them knocks on my door a few days later and asks me for a reading. I've got a lot of regular clients from her, tickles me pink every time I think about it.'

The day was sunny and bright and though it was cold enough for a thick jumper, neither Magda nor Sal felt the need for a cloak as they set up their altar things in the garden. They worked easily together, as they had done so often before, to create their magic circle, that wonderful place between the worlds where all things were imaginable and even more were possible.

'Banishing magic, I think.' Magda said.

Sal shook her head. 'It's mid-day and it's sunny, we need things to come to us, we should be invoking.'

'Waning moon, it's past Samhain now, the leaves are dying off and the weather is turning to winter, it's actually half-past twelve, learn how to read your watch girl, and we want to get rid of the obstacles in our way. See? Banishing magic, letting go of things.'

Sal submitted to the older witch's wisdom as usual, and grudgingly admitted she was right, as usual. It wouldn't be as bad if she didn't look so smug about it, Sal thought. Nevertheless, she circled three times with Magda, walking anti-clockwise, the widdershins direction of banishing. An act of releasing any self-doubt or negative energies, a way to remove obstacles and blockages that are stopping you from moving forward and getting what you want.

Magda took two long white cords from a box and handed one end of each to Sal. They laid the cords out on the ground in a labyrinth and put candles with glass jars all around, lighting them as they went into the centre of the labyrinth.

Then, with purpose and focus, Magda led Sal out of the labyrinth, chanting as she went.

We ask for the blessings of the Goddess of the earth. We ask for the blessings of the Old God of the sun.

Magda walked slowly, saying out loud all the things that they wanted to get rid of, everything was stopping them from moving forward, and Sal followed her, dutifully repeating each little phrase.

'We release all these things which are in the path of our goals, we let go of worry and doubt.' Sal focused on letting go of that small voice in the back of her mind that was full of doubt and unhelpful thoughts. When she reached the end of the labyrinthine path, Sal shook her hands and stamped her bare feet on the earth, grounding herself.

Magda passed a pen and paper to Sal. 'Write down any problems you want to get rid of and we'll burn the paper in the cauldron.'

Sal thought about what her obstacles were – lack of space, for living and working in, was definitely one problem she no longer wanted to put up with. She wrote that down. Something else that was bothering her was the paperwork and the tedium of having to plan, research and organise everything herself, her mum hadn't shown any signs of getting involved yet, despite her initial interest. So that needed was another problem she didn't want.

Facing each other, the two women circled the altar anti-clockwise and after their third time, Magda lit the candle she'd set out in her cauldron and burned her folded paper in the flame. She giggled as the flames caught hold and Sal closed her eyes briefly with worry and pursed her lips, hoping her gran hadn't wished for something ludicrous and out of the ordinary. She lit her own paper, letting the flickering yellow and blue flames turn her obstacles to ash and as the flames in the cauldron died down, leaving only soot and ash and molten candle wax, it began to rain.

Magda and Sal had a mad moment of paddling their bare feet, which Magda insisted on for rituals at every opportunity, in the grass and feeling the beginnings of sludge and water squeeze up between their toes. Sal felt the dirt under her feet and the rain pelting her skin and she feel alive, connected to the very core of the earth itself, filled with a vibrancy that was almost electric. Her whole body hummed with the buzz of magical energy and she yelped and sang and danced with delight because sometimes, she realised, sometimes you just have to dance barefoot in the rain when the mood comes upon you. Sometimes the rain was healing and it washed away your worries and your doubts and sometimes, it was just bloody good fun.

'We feel the earth beneath our feet.' Magda started a chant and Sal took it up, the pair of them spiralling again around the labyrinth and dancing, arms waving in the air. 'We feel the rain upon our skin, we feel the call of the Goddess of Old.'

A peal of thunder made Sal squeal and she spun round to see that it wasn't actually thunder but the roar of a motorbike pulling into the driveway at the side of the house. Stuart heaved the machine up onto the kick-stand and saw the two of them dancing madly in the garden in the rain that was now pouring heavily.

He waved and they waved back but while the biker had clearly had enough of the weather and wanted nothing more than to get in the house to change out of his leathers, Magda and Sal kept up with their dance until they were soaked through to the skin, feeling the cold in their bones and exhausted.

'They're both mad.' Stuart watched from the kitchen window, standing next to Jasmine who was making a hearty stew for dinner.

'Oh yes,' she agreed, 'completely. See what I have to put up with? I might take up crochet or knitting so that at least there's one sensible woman in the house.'

'A house with a sensible woman in it?' Stuart grinned, watching the frolicking women. 'That wouldn't be any fun, though, pet. Would it?'

*

'Oh, that is good news, Mr Jackoby.' Magda listened and smiled, nodding at Mr Jackoby even though she was speaking to him by telephone and not in person. 'Lovely, I am pleased. Thank you for letting me know, good bye.'

'Wonders will never cease.' Reverend Granger was paying Magda another one of his visits, though he assured her, as he'd arrived, that this time it was purely a social call. 'You're a marvel, Magda.'

'Looks like he's coming back to reclaim his garden shed. Will you miss having that daughter of mine helping you out in the churchyard?'

'I suppose so, yes.' He mused. 'She's been very helpful. Where is she, by the way? I thought I might say thank you to her while I was here.'

'Actually, she's out with Sal. They've gone over to Stoke for a day out, shopping and what-not. Apparently Jasmine doesn't appreciate my taste in mugs. Wish I could get her to do a bit of my gardening,' Magda told him, 'my roses need – hey, that reminds me!' She dragged her hand-bag up onto the table and took out a carrier bag which she handed to him. 'Don't put your hands in there, just take a look,' she warned him.

'What on earth?' Suddenly Granger's face was nearly as red as the lingerie recovered from the rose bushes.

'Remember we saw you outside the church, coming back from a walk? I meant to put these in the bin but I forgot. You'll never guess where I found them. Go on then, guess.'

'I wouldn't like to speculate but assume they are not yours.'

'Your rose bushes!' She said, folding her arms across her chest with a smug look of satisfaction. She nodded her head. 'That's right, on the church side of the stone wall. Caught up in the thorns. Now, Mister Vicar, let's think about this, shall we?'

Granger put a hand to his brow and groaned out loud. 'Do we have to?'

'Who do we both know who has recently admitted to snooping around the rose bushes in the churchyard in the middle of the night? That's right,' she jabbed a finger in the air to make her point, 'our lady baker. Only does this look like something she might wear? I think not, she is a confirmed singleton, after all. Well, what say you? Look at that skimpy lace.'

'I honestly don't know what you're telling me for, woman.' Exasperated, reverend Granger drained his mug and shook his head again. 'Probably some kids mucking about.'

'That's what you think, but this is an expensive brand of lingerie, not the sort of thing kids would leave lying around, even if they were doing the deed.'

'Really, Magda!' He thumped his hand on the table. 'It's neither your business nor mine.'

Magda huffed and sighed. 'Very well, as you wish.' She picked up the bag of scandalous underwear and dropped it in her own bin. 'I shall drop the subject for now, but one day I'll get to the bottom of it, you'll see. Pun intended, by the way.'

'Yes,' Granger glanced upwards as if asking for strength to help him deal with this woman once and for all. 'With you, Magda, there is always a pun intended.'

*

Sal's feet were starting to ache, her hands were freezing and yet her mother still insisted they had to visit Hanley to browse the pottery shops. She didn't have much choice, however, as Jasmine was in a brighter mood today than she had been for a long while and Sal didn't want to complain or protest in case she upset her again. She was underwhelmed by the potteries, shelf after shelf of glazed mugs, finely turned vases and amusingly shaped animal money-boxes.

'Mother, please can you just buy the wretched thing already so we can go and have lunch?' Her patience had finally run out and Sal stood impatiently by the door as Jasmine made her purchase and the counter assistant wrapped the piece carefully in layer after layer of tissue paper before handing it over in a paper bag. At last, they were out of the shop and Sal dived past people in the street swiftly, making her way straight for Costa and before long they were seated with refreshments and Sal sank back wearily in the faux-leather seat, sipping a large Americano with hazelnut syrup. Not a great coffee, for a great coffee, she would have had to trek across town to her favourite independent café, but it was still good enough.

'I can't believe you've actually paid money for that ugly mug.'

'I like it.' Jasmine shrugged. 'Besides, all the ones at home have got witches, unicorns, cauldrons or slutty slogans on them.'

The barista came over with their hot paninis and Sal tucked in gratefully. 'You know,' she said between bites of melted cheese and mushroom, 'I do think my idea for a therapy centre could work. I just can't get my head around the thought of business loans and having to do all the paperwork involved as well as actually doing the massages and things.'

'Go on, I'm listening.'

'I want to stop mucking about, Mum, and start getting on with it. I know Gran's up for it but she already said she's looking to retire completely over the next couple of years. If you come on board too, it could be such a success. I see it as needing three, hopefully four rooms. One for the reception and display area, two rooms for therapies and readings and we must have a storage space with a workshop or kitchen where I can get on with making all the creams and oils and candles and incense.'

'I have been giving it some thought, Sally. We can go over your ideas and make a start on the paperwork this evening, if you like.' Jasmine nodded, thinking over the rough outline of the centre. 'There's a lot of research involved, commercial properties aren't easy to come by so the bank loan will be significant. It took me years to get a decent amount of savings and I took a lot of risks keeping it secret from Paul, but I can put in some capital up front as an investment.'

'Speaking of the slug, how are you feeling today?' Sal remembered it was the day of the funeral and now she wished she hadn't asked.

'Strangely, I feel happier than I have in ages.' Jasmine finished her cake, licking her fingers to savour every last smidgeon of white chocolate. 'Not laugh out loud happy, more content perhaps. It feels good to know it's all over with, once and for all.'

'And his sister's not been in touch again?'

'She saved a few things of mine after all and promised to send them in the post but I can't think of anything left in the house I could possibly want so I refused to give her an address. It's liberating, I feel like a new woman.'

'That's good, Mum.' Sal said, meaning it. 'You do seem a lot better.'

'Is that your phone or mine?'

'Hello?' Sal answered her mobile and listened while Jasmine drank the last of her Lady Grey tea. A woman's voice greeted her and she recognised it at once but why was she ringing? 'Yes, he's doing really well, thank you. Oh, I see. No, no problems at all, yeah, he's adorable. I definitely made the right choice. No, not at all, good to hear from you. I mean, thanks for checking. Yes, you take care too. Oh, okay. Bye.'

Sal was puzzled and as she and Jasmine gathered up their shopping bags and coats, she was quiet until Jasmine prodded her.

'That was Alex, from the cat rescue centre, wanting to check up on Percy, I mean, Bran.'

'That's a bit strange, Sally,' Jasmine said, 'they don't normally do that, do they? Not for cats.'

'That's what I thought.' Sal headed out of the coffee shop and they walked through town to the car park. She knew it meant nothing, it was a routine courtesy call. 'I guess their policy has tightened up a bit.'

'You what, love?' Jasmine was concentrating on the traffic, pulling into the relentless stream of cars on the inner ring road. 'Wasn't listening.'

'Nothing, Mum,' Sal tried to forget about the phone call on the drive home but for some reason, the woman's voice had got under her skin and left a flush of butterflies in her stomach. 'Maybe I just need some more of Gran's perioditea.'

Jasmine found this hysterical and burst into fits of contagious laughter. 'Can you feel your womb, Sally?'

*

Magda hummed along tunelessly to The Archers theme tune while she set places for dinner, clearing wax moulds and bottles of essential oils out of the way to make space. The now familiar and homely purring noise of the bike pulling up sent a flutter through her belly and she patted her hair, made sure her blouse was tucked in and tried to look seductive when Stuart walked in.

'You do know I'm sitting right here, Gran?' Sal told her. 'I can see what you're doing and it's not very subtle.'

'Evening, pet.' Stuart's voice was muffled and Sal pointed at his head. 'Sorry.' He took off his helmet and shoved it out of the way on a shelf he had installed high up on the wall, out of reach of the kitten. 'Something smells good. I'll cook tomorrow, though. I don't expect to be waited on, I told you that.'

'This isn't for you,' Magda shook a spoon at him, 'it's for me. No way am I waiting for you to come in and cook. We wouldn't be eating till eight or nine, I'd starve.'

'Still, I'll get the vacuum out or something.' Stuart insisted. Sal called Jasmine through from the lounge where she'd been working on her laptop researching potential grants and business loans.

'I think my old bank might offer us a good deal,' Jasmine said. 'Interest rates are good at the moment but it's finding the premises that's going to be the hardest part.'

'I have been to every estate agent I could find today,' Sal

complained, 'there's no commercial properties anywhere near here that looks suitable, either for sale or rent, not at a decent price.'

'How about setting up an online shop in the meantime? You make the products and come up with the text, I'll do the photographs and upload them and keep track of sales and maybe do a bit of marketing and advertising. It'll be a start and if people like the sachets and candles they'll recommend us and when the centre opens, we will already have a customer base.'

Sal thought an online presence would be a good idea and said so, 'but we'd need to come up with a name first. Something that suggests massage, relaxation.'

'That reminds me,' Magda said, dishing out bowls of soup and chunks of fresh bread, 'one of Bonnie's friends rang this afternoon for you Sal to arrange a massage, I said you'd ring back.'

Sal listened to the conversation going on around her and realised that for the first time since she'd lost her job at the women's refuge, she wasn't worried about her future. Things were coming together nicely in ways she would never have foreseen. She thought back to the cards she had pulled out of the deck for herself, the magician, the empress and the chariot, along with the banishing ritual to get rid of any problems, it was all working out as predicted and it was starting to flow and grow and the progression of it all felt natural and easy now her mum was helping her navigate the way.

'Of course, we could really use a loan to spruce up the house a bit,' Magda worried, 'we could desperately do with an extension for a workshop if nothing else.'

'I might have an idea about that.' Stuart sat up straight and stroked his beard with his left hand. 'My garage, see. Needs a lot of work doing to it, roof needs redoing – part of it actually caved in today at the back, nothing major but it needs a few other things doing as well so the roof tiles this afternoon was a turning point. I've got to let the building go. I can't keep running a decent shop out of a building like that.'

'How does that fit in with everything?' Magda looked at him

blankly.

'I'm not running an aromatherapy centre in a clapped out old garage.'

'I need some new premises too, that's what I'm getting at.' Stuart said.

'Oh bloody hell.' Sal stood up, feeling overwhelmed. 'Stuart, you're lovely, really you are and I'm glad you're making Gran so happy but we haven't got room.'

'I thought we might join forces.' Stuart continued.

'Join forces? I can't make sterile creams and massage oils in a garage with greasy bike parts all over the place, I told you. I just can't.'

'No, wait.' Magda held up a hand. 'I think I can see where you're coming from, Stuart.'

'This is crazy,' Sal shook her head and moved away from the table, Jasmine looked awkwardly from her daughter to her mother and then at Stuart in the middle of them both and decided to keep her mouth shut. 'We haven't got space to keep out of each other's way as a family, let alone running two businesses from the house. It's not going to work.'

'Give me a chance to …'

'No, I can't think about this right now.' Sal was starting to feel tears pricking at her eyes now. 'I finally thought I'd found something I wanted to do with my life and I – oh, I give in!' She left the room and darted into the hallway, determined not to cry in front of everyone. She heard her mum calling after her but ignored the platitudes and went up to her room where Bran, curled in a little ball on her bed, woke up and miaowed at her.

Sal shut her door and picked up the kitten, nuzzling his velvet fur into her face and wiping her tears. 'I'm pathetic, aren't I?'

A soft rapping on her door. 'Come in.'

'I'm sorry, love,' Magda sat beside her on the bed, fingers loving caressing the patchwork quilt she had made herself when Sal was a baby. 'I don't mean to side against you, I promise. Stuart's got some decent brains behind all those whiskers, you know. Come and hear him out, please.'

'I'm such a prat, Gran.' Sal apologised. 'I can feel everything coming together in a flash and then something always seems to stir up trouble and it slips away.' Something dawned on her then. 'What did you wish for? Tell me, what did you write on that piece paper we burned? You said you wanted to stir things up. Oh, Gran. What have you done this time?'

'Oh it's not me you need to worry about this time.' Magda said with a girlish grin. 'It's that biker boyfriend of mine.'

Sal followed her gran out of the room and downstairs, the kitten nagging and pawing at her hair. She thought, not for the first time, about getting it cut off.

'He's got an idea, Sal.' Magda nodded proudly, leading the way downstairs. 'And it's a doozy!'

Chapter Sixteen

'The old Turner farmhouse has just come on the market.'
Stuart produced a glossy brochure from the estate manager and
opened it reveal photographs of a large, sprawling building which was
the farmhouse itself, surrounded by open countryside. There was a
large courtyard with outlying brick and timber barns and outhouses
and old stables.

'I know it'll be a stretch, but look at that.'

The Howard women cooed and ahh-ed over the photographs
and descriptions of the farm. 'It's being sold in two lots so most
of the farm land itself would be taken over by neighbouring farms
and we would be left with the house, the courtyard and this bit of
land here,' he pointed to a large grassy area of meadows, 'and these
outhouses and buildings here.'

'How do you see it working?' Jasmine asked. She'd already
started to make notes on the back of an envelope. 'Assuming we can
finance it.'

'The garage has been doing really well, I've been turning work
down and we've had a lot of super bikes in lately, they bring in decent
money for what we do. I'm also doing a lot of trikes and choppers
and if I can get another good mechanic to work full-time I can
expand, maybe even take on an apprentice. These two buildings here
would give plenty of space for what we need.'

'Leaving these ones on the other side of the courtyard for
a therapy business?' Jasmine butted in. 'With a bit of work, this
outhouse could be a workshop and kitchen and this could be divided
up for the therapy rooms and the reception area.'

'See?' Stuart grinned. 'Don't you love it when a plan comes
together?'

'What about the house?' Magda wanted to know. 'I went
round there once, when it was owned by the Kennedys', didn't seem
overly big to me.' She opened the brochure to the right pages and
when she saw the internal photographs her mouth formed an 'O'

shape but no sound came out.

'Reckon they didn't show you round properly while you were there.' Stuart pointed out the spacious living areas. 'Five bedrooms, three of them are en-suite and there's a drawing room, kitchen, dining room, two reception rooms, utility and a few little box rooms.'

'Look at that, Sally.' Jasmine had noticed Sal had been hanging back a little, letting the rest of them talk while she thought things through and got over her tantrum. 'I can see it working here, can't you?'

'I – yes' Sal admitted and she finally let out the breath she'd been holding in. 'Thanks Stuart. I'm sorry.' She went over and hugged him, feeling awkward about it at first. Then he stood up and grabbed her, lifting her in the air with a giant squeeze.

'Nothing to say sorry for, Sal pet.' He said, putting her back down and slipping an arm around Magda's waist. 'What do you reckon my little witch?'

'Well, my hairy druid, I think it's a cracking idea but what does our financial whizz-kid think? That's the big question.'

'Give me a couple of hours.' The back of the envelope was full, so Jasmine scurried off to get her laptop, setting it up on the kitchen table once the soup dishes had been cleared away. She insisted on having the kitchen to herself so she could have some peace and quiet while she went through a few things. Magda encouraged Sal to practice her tarot reading skills on Stuart in the lounge, while she read a book and Jasmine worked away on the laptop, frantically creating spreadsheets and googling for information and statistics.

'More tea' she muttered, pouring the last dregs from the pot into her new mug. 'God, Sally was right, that is one ugly mug.'

Jasmine was in her element, working out costings, outgoings, comparing interest rates and loans and by the time she looked at her watch it was nearly midnight and the house had fallen quiet without her realising it. Jasmine switched off her laptop and shut the lid, rising from the kitchen table to get a glass of water. She rubbed her aching behind and yawned loudly, reaching into the cupboard on the wall for a glass when she heard a noise behind her. She looked around but couldn't see anything.

'Hello?' Jasmine hunted under the table and among the coats and chairs, assuming Sally's kitten had fallen asleep somewhere and was shifting in his sleep but there were no more noises so she drank her water and rinsed the glass at the sink. A dark shape caught the corner of her eye, so fleeting that Jasmine wasn't sure if she had seen it all. She stood still and slowly looked up out of the window. She'd seen something, all right. There was somebody snooping about in the garden, among the shrubs and bushes at the far side, past the clear area her mum and Sally used for rituals. Her first thought was to run and hide but she didn't need to do that anymore, not now that she was freed forever from that monster her husband had turned into. She didn't have to be scared anymore so she took a deep breath and plucked up some courage.

As quietly as she could, Jasmine prised open the back door and tiptoed out. She wasn't wearing shoes and the cold flagstones on the path turned her feet to icicles. She kept to the edge of the garden, using the bushes as cover and crept slowly along, keeping an eye on the dark shape ahead. There was a muffled noise, a shuffling sound and Jasmine saw that whoever this midnight visitor was, they were heading towards the house. She kept still, hidden from view by the wishing tree and watched as, bold as brass, the intruder trotted across to the side of the house and seemed to see what they were looking for.

Jasmine followed at a distance and saw whoever it was carefully lifting the dustbin lids off, one by one. First the recycling bin was raided, next the green bin which contained only garden waste and then the household dustbin was sorted through. A sound like the rustling of a plastic bag, the lid replaced and that was it, their nocturnal bin-raider scarpered off down the driveway and Jasmine snuck down to the end of the driveway to see the person half-waddling, half-running up the road towards the village, some small package clutched tightly in their left hand.

Stuart was furious in the morning when he found out. He barged about the kitchen and couldn't keep still for a second. 'Why didn't you come and get me?' He complained. 'I'd have caught the rotten –.'

'Stuart!' Magda chided, 'mind your language. He's got a fair point, however, Jasmine.'

'It was just so odd, I didn't think. All they did was go through the bins and then run off.'

'And you've no idea what this person managed to sneak off with?'

'Was it a man or a woman?'

'How tall were they?'

'Stop, please.' Jasmine held her hand up briefly to hush everybody. 'It wasn't a big deal, all right? It could have been anyone but I'm fine, they haven't broken into the house or damaged anything.'

'Very brave of you, Jasmine.' Magda said. 'Especially after what you've been through.'

'Thanks Mum.' Jasmine smiled. 'I hadn't thought about it like that, I knew it wouldn't be him so I didn't need to be frightened.'

'Bugger, look at the time, I'm off.' Stuart grabbed a piece of toast and took his helmet down from its perch, high on the wall. 'I don't believe it.' He pulled the kitten gently free from his resting place and handed him to Sal before dashing out of the house.

'How did you get up there, Bran? I think he's learned how to levitate.' Sal said, fussing Bran's fur and feeding him scraps of bacon that were left on her plate.

'I still want to know what they've nicked from our bins.' Magda said grumpily. 'I won't let them get away with behaviour like that in my territory.'

'Territory?' Jasmine scoffed. 'You're not a guard dog, Mum.'

'Oh you should have seen her last summer, when those hippies wanted somewhere to pitch a tent for the night. They were in the field at the back and Gran went crazy, chased them off.'

'Only because they interrupted my solstice ritual.'

'I'm surprised you didn't invite them to join in.' Jasmine said.

'I think she would have done but they screamed when they saw her in the buff and that's when she ran after them with her broom.'

'Remind me why I came back here.' Jasmine snorted. 'It's like living in a zoo.'

'They deserved it, bunch of perverts.' Magda nodded, 'anyway, rubbish thieves aside, how did you get on last night? Any news for us, love?'

'Well, if we take into account the estimated valuations of our collective assets and comparable market prices for… what?' Jasmine noticed both Sal and Magda were gawping at her open-mouthed. 'I did do this for a living, for nearly thirty years, in case you forgot. Can I carry on now?'

Mouths closed once again, they both paid attention as Jasmine went through her findings. They talked about mortgages, re-mortgages, extensions, conservatories, funding, grants, loans and start-up costs. Jasmine had been thorough in her endeavours to finance the therapy centre and agreed with Stuart in principal that selling the old house and his garage and moving to a combined business premises and family home would be a good idea. Selling up the old house and Stuart's garage to get somewhere large enough for all their needs wouldn't be any more or less of a financial stretch than renovating and extending their current house. Now she had some facts and figures to back it up and Sal was amazed.

'You did all of this last night?' She marvelled, suddenly seeing her mum in a different light altogether. Jasmine was normally an emotional train-wreck, unstable, flighty, overly dramatic and went off to live with the nastiest of men at the drop of a hat but now here she was, laying out a well thought out proposal for a therapy centre that Sal had been struggling with for weeks.

'I'm not finished yet, but my initial findings say yes, we can do it. I'll have to come up with something a bit more formal for the banks though.' The letter box rattled and Jasmine retrieved the day's newspaper, spreading it open to read her horoscope at the table. 'The estate agent opens at nine, if you want to, we might be able to view the farmhouse today.'

'As simple as that, eh?' Magda eyed her daughter up in pretty much the same way that Sal had done only moments earlier and realised that she had probably done a pretty good job of raising her after all. 'Well done Jasmine, I'm proud of you.'

'What?'

'I'm proud of you.' She drew her chair up next to Jasmine and gave her a quick hug. 'You too, Sal. This therapy centre of yours is a grand idea, especially now I'm starting to get on a bit, I could do with somebody else around to look after things.'

'There will be plenty of time for you to retire in a few years, Gran, I can't do this without you.'

'Still, you're going to be doing some of the readings, aren't you? Speaking of which, it's half past eight, you know what that means.'

'Here we go again.' Jasmine should have known it was coming. She read out each of their horoscopes while Magda shuffled her tarot cards and laid them out.

'Virgo, the full moon is in your sign this week, giving all areas of your life a significant boost.'

Magda tapped the paper. 'Even you've got to admit that's a bit woolly, I'm going to write my own column and send it to the paper, that'll show 'em.'

'All right, and what do you predict, oh high and mighty tarot queen?'

'Let's see...' Magda turned over her first card and immediately scooped it back up again before Sal or Jasmine had a chance to see it. She shuffled the deck a second time and tried again, laying out a new card and then covered it straight away, picked it up and put it back in the deck. 'Don't think I like the look of the cards today,' she hurriedly put the pack of cards back on the shelf, 'let's see about giving that estate agent a ring, shall we?'

Sal frowned, that wasn't like her gran at all. She worried about it briefly – why would Magda scuttle the cards away so quickly unless she had seen something horrible? But soon she was caught up in the excitement and potential of her business and coaxed her mum into going through all the information again, making sure she understood and listened properly this time. They arranged to meet someone from the estate agency's office in the afternoon and Magda rang Stuart to let him know so that he could meet them at the farm.

Sal had planned on making some more herbal tea as her monthly cycle was making itself known again but as soon as she took down the first jar of herbs she needed, there was a knock on the front door. She answered it to find a short, dumpy woman with a thick coat and scarf on. She ushered the lady through to the kitchen where Magda was already filling the kettle. Another tarot reading, by the looks of it. Sal made herself scarce and joined her mum in the lounge where they put their heads together and reviewed their list of questions for the estate agent.

*

The farmhouse, officially called Turner's Lodge and Farm Holdings, was a sprawling mess of buildings and turned out to be nowhere near as tidy, modern and pristine as the photographs had led Sal to believe but it was still like nothing she had ever dreamed of living in. The courtyard with its barns, sheds and old stables would be ideal for the relocation of Stuart's garage and workshops. On the other side of the courtyard were more buildings and an old loose box area which was large enough to provide three rooms for the treatments and reception area and Sal had her eye on one of the barns on the side she had come to think of already as the garage side of the courtyard.

'I can turn this into a kitchen and workshop, there's already water in here.' She looked up. 'And electric. Hey, look at this.' She ran her hands over the worn rungs of an old ladder which led up to a small hay loft.

'Don't go up there!' Magda screeched across. 'I mean, that ladder doesn't look safe.'

'I wasn't going to climb it.' Sal wondered if her gran was losing the plot today. She had already given Sal warnings about hot kettles and sharp knives in the kitchen and now this. What exactly had she seen in those two, unread tarot cards this morning?

'Can we see the house now?' Jasmine asked, eager to search through the empty, old property. 'Stuart, are you happy with what we've seen so far?'

'Bit nice, isn't it?' He said, hands in his trouser pockets. He had put on a plain shirt and blue jeans and looked quite respectable and his beard was combed through with sandalwood and patchouli oil. Magda sidled up to him and linked her arm through his and the four of them wandered through the house.

Five bedrooms seemed excessive but again it turned out that the brochure had not provided an accurate picture of the size of those rooms, two of which were small box rooms. The three main bedrooms were large enough and there was more than enough room for them all through the rest of the house with two sitting rooms, a large dining room and separate drawing room, a colossal kitchen with attached utility area and a cosy study.

'I can use this for readings to start with,' Magda announced, claiming the study space before anyone else could. 'Just until we get things up and running properly.'

'Do you think people will come out this far, though?' Sal worried, 'it's a bit out of the way.'

'We walked here.'

'Yes,' Sal argued, 'but this is on the other side of the village, further away from Stoke.'

'Of course they will.' Magda nodded firmly. She opened cupboards in the kitchen, checked under the stairs and nosed into every possible nook, cranny and crevice in the house. 'This place could have been made for us.'

'Don't speak too soon.' Stuart had been exploring and told

Magda what he'd found. 'The outhouse and barns will take a lot of work to get them up to standard, lots of damp and loose or missing roof tiles, in the house too. We're much closer to the flood plain here, maybe even on it, so that's a big risk and let's not forget the land around here is being sold off. If the adjacent farms don't buy, that could be development land. Would you be as happy here if your view was a new housing estate instead of open fields and countryside?'

'How much is the land going for? Could be a great place for a pagan camp in the summer.'

'I never thought of that.' Jasmine said, not put off by any of the possible issues Stuart had mentioned. 'We've got a lot to think about, I'm starting to get excited though, what about you Sally? Sally?'

'I'm here,' Sal came into the kitchen from outside. 'Guess what? There's even a secret tunnel.'

'They didn't put that in the brochure.'

Sal led them to one of the outbuildings where a short, dark wooden door led down a stone stairwell into a large underground room. The room had an earthen floor with no lighting so Sal wedged the door open. On the other side of the room, an identical stairway led upwards and the door at the top opened into the area between the house and the outbuildings.

'That's what normal people call a cellar, Sally.'

Sal stuck her tongue out at her mum. 'I used it to travel from one place to another, therefore it's a secret tunnel. Besides, a secret tunnel sounds much cooler than having a cellar with two doors.'

The four of them took another quick look through the various buildings dotted around the premises and Magda and Stuart walked round the gardens at the back of the house itself. She could picture herself living here very happily and she leaned on Stuart's arm, feeling satisfied that after the warning this morning, that leering death mask grinning at her twice in a row, nothing untoward had happened. It was turning to be a good day, after all.

Stuart had a job to finish at work but the three Howard women met up with the estate agent, who recognised Magda and trusted her with the key rather than show the place himself, and said they were very interested in the property.

'We'll talk it over, Mr Johnson,' Jasmine shook the man's hand and spoke with a clear, crisp tone of authority, 'I shall be in touch if we wish to make an offer.'

Outside the office, Sal and Magda stared at Jasmine. 'We could have put an offer in now,' Sal said, 'we talked about it this morning.'

'But that was before we saw the state of the place.' Jasmine countered. 'Needs a lot of work doing, I'm no estate agent, but even I know the essential repairs aren't going to be cheap. We'll haggle him down a bit.'

'Did he say if there had been any other offers?'

'Only one, the vendors refused and the buyers didn't want to make another bid. If we do some enquiries into costs I think we have a bit of wiggle room on the asking price. As long as we stay above that first offer, this place could be ours within a couple of months.'

*

At the end of the day, Magda and Stuart nipped out to the Black Swan for a pint and were joined by Bonnie and Sal. Bonnie was delighted by the old fashioned pub and kept putting tokens into the juke box so she could listen to retro tunes from the 1980s.

'Spandau Ballet, in a place like this.' The red-head had stood at the bar talking to the land lord for twenty minutes before sitting down with her pint. 'Stevie actually picked all these tracks himself, back in the day.'

'Are you old enough to remember the eighties, Bonnie?' Magda queried.

'Not really,' she confessed, pulling off her leather jacket and hanging it over the back of her chair. 'Some of these bands are still going though. Oh, Sal, did my mate give you a ring, by the way?'

Sal looked back at her blankly and Magda apologised. 'Sorry, meant to tell you, somebody called the house for you about a massage, I wrote the number down somewhere.'

'Thanks, this is great Bonnie, I'm so grateful to you for

recommending me. Hopefully some of your friends might be able to give me a testimonial for the centre, when I start advertising.'

'Sure, I can ask around. I'll do a review for you too if you want.'

Sal nodded and drank her beer. She would have preferred wine but the selection in the Black Swan was about as outdated as its music and Blue Nun was about the best she could hope for unless she fancied a repeat of the badly made cocktails with saucy names.

'What do you think of the farmhouse idea, Bonnie?' Magda asked.

'Sounds brilliant,' she nodded, 'so long as Stuart doesn't start wearing tweed and a flat-cap.'

Stuart's answer to that made even Magda blush and she punched him lightly on the arm. 'Even I don't say words like that.'

'You said words like that the other night.' He reminded her with sly chuckle and Magda blushed again.

'Not in public, though and not in that kind of context.'

'Stacy said she's got a new tenant for the flat already, by the way.' Jasmine said.

'That was quick.' Magda sipped her drink. 'Glad to hear it, after the work Mark put into last month.'

The evening wore on with more old-school classics belting out from the juke box and Bonnie impressed everyone with a close-up coin trick. Sal and Magda cooed again over the brochure from the estate agents and Stuart made a list of everything he had noticed that needed repairing or replacing so that Jasmine could decide how much to offer.

'It's decided then?' Bonnie looked surprised. 'Are you sure this isn't a bit too much too soon? Stuart, we talked about this.'

'Yes, and what did I say?' Stuart grabbed Magda's hand under the table and held it tightly, seeing the worried look flitting briefly across her face.

'You said you'd been waiting years for someone like Magda to come along and neither of you is getting any younger so you're not wasting another minute.'

'Why don't you come over for dinner tomorrow, Bonnie? We can always make room for one more round our table.' Magda offered and Bonnie was pleased to accept.

After a pleasant night out, Magda and Stuart left the others in the pub and headed home early. Despite the teasing calls of 'we know what you're doing' from Sal, who was a little bit drunk, Magda had only sleep on her mind. Despite now sharing a bed with Stuart, he was usually exhausted at the end of the day and with constant interruptions in the house, they still hadn't found the right opportunity to enjoy it properly. She was feeling quite tipsy and wobbled slightly as she reached down to slip off her shoes. She shoved them in the cupboard under the stairs and then went up, pushing past Stuart so she could head up first. She'd deliberately worn a dress that clung to her figure and was thrilled to think of him watching her as she climbed up. An appreciative noise behind her indicated that was exactly what he was doing and she wiggled her way slowly to the bedroom that they now shared.

'I thought you were tired.' Stuart said, closing the door and putting the bolt across. 'That was not the walk of a lady who wants to go to sleep.'

'Well, I may have perked up a little bit, fresh air and all that.' She said, eyeing him and licking her lips. 'I've been wondering about our, situation, shall we say?'

'And what have you decided?' Stuart was a patient man, she knew that, but she thought they had waited long enough.

'My hips are not good, but they're not bad either and I wonder if tonight might be our lucky night at last. The girls are out for another couple of hours and we've got the place to ourselves for a change.'

Stuart held her closely and tenderly and then began to kiss her. Soon they were clothed only by the night and Magda felt a heat rising up from her belly and filling her with anticipation as Stuart's warm hands caressed her.

202

'Magda.' He said, his voice sounding stern.

'Yes, my love, yes.'

'Magda, your breast.' He sounded insistent now, she thought.

'Oh you devil, go on.'

'No, woman, open your eyes.'

Magda did as he asked and looked down to where his hand was cupping her breast. 'That bloody card this morning, I knew something would happen.'

There was a hard, firm lump in her breast that showed clearly beneath her skin and she wailed with horror.

CHAPTER SEVENTEEN

'The one time we are both finally ready and now this.' She cried and leaned into his chest, feeling weak and helpless as he wrapped his strong arms around her. Breakfast was not a happy affair but Magda had made a decision not to tell Jasmine or Sal just yet. She moped in the kitchen and watched the clock carefully, waiting for the hands to show eight when the doctor's surgery reception opened for booking appointments.

'Doomed, we are doomed to never have – Sal, didn't hear you come downstairs.'

'Doomed to never have what?'

'Scrambled eggs and toast.' Magda said, pulling herself together. It was a benign lump, a cyst, nothing to worry about. She pushed it to the back of her mind but the hands of the clock ticked slowly, slowly, slowly.

'What's up Gran?' Sal asked, her gran looked like she might have been crying. She looked at Stuart and shot him a querying look but his expression stayed resolutely neutral. 'You're not regretting inviting Bonnie over, are you? I can cook if you want. What about a lasagne?'

'That would be good of you, yes please.' Magda patted Stuart's hand and sat beside him at the kitchen table for a few minutes before he went off to work, taking his car today because the weather was foul.

After a little while, Sal still hadn't coaxed any information out of her gran apart from the phone number for Bonnie's friend. 'You didn't get a name, did you?'

'Sorry, no, she didn't say.'

'Bit early to ring, I'll phone her later on. Shall I get the cards down for you, Gran?'

'Not this morning if you don't mind, Sal.'

Sal was grateful to hear the clattering of the letter box as the postman did his rounds. 'Oh, I'll go.' She reached the front door and the bottom of the stairs in the hallway at the same time as Jasmine was coming down. 'You might want to wait a few minutes, think they've had a spat, Gran does not look happy. I think she's about to bite somebody's head off.'

'Never mind that, come with me.'

Sal picked up the small collection of envelopes and reluctantly headed back into the kitchen where her gran was standing by the telephone and looking at the clock.

'Sit, come on. Sit down.' Jasmine pushed her way into the room and pulled an A4 wad of paper out from behind her back and displayed the front page. 'I couldn't sleep last night, my thoughts kept churning over the farmhouse. You're both right, I need to get back to work to help me get better and you two haven't got a clue what you're doing. So I did this. Our business proposal.'

'Wow!' Sal was thrilled, the thick wad of paper must have taken hours to prepare. It was a professional looking affair with different sections for finance, business development, training, health and safety, and planning. 'Planning?'

'You have to have planning permission for a change of use from farming but there are two precedents in the area already and the local council shouldn't find anything wrong with it.'

'This is amazing, thanks Mum.' They hugged each other and smiles lit up around the kitchen, even Magda shook off her earlier foggy thoughts, Sal noticed happily. 'Take me through it, please?'

They spent the morning going over the proposal and checking the facts and figures Jasmine had come up with. 'It means we need a huge loan, but with Stuart's motorbike garage as back-up and yes, mother, I already checked with him and it's fine, I promise, and I've got some money I can invest, not loads but...'

'It's brilliant.' Sal said yet again, 'so we can put an offer in for the farmhouse?'

'We need to secure the finances first, Sally, one step at a time.' Magda cautioned her.

'I don't think that will be a problem, Mum. We're seeing a Mr

Harper at two o'clock at the local branch of the bank I worked for. I've met him at other branches a few times and he seemed all right. We've got a sound idea and we can prove it's workable so I can't see any reasons why he would turn us down.'

'I can't believe it, Gran,' Sal felt giddy with a haze of excitement and anticipation. 'This could really happen. Thanks so much, Mum. You must have been up all night.'

After a successful meeting with the bank, Sal felt even giddier and she threw herself into cooking a feast for them all, just to give herself something to do with her hands. She listened to the radio while she diced onions and carrots and hummed to herself while keeping half an ear on the muted conversation going on in the background.

'I hope you won't be offended, Mum, but I've signed up to Peter's course.' Jasmine confessed. For a moment Magda looked at her blankly.

'Who the devil is Peter?'

Jasmine snorted and nearly spat out her drink. 'Not quite the response he would probably like.'

'Ah, you mean our dear Mister Granger.' Magda cottoned on. 'I don't often hear him called by his first name, threw me a bit. When does that start then? Do you think you'll learn something?'

'Next week, we're having a bit of supper first then a presentation. I think there's going to be a DVD by the guy who came up with the course in the seventies.'

'Now why would I be offended by that? It sounds like a good idea to me.'

'Do you mean that?'

'I can hardly object to my number one daughter going astray, yes I know you're my only one, but still. If it makes you feel at peace, Jasmine, you go right ahead. He is a good man, you know, that vicar of ours. Besides, it was Granger's interfaith event that got me an introduction to Stuart in the first place so I'm in no position to judge.'

Dinner was ready at seven and everything was laid out nicely, the food was good and the conversation was going well between the younger women but Sal noticed that her gran was quiet and started to worry that something was wrong. As soon as she got the chance, she was determined to find out what, but the chance never arose that night because Stuart never left her side, not even to nip to the loo.

Another day passed in relative harmony and Sal and Jasmine went off to the estate agency to put in their offer for the farmhouse and within a few hours they jumped about like lunatics when a telephone call informed them it had been accepted.

'This is like a dream come true.' Sal said to her gran.

'A dream you didn't even know you had until recently, though.' Magda said. 'Where's your mum, love? Something I want to tell you both.'

'She's at the church, I think.' Sal replied. 'She wanted to point out her handy work to Mr Jackoby so he doesn't have to bother with that area.'

'Well, I can't keep it to myself any longer. She can hear it later on.'

Sal felt a cold chill rising through her. Whatever it was, this didn't sound good. 'What is it, Gran?'

'I've found a lump, Sally, in my breast.'

Silence.

'I'm seeing the doctor tomorrow to have it looked at and I'm sure it's probably nothing serious but, still, after losing June and your great-grandma to the big C, it's best to be on the safe side, eh?'

'I'll come with you.' Sal offered but immediately Magda shook her head. 'No, I won't hear of it. You've got enough on your plate with this new business of yours. I've got a biker boyfriend now and he is very good at holding hands.'

'Fancy a walk?' Sal suggested, 'might be raining tomorrow.'

'Now that is a very good idea. We can nip to the grocery on the way back and pick the mead I've ordered in for our Yule feast.'

'If you're getting it today, you'd better order some more because we both know it won't last that long. Are we getting together with the group from your pub moot again? I really enjoyed that at Samhain.'

'Sounds like a good plan, my love.' Magda agreed, 'I'll give Mel and Agnes a ring later. That reminds me, are you seeing that new aromatherapy client Bonnie's set you up with?'

'Yes, she's in my diary for next Tuesday, she's busy with work till then.'

The high street was busy and Magda, as was her custom, stopped at the bakery to nosy in through the window at Mrs Beers. She waved at the woman, who was stood behind her counter putting pastries and tarts into paper bags. Ever watchful of the village gossipers, Mrs Beers made sure she was seen when she smiled and waved back.

'What a fraud.' Magda huffed under her breath, assuming it was Sal who was standing right beside her.

'You've got that right, the slapper.'

'Mrs Owen?' Magda spun round, horrified that she'd been caught saying such a horrible thing out loud. 'I didn't mean…'

'No, you're absolutely right about her, Mrs Howard.' Mrs Owen took a turn at waving to Mrs Beers through the bakery window. 'Remember David's little issue the other month?'

'Oh yes, I hope he's recovered?'

'I found out why he had it in the first place.'

'And you think it was…' Magda and Mrs Owen turned their heads and looked in through the window, eyeing up the lady baker.

'Oh I know it was,' Mrs Owens confirmed it, 'he told me. And you know what makes it worse? They only did it in the churchyard, of all places. Disgusting.'

'Oh, I see. Oh dear.' Magda shook her head. 'I'm sorry.'

'Never mind, he'll get what he deserves with a harridan like that. No, she's welcome to him. Her poor Tony would turn in his grave but she's welcome to him. Well, bye for now, Mrs Howard.'

'Yes, you too,' Magda said, 'you will call on me, won't you? If you need anything. You know.'

'Thank you.' Mrs Owen went on her way with a final, nasty stare at the woman in the bakery. Well, Magda thought to herself, that solves one mystery.

'Gran?' Sal called to her from the doorway of the grocery a few doors further up the street. 'Stacy says do you want this mead or not?'

*

'Stuart was such a gentleman,' Magda told Sal and Jasmine after her doctor's appointment. 'He held my hand the whole time and refused to leave me alone for a second.'

'And what has Doctor McKenna said?'

'Is she gay, do you think? She had a fair old grope, I can tell you.'

'Gran, be sensible for once.'

'I have never been a particularly sensible woman, Jasmine, and I don't intend to start now. She reckons it's a cyst, quite common, she said but she'll get me referred to the hospital to be on the safe side. I'm relieved, I think.'

'You will be, Gran, once you've got it out of the way.'

'Stuart will be too,' Magda chuckled, feeling much better about it now that she'd had some reassurance from the doctor. Whatever came next, she had her family to support her through it and they would face it together. She was looking forward to laughing about it when it turned out to be nothing.

'Here comes trouble,' Sal pointed to the back door. 'Your friend and neighbourhood rector, I'll leave you to it.'

Jasmine let Reverend Granger in and switched on the kettle, making tea in a pot and pouring it out in mugs. 'Milk and sugar?'

'Both, yes please. Oh, good God, where has this monstrosity come from? This must be the most singularly ugly mug I have seen in my life, you're scraping the bottom of the barrel with this one, Magda. This is dreadful, even for you.'

'It's mine and I like it, so there.' Jasmine butted in, though she had to agree. Whatever had she been thinking?

'Never mind about that,' Magda smoothed over the awkwardness with her news. 'You'll be red with embarrassment when you find out what I know. And I didn't have to pry; Mrs Owen came straight out and told me herself.'

'Told you what, Magda?' Granger thanked his lucky stars he only saw Magda once or twice a week at most. That was enough for any sane person, in his opinion. How on earth her family coped, he would never know. Then she told him about Mr Owen, Mrs Beers and the red knickers in the rose bushes and the night-time visitor who came to claim them back from her bin.

Granger didn't quite know where to look and Magda couldn't help feeling a little bit sorry for him. Only a little bit though. She put biscuits onto a plate, laughing so much she could hardly keep a straight face.

'More tea vicar?'

THE END

MIDNIGHT MAGIC

CHAPTER ONE

'Where do you think you're going dressed like that on a weekend?' Magda peered over the edge of the newspaper and eyed Jasmine suspiciously.

Always a carefully dressed woman even in her casual attire, Jasmine wore a pair of well-tailored grey trousers with a crisp white blouse, more suitable to her old job at a High Street bank than milling around the house at breakfast time. High heels clicked on the stone-tiled floor and Magda snorted, spitting out coffee. 'Ha! You sound like a horse.' Magda had never been one to mince her words.

'What a kind thing to say, Mother.' Jasmine replied. She leaned over to Sal who was sitting meekly at the table with a large mug of steaming hot coffee, and gave her a quick peck on the cheek.

'See you later, Mum.' Sal said. 'Are you still up for a night out later?'

Jasmine picked her bag up from the corner of the table and smiled. 'The Black Swan's first live music night in ages? Try and stop me.'

'Don't spend too long mulling over what to wear, Jasmine,' Magda retorted, 'you're over-dressed for a night out in this village, let alone any kind of day-time shenanigans. What are you up to?'

'What's got into you, Gran?' Sal asked, wondering what it was this time that had set the witch off on her high-horse. 'You'd be the first to tell me off if I was rude to anyone like that.'

'Good point, Sal. Besides, dearest mother, it's not the weekend yet, it's only Friday morning.' Jasmine ignored her mum's interjections. 'Now can I please just go to work in peace without the two of you bickering like a couple of old women?'

'It may have escaped your attention,' Magda patted her iron

grey hair, 'but I am an old woman and therefore I shall bicker as much I please. Work, eh?'

'Yes, I told you. I've taken up Stacy's offer of working one day a week doing book-keeping for her shop. I'll be back around five.' Jasmine picked up a slice of toast and took a large bite out of it as she walked to the door and left for the day with a wave of goodbye.

Sal drank her coffee while Magda muttered quietly and read the paper. 'Right, that's it.' Magda slammed her fist on the worn oak dining table and put down the newspaper that seemed to be offending her. 'I've had enough of this rubbish. I could do better with my eyes closed, I'm never reading it again.'

Sal sighed and picked up the paper, pulling it out of the Magda's reach. 'You say that every time, Gran. I don't see what the big deal is, nobody expects horoscope columns to be accurate. If it bothers you that much, why don't you do something about it this time instead of making my ears bleed for the next half an hour, complaining about it?'

'I'm going to Sal.' Magda stood up, paced over to the welsh dresser and pulled open a drawer, taking out a pad of paper and a biro. 'By jingo lass, I'm going to.'

Sal watched with mild amusement as her gran stared at the blank sheet, chewing on her lip, pen poised over the paper. 'Having trouble, Gran?'

'No,' an indignant response. 'No, I'm just thinking. Can't just write down any old codswallop, can I? Otherwise, why bother?'

'Yes, of course.' Sal smirked. She picked up the newspaper and read the offending astrology column. 'Mine says the new moon's passage through Sagittarius should bring resolution of past hurts and I should expect an invitation from a handsome male stranger.'

'See what I mean? Utter rubbish.' Once again, Magda focused on her blank sheet of paper. 'Dear editor,' Magda spoke out loud as she wrote it down, 'I am writing to protest against – no, I am writing to *vehemently* protest against the trashy column which you dare to call a horoscope. As a practising witch and tarot reader of some experience, I could do better standing on my head. Please see attached an example of how, in my experience, no. Already used the word experience, that won't do at all. Hmm. Ah! How, in my opinion – my *considered* opinion – your column of predictions *should* be written, yours sincerely, Mrs Magda Howard, Professional Witch.'

'Brilliant, that should do it, Gran.' Sal said, raised her eyes over the newspaper and eyed her gran with a hint of sarcasm. 'What are you going to send them?'

'Haven't got the foggiest, Sal, you know I don't have anything to do with astrology, all those bloody planets milling about up there and don't forget all the asteroids whizzing across the sky, all willy-nilly and crashing into things. It's a disaster waiting to happen, you mark my words. Great bears made up of tiny light specks billions of light years away. How exactly is all of that supposed to relate to us pathetic little creatures down here on our tiny planet?'

'You could always just make it up.' Sal shouldn't have been surprised that Magda was taking it all so seriously. Some trivial nonsense like this was probably just what was needed to take her mind off the impending hospital appointment looming on the near horizon.

'Wash your mouth out, girl!' Magda spat tea all over her neatly written page. 'I shall do no such thing.'

'What about a tarot card for each month, then?'

'I'm doing this, not you. Why don't you go off and play with your dolls or something?'

'Very funny, Gran. I'll just go and carry on with the packing on my own, shall I? Three weeks, Gran, three weeks till we move.'

'Go, shoo, out. I can't work with you watching over me.'

Sal laughed as her gran waved her hands at her in a dismissive gesture. She wandered through to the hallway, pulling the door behind her but not entirely closing it. She waited a few moments and then peeked into the kitchen through the narrow gap. Sure enough, her gran was taking a well-thumbed deck of tarot cards down from their customary place on the dresser shelf. Magda unwrapped the black silk cloth and the cards tumbled gracefully into her nimble fingers. With a practised shuffle, the wavy-haired crone mixed the cards and muttered several short sentences, not quite loud enough for Sal to hear. Her tarot mantra, no doubt. A quick plea to the powers to bring clarity and accuracy to her readings. Sal's own card readings over the past few weeks had been getting better as she practiced but she had a long way to go before she reached the level of proficiency her gran possessed. The day was looming when Sal would have to come up with a tarot reading mantra of her own to give her readings a much needed boost, especially if her plans for the holistic centre came to fruition – she could just imagine the look of horror on the faces of paying clients if she didn't improve past her current level which Magda described as fair but Sal herself knew she'd got a long way to go.

'Blast you, Hanged Man, I'm not writing that down!' Magda's muttering drifted through the doorway to her and Sal tried hard not to giggle to herself as she walked away quietly and left the wise woman to her own devices.

Sal picked up a cardboard box from the pile stacked up in the hallway and took it into the lounge. Looking around the room, she wondered where to start. The book shelves were crammed not only with books but with a wide range of ornaments and the assorted sundry knick-knacks of a witch's life. There were jars of incense, a small vase full of long feathers, crystals and dragons, a set of three porcelain witches in descending sizes brought back from a visit to Glastonbury last summer, a crystal ball sat next to a miniature cast-iron cauldron and packs of tarot cards were scattered here and there in neat little piles. She ought to start with the books and ornaments, she decided, because although Gran had a favourite set of cards she kept in the kitchen, it wasn't unusual for any of the dozens of sets lying around the house to be called into action at a moment's notice.

By mid-morning, Sal was covered in dust, gasping for a coffee and was thoroughly fed up of lugging boxes into the hallway; at least they were labelled and ready to be shipped over to the new place in a few short weeks. Her plans for a refreshment break were scuppered when she entered the kitchen to find her gran seated at the table with a lady guest.

'Ah, here she is now.' Magda waved for Sal to come in and ushered her to sit with them. 'Sal, this lady has a bit of problem – probably more your kind of thing than mine.'

Without saying another word, Magda left them to it and Sal chatted with the lady for a couple of minutes and thought that a new moon spell casting would be in order, backed up with a charm bag of crystals and some dried herbs.

'Can you come and pick it up tomorrow, Mrs Fortune?' Mrs Fortune sighed softly. 'I'm just so glad you can help me,' the woman said, her face visibly relaxing. 'And you will be, you know, discreet?'

'Of course.' Sal reassured her. 'I'll give you a ring when I've got it ready for you.'

Magda crept back in at the sound of the back door closing behind the woman and let out a little giggle. 'Can you believe it? Anyone would think she was hiring an assassin, the way she carried on.'

'And all she wanted was a bit of fertility magic.' Sal smiled. 'Tell you what though, she's insisted on paying double what I asked her for. She said if it works, it'll be worth her weight in gold.'

'Very good of her,' Magda agreed, 'so how is the packing going? You've got cobwebs in your hair, by the way.'

'Hmm, thanks.' Sal brushed a hand through her hair and shook it out. 'Feels like I've hardly made a dent in it. How's the newspaper column going?'

'You know me, don't like to blow my own trumpet,' Magda twirled a finger round the gaudy plastic bead-string that hung down over her ample bosom. 'But let's just say that the cards have been very helpful and with a bit of midnight magic this evening, the editor won't be able to resist my charms.'

'Is that right?' Sal grinned. 'You can't help yourself, can you? Any excuse for a bit of spell casting. Let me guess, you managed to find out what star sign the editor is and made sure he's got a decent forecast in his new column?'

'Pah! As if I would stoop to such lengths!' Magda laughed indignantly and a flush of colour rose in her cheeks.

Sal stepped over to the kitchen window and gently fussed over the ginger kitten who sat there purring loudly, demanding her notice. 'Who's my pretty boy, then?'

The cat pushed his furry head into her hands, clamouring for greater attention and Sal supressed a chuckle as she heard a small voice behind her.

'He's a Leo, as it happens.' Her gran said quietly. 'Good things are happening to Leo's this month. Coincidentally, of course.'

'Oh, yes, of course. Funny how these sorts of coincidences crop up a lot when you're involved.'

Sal wasn't sure how her gran had managed to find out this snippet of information about the editor of the local news-rag but one thing was for sure, with Magda on his case, the poor man didn't stand a chance. Sal wouldn't be in the least bit surprised if the next edition of the paper included a new column of predictions penned by their very own witch-in-residence.

TO BE CONTINUED ...

An Interview with the Author

Wild Women is very different to the kind of paranormal and fantasy novels that normally feature witches. Do you think there is a need for fiction featuring real witchcraft set in the everyday world?

Yes, absolutely. I adore reading paranormal romance and I've written some myself, but the shelves are swamped with it and the protagonists are, almost without variation, young women barely out of their teens. They suddenly 'come into their power' with magical gifts and fall in love with a vampire or the alpha werewolf or start working for a covert paranormal government agency. It's very hard to find fiction I can relate to as an adult woman with an interest in paganism and witchcraft. I know I'm not alone in this desire to read fiction featuring real witches and pagans set in this mundane, everyday world and with very few authors writing anything like that, there is definitely a market for books like this.

You wrote the short story first, Sugar and Spice. Was it always your intention to write more about the Howard family?

Yes, Sugar and Spice came first but it was always going to be part of a much larger story arc featuring the three women. As soon I had the idea the characters really came to life in my head and the novel took shape very quickly so it didn't take long to come up with the overall plot. I'm looking forward to working on the sequel and developing the characters a bit more.

Where does your inspiration come from and are any of the characters or situations in the book based on your own life?

Inspiration is a tricky thing to pin down – who knows where ideas come from? I think there's a giant cloud that circulates around us all, like an astral plane where ideas live. They mill around for a while then get bored and float down to our realm. If we catch them, the ideas are ours to use. There are certainly some aspects of the book, some of the events, which I write from the perspective of

217

personal experience, such as Magda's close friendship with the local clergy, environmental protests and retreat weekends and obviously there's the witchcraft connection but I have very little in common with Sal or Jasmine.

Without giving too much away, can you give us a little bit of insight into the sequel and what we can expect next with Magda, Jasmine and Sal?

There are likely to be three books in total featuring the Howard women. There will be a few obstacles to overcome for all of the ladies and Magda has fun writing to the newspaper about the dreadful horoscopes, Jasmine makes a new friend and Sal... well, Sal has adventures of her own to look forward to. It won't always be pretty and things aren't straight forward but there will definitely be a lot of fun and games to enjoy along the way.

The Children of Artemis had never published a book before Wild Women. Can you tell us how that came about?

I had a crazy idea while I was writing Sugar and Spice that I would persuade Children of Artemis to print the short story in the magazine and then publish the book as a follow-up. I knew I had to persuade them that this was a good idea so I did some research into current market trends, what other authors were writing in this new genre, what sources we could use for publicity and why I thought Children of Artemis could make it work. Children of Artemis were already publishing my articles in Witchcraft and Wicca magazine and I had been a guest speaker and panellist at the Artemis Gathering and Witchfest so I said it would be a logical step for them, as pioneers of stunning witchcraft events, to branch out into publishing. I put everything together into a ten page proposal and sent it off with the first chapter of the book, a synopsis and the short story. I proposed the story for the May edition of the magazine with the book itself to be released after that. It was completely off-the-wall but I had nothing to lose so I pressed 'send' and began waiting. I am very fortunate and grateful that Cath and Dave took the idea and ran with it and I didn't have to wait long because Dave and Cath phoned me the following day to tell me how much they both loved it.

You're already known as a public speaker and non-fiction author in the field of witchcraft and paganism, what was it that made you turn to writing novels?

Actually, writing fiction is my first love. I've always enjoyed reading and my parents used to read or make up stories for me, my sister and my brother when we were very young so I have this deep, ingrained passion for a good story. When I was around five and started school, every kid was given a tri-fold magnetic folder with hundreds of words on little magnetic stickers and we were supposed to select the right words for a sentence written on the blackboard but I used them to make up my own stories and I haven't stopped writing since. I've had articles and non-fiction books published and I have had short stories read out on local BBC radio and some of these are available as free e-books. Being an author and writing fiction has always been my primary ambition, I love creating stories that leave people wanting more.

Writing is often seen as a very lonely and solitary profession. Can you tell us something about your writing process?

I have a full-time job and like everyone else there are plenty of things I fill my time with so I have to fit my writing in around all of that. Usually, stories start with an idea, maybe a character talking to me or doing something in my mind and over a few days, weeks or months, that idea becomes more solid. I'll probably jot down a few lines about the story and then start filling in the gaps. I used to start with a blank page and see where it led but it's not a very structured or easy way of writing. After taking advice from some of my favourite authors, I now write a short synopsis and base my detailed outline around that, which is a much more productive way of writing. Then

I crack on with the actual writing with a very simple process of glue-backside-seat-laptop-type. I write at approximately 1,000 words an hour when I'm in the zone so the pages can fill up pretty quickly. Once I've finished a section I usually persuade my husband to read it and when he likes it, I know it must be okay because he is a picky reader, like me.

What kind of books and authors do you like to read?

When I was in my teens and my friends were reading things like Mallory Towers, I was on the edge of my seat with James Herbert, Stephen King, Kingsley Amis or Dennis Wheatley and I'm still a fan of modern horror. However, Phil Rickman is definitely my favourite author to date (he follows me on twitter, which is very cool) but I do read a bit of steampunk fiction too, my favourites being Jamie Sedgewick and Lindsay Buroker. I love a good ghost story or a post-apocalyptic zombie thriller and, if it's done well, some urban or paranormal fantasy. Other authors I enjoy reading are Kevin Hearne, Alan Dean Foster, Charlaine Harris, Joanne Harris and of course, Sir Terry Pratchett.

What do you do when you're not writing books?

I have an office job with the local council which steals most of my time. As a family we enjoy field archery and we do a lot of camping around the UK. I attend several pagan festivals and conferences each year, often running a workshop or as a speaker and I have my personal Wiccan practice to keep me busy. I love wild, open spaces and have several standing stone circles within an hour's drive from home. I live just outside Sherwood Forest with my family so I'm surrounded by ancient oaks and can't resist a walk in the woods.

And finally, what else have you written and where can we find out more?

My first non-fiction book was The Witching Path, published by Capall Bann, then I have The Witch's Journey and Living Witchcraft published in 2017 by Thoth. I've written feature articles for Kindred Spirit, Prediction, Paranormal Magazine, Spirit & Destiny and Witchcraft & Wicca. Current writing projects include the next book in this series and a non-fiction title on the folklore and magic of dolls and poppets.

For more about me and links to all my writing visit: www.moirahodgkinson.com or check with Children of Artemis at www.witchshop.org or www.witchcraft.org for more updates on Wild Women.